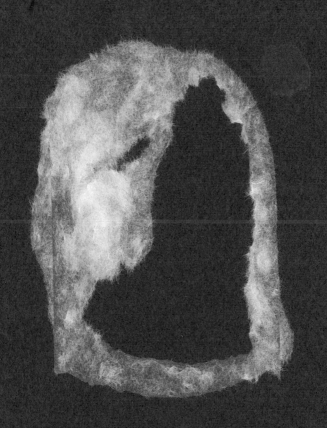

Drama and
COMMITMENT

Drama and
COMMITMENT

POLITICS IN THE AMERICAN
THEATRE OF THE THIRTIES

by Gerald Edward Rabkin

INDIANA UNIVERSITY PRESS
BLOOMINGTON   1964

Second printing, 1964

ACKNOWLEDGMENTS

I am particularly indebted to Professor Harold R. Walley, under whose supervision this study was originally undertaken and whose keen insights into matters dramatic and theatrical helped clarify the issues at hand. I should also like to thank Professor Robert G. Shedd, who planted the initial seed from which this book emerged, and Mr. Lou Polan, who generously placed at my disposal many invaluable theatrical documents of the 1930's. I would like to acknowledge the assistance given me by the Graduate School of Indiana University and the editors of the Humanities Series, in particular Professor Edward D. Seeber, and I am most grateful for having as astute and gracious an editor as Mr. Walter Albee of the Indiana University Press. I would also like to thank the following for permission to quote from books which they have published or control: Alfred A. Knopf, Inc., for citations from The Fervent Years *by Harold Clurman, and the Viking Press, Inc., for citations from* Exile's Return *by Malcolm Cowley.*

5352

to My Mother and Father

CONTENTS

THE PROBLEM OF POLITICAL COMMITMENT

A drama of "no comment" is a drama of no future. Art of any kind that turns its back on the world is uncivilized in the precise and single sense of the word.

KENNETH TYNAN, "Theatre and Living"

In the conflict between the poet and the politician the chief honor the poet can hope for is that of remaining himself. Life and reality, on the one hand, and politics, on the other . . . are not interchangeable terms.

WALLACE STEVENS, response to questionnaire in *Partisan Review*

PROLOGUE: ONE

SINCE the end of World War II, a new word has entered the lexicon of English and American criticism. Perhaps "new" is not quite the appropriate adjective, for the word, "commitment," is obviously not of recent vintage. Yet an examination of contemporary criticism reveals that "commitment" and its various adjectival forms have recently assumed new literary connotations. For example, in a review of Henry Miller's *Colossus of Maroussi*, Richard West writes: "Good luck to his lonely stand against a score of modern idiocies! He remains the last great un-American, uncommitted, status-spurning, disorganization man."[1] And the new usage has even found its way into fiction. The following exchange is from James Baldwin's *Giovanni's Room*:

> "You may laugh," she said, humorously, "but there is something in what I say. I began to realize it in Spain—that I wasn't free, that I couldn't be free until I was attached—no, *committed*—to someone."
> "To someone? Not some*thing*?"
> She was silent. "I don't know," she said at last.[2]

The hesitancy of Baldwin's heroine has not been shared by her generation. Not only has "commitment" emerged as one of the most frequently used literary terms, but it has raised a number of literary problems, one of which has been the subject of recent critical debate. In an editorial of November 27, 1959, the *Times Literary Supplement* noted that "a word like 'commitment' was unwrapped one day from its continental wrapper . . . and was found not to be the

3

blank cartridge of foreign intellectuals, but to contain ex-
plosive charges that might go off here too."[3] The charges did
go off, and British writers have, for the past decade, heatedly chosen sides on the problem of whether or not the
artist should be "committed." Hugh Thomas, for example,
maintained strenuously that *"engagement* is essential" for
the artist,[4] and Kenneth Tynan argued that "if all art is a
gesture against death, . . . it must commit itself."[5] Tynan's
argument is typical of the case for commitment; in an essay
entitled "Theatre and Living," he argues that there are
three attitudes toward life open to the dramatist: he can
record it imitatively, he can withdraw from it, or he can
seek to change it. Great art, he continues, must, by definition, deal with more than the recording of detail; it *must,* in
the nature of the case, comment, and drama, in particular,
demands not only explanation, but *resolution* as well.
Therefore, the artist, and particularly the dramatist, is
forced to involve himself with political issues, to immerse
himself in the world of which he is a part. Art which ignores
social questions "is a shrinking flower that conspires at its
own death by ignoring the soil in which it grows."[6]

Other defenders of the necessity of commitment, however, have pointed out the dangers inherent in a too-strenu-
ous dedication to political action. Doris Lessing, speaking
from years of experience in the political vicissitudes of the
left, counsels that the point can easily arrive when commitment sells out to expediency, and art may be replaced
by "the little tracts about progress, the false optimism, the
dreadful lifeless products of socialist realism."[7] Despite
these real dangers, however, she stresses the importance of
commitment. Commitment to what? To the efficacy of political action, to the humanistic gesture. Art is a social act
with social consequences: "The image of the pretty singer in
the ivory tower has always seemed to me a dishonest one.
. . . The act of getting a story or a novel published is an act

of communication, an attempt to impose one's personality and beliefs on other people."[8] Similarly, K. W. Gransden sees the problem of commitment as a necessary reassertion of humanistic values in an empirically-oriented, apolitical society. To Gransden, the committed writer represents the voice crying in the wilderness that something *can* be done, that something *must* be done. He agrees with Miss Lessing that *what* the writer is committed to is less important that the *fact* of commitment. What is the writer committed to? "Everything. Nothing. . . . It is the attitude, the generalized nature of the protest they feel impelled to make which is significant."[9]

A similarly ambiguous endorsement of commitment has been extensively affirmed in the first book-length consideration of the problem. In *The Writer and Commitment*, John Mander continually asserts the importance of commitment for the writer. "What matters in art," he states, "is the quality and nature of the artist's commitment."[10] But Mr. Mander is never quite successful in defining just what this "commitment" entails. Throughout his detailed analyses of such varied writers as Auden, Orwell, Angus Wilson, Arthur Miller, and Thom Gunn, Mander offers several definitions which apparently are rooted in Sartrian Existentialism:

Before we ask in what the commitment of a writer consists, we must be convinced that he *is*, in fact, committed, that he is in the existentialist's sense *responsible*.

.   .   .   .   .   .

Commitment stands, then, for the basic cast of mind, the fundamental convictions of a man, still perhaps in pre-philosophical, pre-conceptual form, to which he has come in the exercise of this existential responsibility.

.   .   .   .   .   .

Commitment is what remains in the work of the author's subjectivity after the author has done his utmost to eliminate it.[11]

In addition to their catch-all vagueness, Mander's definitions lean toward tautology, a difficulty of which he is not
unaware: "All art is committed, it would seem, to something
beyond itself, to a statement of value not purely aesthetic."[12]
If *all* art is committed, has the term not been robbed of its
critical validity? We shall deal with this problem shortly.
At this point the significant fact is that the problem of commitment has aroused such interest among British critics.[13]

In contrast to their British counterparts, American
writers, since the war, have consistently reaffirmed the
liabilities of political commitment. They have become loath
to involve themselves politically, a trepidation several at-
tribute to the bad experience of "position-taking" in the
thirties. For example, a questionnaire sent to a number of
writers by the *Partisan Review* in 1948 asked about the
artist's relationship to the then growing tension between
the Soviet Union and the United States: "Do you think a
writer should involve himself in it (as writer? as person?)
to the point of commitment?" The responses affirmed the
necessity of the writer's detachment. John Berryman answered defiantly: "The writer 'should' do any damned thing
he can think of to keep on writing, writing well."[14] Wallace
Stevens pointed out that "in the conflict between the poet
and the politician the chief honor the poet can hope for is
that of remaining himself."[15] Clement Greenberg seized
upon the distinction posed between writer and person, and
asserted that while the *person* might have political obligations, the writer had obligations only to his art: "*Qua* writer
he is only interested necessarily in what he can write about
successfully."[16] And Leslie Fiedler seconded this distinction: although the writer may at times be *forced* into a position of political commitment, he is so at the sacrifice of his
role as writer, for "a successful poem is a complete and final
act; if it leads outward to other action, it is just so far a
failure."[17]

This apolitical position has remained constant for the past decade and a half. *Anvil,* a socialist periodical, in 1960 asked Lionel Abel, Arthur Miller, Paul Goodman, and Harold Rosenberg three main questions: "Is there, in fact, a drift away from politics on the part of writers; does the writer have an obligation to political commitment; is there a conflict between art and political commitment?"[18] All agreed that political activity is at present in the United States bankrupt, that political stands are futile, that "there is an inherent conflict between artistic integrity and any commitment."[19] Rosenberg put it this way:

Writers will rise to issues only when these issues are handed to them ready-made by others with instructions on how to react to those issues. But, then, . . . the writers will not be acting as writers but as cohorts, and their activity will be in fact only another species of passivity.[20]

I think we may observe from these various statements that one specific aspect of the concept of commitment has emerged as the subject of debate. The issue under contention involves the importance of *political* commitment for the artist, the significance of his conscious involvement in the social issues of the age in which he belongs. This problem is, of course, by no means a new one. It was, in fact, heatedly debated in the 1930's as the problem of "social significance." That it should arise anew in our time as the problem of political commitment is not surprising when one considers the origin of commitment as a term in literary criticism.

The concept of commitment arises in response to the widespread postwar dissemination of Existentialist philosophy. The *Oxford English Dictionary* tentatively lists the date of the initial appearance of "commitment" as a term in literary criticism as 1954, and also cites 1952 as the earliest date for the appearance of "committed" (in a similar sense) and "committedness."[21] But the *Partisan Review*, in the questionnaire on the state of American writing cited previously, had already used the term in almost its specifically modern sense as early as 1948 ("Do you think a writer should involve himself in it [i.e., the cold war] as writer? as person? to the point of commitment?"). The absence of qualification is significant, and several contributors to the symposium were indeed puzzled.[22] Perhaps it might not be deemed arbitrary if we found some connection between the emergence of the term and the fact that *Partisan Review* had, in the previous issue, just finished the serialization of the translation of *Qu'est-ce que la littérature?*, Jean-Paul Sartre's attempt to demonstrate the necessity of an engaged or committed literature.

Although Bernard Frechtman, the translator of *What Is Literature?* continually uses the English cognate of *engagement*, the word in English does not entirely subsume the implications of its French counterpart. "*Engager*," writes Hazel Barnes in her glossary to terms in Sartre's *Being and Nothingness*, "includes both the idea of involvement and the idea of deliberate commitment,"[23] and most translators have preferred to use the latter word.[24] F. H. Heinemann refers to Sartre as "the philosopher as well as the artist of commitment,"[25] and in the current literary debate, the terms *engagement* and "commitment" are frequently interchanged. Lionel Abel, in the symposium in *Anvil*, notes: "The word 'commitment' appears in *Anvil's* letter, and I presume was used in the same sense Sartre gave to the French word *engagement*."[26]

The concern with commitment, then, reflects the vital contemporary influence of existentialist art and theory. *Engagement* or commitment arose as an esthetic problem when the French existentialists—Sartre and his disciple Beauvoir—attempted to redefine the purpose of art in terms of their general philosophical position. It was not an arbitrary redefinition, for in existentialism the traditional philosophical categories—ethics, epistemology, meta-physics, etc.—are not mutually exclusive; on the contrary, they are inextricably intertwined. Since French existential-ism is an activist philosophy, ethics is not a by-product of more basic philosophical concerns; it is the category from which all else follows. Sartre's position is not one of detach-ment; man is in the world here and now, and must act upon this existentialist fact in order to achieve freedom and self-realization.

Notre liberté aujourd'hui n'est rien d'autre que le libre choix de lutter pour devenir libre. . . . Il ne s'agit pas . . . d'encager mes contemporains: ils sont déjà dans la cage; il s'agit au contraire de nous unir à eux pour briser les barreaux . . . pour mériter le droit d'influencer des hommes qui luttent, il faut d'abord participer à leur combat, il faut d'abord accepter beaucoup de choses, si l'on veut essayer d'en changer quelques-unes.[27]

Logically, therefore, the existentialist as both theoretician and artist cannot cite the inevitability of *engagement* in the human condition without recognizing its necessary exten-sion into esthetics. If, as he tries to establish, the individual is of necessity involved in the fact of existence, and to sur-vive this involvement must commit himself to certain ac-tions, however absurd, must not the artist by logical inclu-sion be involved in the same existentialist dilemma? And since his actions are manifested in the works of art which he produces, does not commitment as an ontological or ethical category lead inevitably to commitment as an esthetic category?

In *What Is Literature?*, Sartre attempts his most explicit esthetic analysis in order to demonstrate the necessity of a committed literature. His process of argumentation is cumulative; he does not construct, throughout the work, a logically consistent position, but attempts rather to demonstrate his thesis through various approaches (formal, functional, and historical), all of which end with the affirmation: literature must be committed. Yet whether we consider *What Is Literature?* as an attempt at serious esthetic argument or, as Iris Murdoch does, "a recommendation to writers concerning their craft, not a demonstration of its essential nature,"[28] the fact remains that the concept of commitment arises in the late forties with the intense interest in existentialist problems.

It is reasonably clear from Sartre's work that *engagement* is conceived as a social and political activity. The writer, he maintains, must commit himself to the political arena in order to retain his artistic integrity. However, when the concept made the journey across the Channel and the Atlantic, it suffered a slight sea-change. Much of the confusion which has arisen from the term "commitment" in recent years derives from ambiguities bred by the connotations of the word in English. We speak of commitment in common usage as a pledge, a bond, an obligation; we speak of noncommitted nations and candidates. It is not difficult in English usage, therefore, to extend the concept of commitment to include any belief which incurs obligation, whether individual or social; for by inclusion it is possible to say that we are all "committed" to some moral, religious, political, or esthetic belief. The extension to nonpolitical areas of consideration was thus easy, and Anglo-American critics began to investigate the literary implications of all sorts of "commitments," such as the moral and the religious. The horizons of *engagement* were, therefore, greatly widened.

Since the concept of commitment has been extended by English and American critics into considerations of the literary consequences of many varieties of belief, it is perhaps difficult to speak of a single problem of commitment. The term "commitment" as such is necessarily ambiguous, for it is obvious that neither in common nor existentialist usage is it possible to speak of the act of commitment without predicating an object to which one is committed. The question which inevitably arises is: commitment to what? Since all art is by definition "committed" to human or esthetic values, an abstract discussion of the concept of commitment in art is obviously tautological. Insofar as the artist is primarily concerned with esthetic commitments, there is no problem. The *problem* of commitment arises when the artist is committed to values or actions extrinsic to the immediate concerns of his art, when the moral urgency of outside imperatives forces him as artist into nonesthetic areas of consideration. This problem, implicit in the contemporary debate and explicit in the Sartrian origins of the concept, is most clearly defined in terms of social and political commitment. The former, moreover, inevitably predicates the latter; if an individual is committed to certain social objectives, he is necessarily involved with considerations of means to realize them. It is, then, this specific aspect of the relationship between art and commitment which may be profitably examined. The problem of political commitment is not only of sufficient literary importance to justify such an investigation, but may also throw light on the larger problem of the esthetic consequences of any nonesthetic belief.

Certain facets of the problem became apparent when the Bollingen prize for poetry was awarded in 1948 to Ezra Pound. Many critics were troubled by the prospect of conferring literary honors upon an individual who has supported the fascist cause. Karl Shapiro wrote: "I voted against Pound in the belief that the poet's political and moral philosophy ultimately vitiates his poetry and lowers its standards as literary work."[29] Clement Greenberg took a slightly different position: "Life includes and is more important than art, and it judges things by their consequences.

. . . It is still justifiable to demand that . . . [the artist] be a successful human being before anything else, even at the cost of his art."[30]

We can see the critical difficulties raised by these pronouncements. Shapiro maintains that a bad man cannot produce great art. Greenberg, on the other hand, does not attack Pound as an artist, but merely as a man with despicable opinions. There are certain fundamentals of human decency which must be preserved "even at the cost of art." Irving Howe delineates the moral-esthetic problem involved:

Once you consider extra-literary matters in a literary judgment, where do you stop? You stop at the point where intelligence and sensibility tell you to—that is what they are for. But it would be absurd to deny that there are occasions when esthetic standards and our central human values clash, and even the latter must seem more important.[31]

This debate reveals negatively several of the issues implicit in the problem of political commitment. If, at times, the artist is led to political affiliation and action, what are the esthetic consequences? If we approve of art which takes stands with which we concur, what is the effect on our esthetic sensibility of the commitment we detest? I think we may observe the importance of political commitment as a literary problem; it brings into focus many of the perennial esthetic dilemmas, dilemmas which, while they may lie dormant in periods of formalism, continually re-emerge when life demands of art its due.

With respect to the artist, therefore, the problem of political commitment has two aspects. There is, first, the moral problem: can the artist, as a human being living within a situation which demands political resolution, morally ignore these problems and still retain his integrity as a man? Second, and growing out of the first, there is the esthetic problem: can the artist *qua* artist ignore these problems *in his art* and still maintain *its* integrity?

Since the former aspect lies outside the realm of literary criticism, it is the latter aspect which we shall examine. It is, therefore, necessary to consider in what context the problem may be most advantageously studied. Since light is most often thrown on a present problem by the consideration of an analogue detached from it, we may find it valuable to consider the problem of political commitment in terms of a historical period in which the problem was similarly crucial —if not always defined in exactly the same terms as today. And we are fortunate to have in recent history precisely such a period; for on one point the contemporary debaters concur: the 1930's were a "committed" period, even if they disagree on the suitability of this commitment for our present age. "The last thing one wants in literature now," writes Roy Fuller, "is a phony 'contemporaneity,' bearing as much relation to the committed writing of the thirties as the visit of the four undergraduates to Hungary (in the news as I write) does to the International Brigade."[32] And an editor of the *London Magazine* (presumably John Lehmann), in a questionnaire addressed to several British writers on the question of commitment in the present age, makes the comparison explicit: "During the thirties it was a widely-held view that poets, novelists and playwrights should be closely concerned *in their writing* with the fundamental political and social issues of their time. . . ."[33]

In considering the political commitments of writers in the 1930's, however, it may be advantageous to restrict our field of enquiry. The literary manifestations of the age were too diversified to encompass fully within the scope of this study. Poetry and the novel—although both affected by the particular social climate of their age—were beset by their own formal considerations. One genre, however, was obviously and generally affected by political concerns; in drama of the 1930's the problem of political commitment manifest in all art of the period is most sharply and clearly delineated. It is not surprising that this should be the case, for drama, by its very nature, is an immediate and public art. As Francis Fergusson has pointed out:

The art of the theatre—notoriously an "impure" art—seems to be as close to the art of politics as it is to poetry, painting or music. The theatre artist, whether actor or playwright, depends upon the interest and support of an audience just as the politician depends upon his constituency. . . . The theatre artist cannot practice his art without real people assembled before a real stage; a theatre without an audience is a contradiction in terms. That is why politics and the theatre are necessarily so close to the public mood and the public mind of their times.[34]

Thus, this study will ask the following questions: in a period of intense social change, what influence did political and social forces exert upon an art form necessarily responsive to these forces; what were the *forms* of commitment, the political alternatives chosen by writers living in an age of controversy; and what were the esthetic consequences of their choices?

Since the question at issue is that of commitment, I shall attempt to clarify at the outset the sense in which the term is used in the present study. In doing so, my intention is not to offer any new definition, but simply to clarify the significance of the term in current usage. Employing both its existentialist and its common linguistic connotations, I shall use the term to describe both the conscious *involvement* of the artist in the social and political issues of his age (in contrast to deliberate detachment or political noninvolvement), and the specific political *obligations* which the artist assumes in consequence of this involvement (e.g., the liberal commitment, the Marxist commitment). Let me affirm that I am in full agreement with the distinction made by

Irving Howe in his study of the political novel. When I speak of the problem of political commitment, I have no ambition, in Howe's words, "of setting up still another rigid category. I am concerned with perspectives of observation, not categories of classification."[35]

2

THE COMMITTED DECADE AND ITS DRAMA

Creep, my ember! Blaze my brand!
The end of all things is at hand.
Idlers in the market place,
Make an end of your disgrace!
Here's a fair day's work for you—
To build a world all over new.

FLORENCE CONVERSE, "Bread Line" (1932)

You, who shall emerge from the flood
In which we are sinking,
Think—
When you speak of our weaknesses,
Also of the dark time
That brought them forth.

BERTOLT BRECHT, "To Posterity"

CHAPTER TWO

AT THE END of *Exile's Return*, Malcolm Cowley recounts the series of wild New Year's Eve parties which the generation of the twenties offered in homage to the decade which was passing into history. The decade had really ended the previous October on Black Thursday; the lost generation sensed that it was performing the ritual of self-interment, and was determined to go out with a bang, not with a whimper. "They traveled about the city in caravans of taxicabs, suddenly irrupting into a strange house in a mass attack . . . filling every corner with screeches and guffaws, in half an hour drinking all the punch, then rushing off to another house in a great undisciplined body. . . ."[1] Of all the bacchanalian events that occurred that night, Cowley reports that he was most impressed by the story of a friend who told how after attending four successive parties he found himself in a subcellar joint in Harlem:

The room was smoky and sweaty; all the lights were tinted red or green, and as the smoke drifted across them, nothing had its own shape or color; the cellar was like somebody's crazy vision of Hell; it was as if he were caught there and condemned to live in a perpetual nightmare. When he came out on the street, he said, it was bathed in harsh winter sunlight, ugly and clear and somehow reassuring. An ash-colored woman was hunting for scraps in a garbage can.

That was the way a decade came to its end.[2]

This is the way another decade ends: on New Year's Eve ten years later W. H. Auden—speaking, like Cowley, in the authentic voice of his generation—writes:

Tonight a scrambling decade ends,
And strangers, enemies and friends
Stand once more puzzled underneath
The signpost on the barren heath
Where the rough mountain track divides
To silent valleys on all sides,
Endeavoring to decipher what
Is written on it but cannot,
Nor guess in what direction lies
The overhanging precipice.[3]

Between these two dates was enacted the drama of a generation. For Cowley and his friend the image of the scavenging woman, however pitiful, was "somehow reassuring." This reassurance was born of the conviction that the Big Party was at last over; the unreal phantasmagoria of the cellar club was dispelled by the harsh light of reality. The ruins of social decay were illumined by the testimony of the senses; and it is not surprising that the worlds of art and ideas should themselves be characterized by the search for social enlightenment. "Come into the light, comrade!" was the communist offer of salvation, and it is the metaphor of *illumination* which characterizes the thirties. Man could no longer exist in the shadow of his personal nightmare; the pose of noncommitment, he came to feel, was itself a political act. No less than the striking worker, the artist-intellectual felt compelled to ask—and to answer—the question posed by the union song: which side are you on?

By the end of the decade, as Auden's poem reveals, the light of social illumination had dimmed, and the answers once so clear and bright, the sharp black-and-white images of reality, began to blur and fade. The signpost on the barren heath was no longer clearly decipherable, the path to salvation no longer led in a single direction. But Auden, no less than Cowley, had shared the perils and consolations of commitment; he, too, had found in the necessity for social action a moral imperative which outweighed the esthetic.

Yesterday, the belief in the absolute value of Greek;
The fall of the curtain upon the death of a hero;
    Yesterday the prayer to the sunset,
And the adoration of madmen. But today the struggle.
    .   .   .   .   .   .

Tomorrow, for the young, the poets exploding like bombs,
The walks by the lake, the winter of perfect communion;
    Tomorrow the bicycle races
Through the suburbs on summer evenings; but today
    the struggle.[4]

"Today the struggle," this is the key to the contradictions of the thirties, the source of both its weakness and its strength. An age of tension, terror, and breakdown, it seemed to demand action. But action within the context of an era of convulsive change becomes more than an idle gesture; paradoxically, despite the enormity of conflicting social forces, man in the thirties felt anything but impotent. The act of commitment was crucial because it seemed meaningful. It was not mere hyperbole which caused a Marxist critic to write: "This is a marvelous time in which to be alive. It is immeasurably better than 1890, when literature was devoted to *trivia*. Today we have everything *but* triviality to write about."[5] It is this sense of living on the crest of history —of being a vital element in the age to which one is born— which endows literature and criticism of the thirties with both the virtue of enthusiasm and the liability of temporality.

The fact of economic breakdown brought forth the search for social alternatives. Intellectuals who had remained defiantly apolitical throughout the preceding decade rushed to make public commitment, finding in the failure of capitalism (in Edmund Wilson's words "that stupid, gigantic fraud")[6] not despair, but rather a new sense of purpose. In no document of the period is this compulsion for political action more evident than in the pamphlet, *Culture and the Crisis*, issued by fifty-two artists and intellectuals at the peak of the 1932 presidential campaign. The pamphlet—signed, among others, by Sherwood Anderson, Erskine Caldwell, Malcolm Cowley, John Dos Passos, Theodore Dreiser, Sidney Howard, Lincoln Steffens, and Edmund Wilson—noted that there was only one issue in the campaign, the failure of capitalism. Only one alternative would suffice: the acceptance of a program to overhaul radically the entire structure; and such a program, the pamphlet asserted, was available from only one source, the Communist party. All other alternatives were half-measures, doomed to failure.

Above all, *Culture and the Crisis* stressed the importance of political commitment. The role of the intellectual was no longer seen as one of detached contemplation; he was duty-bound, by virtue of his role, to act.

We who write this, listed among the so-called "intellectuals" of our generation, people trained, at least, to think for ourselves and hence to a degree for our time and our people—we have no faintest desire to exaggerate our talents and our influence. Yet, on the other hand, why should we as a class be humble? Practically everything that is orderly and sane and useful in America was made by two classes of Americans: our class, the class of brain workers, and the "lower classes," the muscle workers. Very well, we strike hands with our true comrades. We claim our own and we reject the disorder, the lunacy spawned by grabbers, advertisers, traders, speculators, salesmen. . . . We claim the right to live and to function. It is our business to think and we shall not permit business men to teach us our business. It is, also, in the end, our business to act.

We have acted. As responsible intellectual workers, we have aligned ourselves with the frankly revolutionary Communist Party, the party of the workers.[7]

George F. Babbitt—former member of Mencken's "boob-oisie," now capitalist exploiter—is still the object of abuse; but he is no longer merely a fool, he has become a villain. It is, however, not inappropriate that he should remain the target, for the signers of *Culture and the Crisis* belonged to the generation that had created him. Their commitment, then, assumes meaning in the context of the political apathy from which they had recently emerged. H. L. Mencken and George Jean Nathan, the editors of the *Mercury*, a characteristic periodical of the twenties, were, in their own words, "committed to nothing save this: to keep to common sense as fast as they can, to belabor sham as agreeably as possible. . . ."[8] Politicians—*all* politicians—were by definition fools and scoundrels, and political concerns seemed supremely irrelevant in the context of prosperity. "If I am convinced of anything," stated Mencken, "it is that Doing Good is in bad taste."[9]

The social enemies of the twenties were, thus, strawmen. The Philistine and the Puritan might be ridiculed, but no one seriously entertained the possibility of replacing them. Escape lay in other directions: in the bohemianism of Greenwich Village, the primitivism of Mexico, or the cultural sophistication of Paris. Expatriation became the characteristic gesture of the age; they sold no beer on Main Street, but wine was cheap in the cafes of Pamplona. And always there was the great anodyne, Art. If the bourgeoisie could not appreciate his efforts, the artist would reciprocate by rendering his handiwork ever more experimentally complex.

The reformist zeal which, in the early years of the century, had exerted a strong and effective political and moral force, did not survive the Great War. The muckraking attacks on the shame of the cities and Standard Oil—the concerted effort to combat corruption in both government and business—disappeared behind the facade of a cynicism bred by overwhelming public endorsement of conservatism. Only one event in the 1920's shook the facade of apathy, but it demonstrated that forces of liberalism and radicalism could be revitalized if awakened by a cause. The arrest and subsequent execution of Sacco and Vanzetti brought liberals, anarchists, communists, proletarians, and intellectuals together in collective protest. But despite Marxist attempts to point the moral of the political martyrdom, the disparate forces brought together by the case were dispersed by the tragic fact of execution; they were not to converge again until the era of the Popular Front. The intellectuals resumed their apolitical stance; the rechanneling of their political energies awaited the catalyst of the Depression.

Six months before the Crash Mike Gold had vainly exhorted young writers to "go left," but in the aftermath of depression little encouragement was needed. Commenting upon a symposium in the independently radical *Modern Quarterly* in the summer of 1932, the *New Republic* noted that the "leftward swing" of American writers was a reality:

Three years ago, these . . . critics and novelists were classified either as liberals or men wholly uninterested in politics. Today, most of them distrust the Socialists for being too conservative. . . . The writers themselves believe that the system is doomed. . . . Their change of opinion seems to indicate that American literature is about to assume a different character.[10]

The prediction was fulfilled; American literature in the thirties was, to a large extent, molded by the influence of the Marxist myth. An acceptance of this fact need not necessarily confirm the theory of the "Red decade." The influence of Marxism in the United States was determined by its lack of any substantial proletarian support. When a European intellectual in Germany in the late twenties or in France during the middle thirties attached himself to the communists, he found himself involved with and sustained by a movement comprised of millions of people. In America, however, it was soon apparent that the revolutionary alternative would not be accepted. After all, William Z. Foster—despite the urgings of many of America's leading intellectuals—received fewer than 100,000 votes in the 1932 elections. But it is difficult to measure the extent of a social myth statistically. The intellectual influence of Marxism in the 1930's—as revealed by the commitments of intellectuals and the work of artists—bore no direct relation to the growth of membership in the Communist party, which reached its peak of 80,000 during the war years when Marxist intellectual influence had substantially diminished.[11]

The influence of Marxism on American letters passed through two distinct phases. In the depths of the Depression the newly radical esthetes of the twenties felt compelled to act, and Marxism as a philosophy, and the Communist party as an organization, seemed the most effective means of realizing this desire; in short, they accommodated themselves to what they felt were revolutionary necessities. For the communists offered a program of action, a disciplined organization, a working model—the USSR, which was embarking upon its first five-year plan and maintaining full employment—and a body of doctrine which placed all social and esthetic phenomena in the coherent philosophical framework of dialectical materialism.

After 1935, however, the political atmosphere changed significantly. The communists, who had gradually alienated the early intellectual converts (by 1936 most of the signers of *Culture and the Crisis* had disaffiliated themselves from the Communist party) now openly sought the support of nonradical, anti-fascist intellectuals. Thus, while the initial burst of Marxist influence had waned by the middle of the decade, this influence was revived by the rise of fascism; for although the economic collapse which had turned the intellectuals of the twenties toward radicalism had been ameliorated by New Deal reform, the fascist threat continued to grow throughout the decade. And after 1935 it was no longer necessary to accept all the particulars of communist faith, for the policy of the United Front—officially decreed in 1935 by the Comintern—no longer viewed all capitalist states as equally warlike. All could unite in opposition to the fascist menace, a change in ideology reflected by the presence at the Second Congress of the Marxist League of American Writers of such noncommunist adherents of the Popular Front as Hemingway and MacLeish. The Congress of 1935 had boldly advocated a program based upon the "fight against imperialist war and fascism,"[12] but the program of the 1937 Congress was hardly revolutionary: "It seeks to restore and raise the living standards of the people, . . . to maintain and extend democratic rights and civil liberties."[13] In short, "Communism," in the words of the party platform of 1936, was "twentieth-century Americanism."[14]

The heyday of the Popular Front, however, was shattered in 1939 by the Nazi-Soviet Nonaggression Pact. The impact was staggering. It had not been difficult for the communist writers to temper their revolutionary commitment to cooperate with the opponents of facism, for many, being middle-class intellectuals, had welcomed the opportunity to forego the necessity of viewing all noncommunists as class enemies; but the pact demanded a total revision of attitude that only the most deeply committed could achieve. To many it seemed the betrayal of all that they had struggled for during the past years. One-third of the officers of the League of American Writers resigned, one hundred of its eight hundred members formally left, and many others drifted away.

With Hitler's invasion of Russia, the Popular Front was

revived; but although public estimation of the Soviet Union was never so high as during the period when it was our wartime ally, for all intents and purposes the Marxist myth had lost its efficacy for the intellectuals. Wartime, in any case, is rarely a time for intellectual vitality; all energy is directed toward the single goal of victory, and art tends towards either exhortation or escape. With the advent of the Cold War and McCarthyism, the radical element in the United States dwindled to insignificance and many found that it was not sufficient to have repudiated the Marxist myth; the act of having once subscribed was itself condemnatory, unless accompanied by the most vigorous demonstrations of patriotic fervor.

The compulsion toward political commitment did not, however, enmesh all intellectuals in the many vagaries of Marxism. Although, in the early days of economic breakdown, many liberals turned left simply because they saw no other alternative, as the decade progressed, it became apparent that Roosevelt's pragmatic reformism, if it had not ended the Depression, had at least ended the crisis. F.D.R. was fond of quoting Macauley's dictum that one must reform in order to preserve, and in order to preserve capitalism experimented boldly. Some efforts, like NRA, failed; others, like TVA, have become unchallenged American institutions. In any case, liberals no longer were confronted by an either/or situation; they found that they could indeed support a government which had undertaken such reforms as WPA and Social Security, which had encouraged trade unionism and, in general, taken an active role in all areas of American life. With the advent of the Popular Front, many liberals found in anti-fascism a cause in which they could affiliate with the communists, since the communists were, in any case, themselves talking very much like New Dealers. The liberal commitment, however, was not related to a single social myth. Like New Dealism, it was itself pragmatic, accepting certain tenets of Marxism while eschewing others. Although the liberal often respected the social fervor of the Marxist, he saw no sense in predicating his anti-fascism upon what he conceived to be another form of totalitarianism. But whatever his politics, the significant fact is that, in the thirties, the writer felt compelled to commit himself, to involve himself in the social issues of the age to which he belonged.

Since drama is pre-eminently a social art, it is not surprising that the social concerns sketched above should find dramatic expression. Indeed, the virtues and defects of American drama of the 1930's are largely due to the intensity of its barometric reflection of social change. Because the Depression and, as the decade progressed, the imminence of war were never far off-stage, the serious American playwright responded to what seemed to him inexorable demands for social and political commitment. This does not mean, however, that most plays produced in the period 1930-41 were social dramas. On the contrary, statistics reveal that the bulk of drama produced during the decade was substantially similar to that of the periods which preceded and followed it; the common fare of Broadway has not varied considerably in forty years. But if we consider *significant* drama of the 1930's—that drama which has had greatest survival value and which has received most critical attention—we find an overwhelming preoccupation with social issues. The work of the major dramatists of the period —Odets, Lawson, Anderson, Rice, Behrman, Green, Shaw, Hellman, Sherwood—unquestionably reflects an intense, active concern with the political and social issues raised by the Depression and the rise of fascism.[15]

To appreciate the change in the direction of American drama in the thirties, it is necessary to view the dramatic contribution of the decade which immediately preceded it;

for the 1929 Crash represented a dramatic as well as an economic watershed. Serious American drama of the 1920's, no less than the other arts, was overwhelmed by various kinds of experiment. The constraints of realism were rejected in favor of attempts to reorder experience through new techniques, new concepts and sequences of dialogue, new versions of characterization, and bold innovations in scenic design. The main vehicle for this dramatic experimentation was the technique of expressionism, newly revealed to American playwrights through the Theatre Guild productions of the works of Kaiser, Toller, and Capek, and through films like *The Cabinet of Doctor Caligari*. Beginning with Lawson's *Roger Bloomer* and Rice's *Adding Machine* in 1923, American drama in the twenties adapted expressionistic devices to its serious needs. Rice's *The Subway*, E. E. Cummings' *Him*, Kaufman and Connelly's *Beggar on Horseback*, all of Lawson's plays of the decade, and, of course, many of the dramas of Eugene O'Neill (*Emperor Jones, The Hairy Ape, The Great God Brown, Lazarus Laughed*) reveal an indebtedness to expressionistic technique. Indeed, the dramatic canon of O'Neill represents a persistent search for new forms of dramatic expression.

The intensity of dramatic experiment in the twenties, however, does not merely indicate the dominance of esthetic over social concerns. That the serious dramatist *was* concerned with society is revealed by the explicit condemnation of contemporary business morality in such plays as *The Adding Machine* and *Roger Bloomer*. But, in general, this social criticism was ill-defined because the playwright could not as yet offer a political alternative. Indeed, one of the attractions of European expressionism lay in its perennial theme of alienation. Man, brutalized by industrial society, was conceived of as a social victim, with little recourse but to accept his extinction at the hands of forces too vast for him to control. Rice's Mr. Zero became the characteristic "antihero" of the age, the embodiment of impotence who is condemned in death as in life.

That serious drama which was nonexperimental, in that it retained the traditional, realistic form, was, more often than not, preoccupied with psychological rather than social man. The moral revolution which followed the Great War was reinforced by the impact of the sexual theories of Sigmund Freud, with the result that much of American drama turned inward to investigate the complexities of the human psyche in such plays as Sidney Howard's *Silver Cord* (1926), Anderson's *Gypsy* (1929), and O'Neill's *Desire Under the Elms* (1924).

American drama of the 1920's was politically uncommitted for the simple reason that there were few specific issues that seemed to demand commitment. Although the Sacco-Vanzetti case brought forth the protest of Anderson and Hickerson's *Gods of the Lightning*, and despite the social experimentation of Lawson, Dos Passos and the Siftons at the end of the decade, in general, the jazz-age playwright, caught up in the dramatic experimentation of his age, preferred the esthetic to the political arena.

The realities of the Depression, however, changed the tenor and direction of American drama. The age of experimentation suffered an immediate demise, for experiment smacked of a frivolity inappropriate to the seriousness that now seemed to be demanded. Although the change is most manifest in the work of Lawson, one of the primary experimenters of the twenties, it is observable in the entire corpus of American drama over the two decades. Those dramatic experiments attempted in the 1930's invariably involved Brechtian technique. The Marxist "agit-prop," the Living Newspaper, and several dramatically presentational productions (Brecht's *Mother*, Piscator's *Case of Clyde Griffiths*) shared the common aim of didacticism, the desire to confront the audience directly with specific social issues and political alternatives. On the whole, however, American drama of the 1930's was primarily realistic in style because it was concerned with centering attention on *what* it had to say, rather than on the *means* of dramatic statement. Protest was now channeled into specific political directions, and abstract condemnations of industrial society were replaced by serious searches for political alternatives. It is significant that the most characteristic dramatic voice of the twenties, Eugene O'Neill, was largely silent in the thirties. His only plays of the decade (save *Mourning Becomes Electra*, produced in 1931 but composed in the twenties) were *Ah, Wilderness*, an exercise in uncharacteristic sentimentality, and *Days Without End*, a confused, semi-Catholic attempt at religious affirmation.

The change in the direction of American drama is first noticeable in the season of 1932-33. Perhaps because drama is a complex and collective art, it takes a while for immediate social issues to find artistic reflection. In any case, the three years immediately following the Crash produced few social dramas. In 1932, however, several events indicated that American drama was taking a new turn. Lawson's *Success Story* revealed him for the first time abandoning his previous experimentalism in a play which savagely attacked the myth of business success against the backdrop of the Depression. S. N. Behrman's *Biography*, produced the same year, also demonstrated the playwright's involvement in new social problems. Behrman had made a modest reputation at the end of the twenties writing high comedies involved with issues no more portentous than the obtaining or relinquishing of a mistress, but in *Biography*, the playwright chooses a political radical for his male protagonist, and the world of the Depression abruptly enters the world of the drawing room. Indeed, Behrman's comic world, as we shall observe in a later chapter, is continually besieged by the social conflicts of his time.

The political awakening of the intellectuals of the twenties, recorded in the initial section of this chapter, is similarly evidenced by the change in the work of several characteristic dramatists of the Jazz Age. In *The Adding Machine* and *The Subway* Elmer Rice had recorded man's impotence before the God of the Machine, but in *We the People* (1933) he emerges in a vigorous, politically committed role, proclaiming that social reform *must* be forthcoming to alleviate the ills of capitalism, and his subsequent plays of the decade reinforce his new-found activism. Social issues also play increasingly important roles in the Depression dramas of Maxwell Anderson and Robert Sherwood. Anderson, despite his concern with reinstating historical verse drama, becomes increasingly involved in the thirties with the themes of liberty and rebellion in such plays as *Valley Forge* (1934), *The Masque of Kings* (1937), *High Tor* (1937), *Second Overture* (1938), and *Key Largo* (1939). Sherwood, on the other hand, eschews the world of comedy—*The Road to Rome* (1927), *The Queen's Husband* (1928) and *Reunion in Vienna* (1931)—for the world of social commitment—*The Petrified Forest* (1935), *Idiot's Delight* (1936), *Abe Lincoln in Illinois* (1938) and *There Shall Be No Night* (1940). Indeed, in the political vicissitudes of their age, the newly committed playwrights found many common dramatic themes: social injustice (*Winterset, We the People*), anti-fascism (*Key Largo, Judgment Day, Flight to the West*), antiwar (*There Shall Be No Night, Idiot's Delight, Second Overture*) and Americanism (*Valley Forge, Abe Lincoln in Illinois, American Landscape*).

If one were to attempt to chart the rise and fall of politically committed drama in the 1930's, one might place the high-point at the mid-decade, 1934-36. This period saw the major productions of the left-wing Theatre Union and the Marxist New Theatre League (which produced, among other short works, Odets' *Waiting for Lefty* and Irwin Shaw's *Bury the Dead*); the Group Theatre's productions of the work of the decade's most important young dramatist, Clifford Odets; the Theatre Guild's productions of such plays as Wexley's *They Shall Not Die*, Sherwood's *Idiot's Delight* and the leftist revue, *Parade* (1935); the production on Broadway of such dramas with social themes as *Dead End, Winterset,* and *The Petrified Forest;* and the International Ladies' Garment Workers Union's socially satiric revue, *Pins and Needles,* which succeeded in placing its finger on the pulse of the period by genially requesting:

> Sing us a song with social significance
> Or you can sing until you're blue
> Let meaning shine from every line
> Or we won't love you.[16]

Despite the major theatrical event of the latter part of the decade, the unprecedented Federal Theatre Project, the record reveals that the period from 1938 to 1941 represents a general decline in social and, in particular, left-wing drama. By 1939, the left-wing theatre movement had died because of a variety of factors, primarily lack of patronage and the change in ideological direction demanded by the Popular Front; the dramas of Clifford Odets became increasingly preoccupied with personal problems after his defection to Hollywood; and several of the twenties' playwrights who had moved left because of the initial impact of the Depression had found reason to be disenchanted with the intransigence of the radicals. Anger at the manifest failure of capitalism gave way to apprehension at the imminence of war, and the mood at the end of the thirties was unquestionably less socially aggressive than at the mid-decade. Perhaps the wistful, almost desperate optimism of William Saroyan accurately reflects the mood of the late thirties, a determined but largely unreasoned faith in the possibilities of man's goodness. Survival was soon to be the only basic social question, and the spirit of political commitment which dominated American drama in the 1930's was largely dissipated by the entry of America into the second World War.

The political commitments of American dramatists in the thirties, like those of intellectuals in general, were generally left of center, either reformist or radical. The 1930's unquestionably represent the high point of Marxist influence on American drama. Even those liberal playwrights who, like Rice, Behrman, and Sherwood, disapproved of radical dogmatism treated the Marxist alternative seriously. Rice, in particular, at the beginning of the decade, made common cause with the Marxists on many issues, and communist characters figure prominently—not always unsympathetically—in Behrman's plays of the mid-decade.

Marxist influence on the drama, as upon literature in general, was greatest at the middle of the decade, a period which witnessed, as we have previously observed, the major productions of Theatre Union, the emergence of Odets, and the brief flowering of "proletarian" drama, the genre which produced such plays as *Let Freedom Ring, Waiting for Lefty, Stevedore, Marching Song,* and *Black Pit.* Indeed, the entire phenomenon of proletarian literature is significant as a reflection of the impact of Marxism on American letters. We may observe that the years 1934-35 saw the publication of twenty-eight proletarian novels and a representative anthology entitled *Proletarian Literature in the United States.* Nor were critical evaluations of the phenomenon restricted to the radical press. The *Times Literary Supplement,* observing the "vitality" of the American movement (in much the same manner as its recent praise for the vitality of "Beat" writing), commented, "An odd outlook, it may well appear, to capture so successfully, in capitalist and individualist America of all places, so many adherents, even among those notoriously unstable beings, artists and intellectuals!"[17] The vitality of the movement had, in fact, waned considerably by the time of *TLS*'s endorsement, but the phenomenon of proletarian literature is significant because it was, briefly, a genuine movement, which had repercussions outside the sphere of its own parochialism; again, like the "Beat" or "Angry Young Men" movements of today, proletarian literature was less important for what it actually produced than for the interest it aroused in literary circles.

Proletarian literature exerted considerable influence upon the drama; for American drama was, and is, New York drama, and New York was the spiritual home of American Marxism. It is not surprising, then, that both the proletarian novel and play should share similar subject matter. Walter Rideout, in his analysis of the proletarian novel, finds such novels may be divided into four main categories: "(1) those centered about a strike; (2) those concerned with the development of an individual's class consciousness and his conversion to communism; (3) those dealing with the 'bottom dogs,' the lowest layers of society; and (4) those describing the decay of the middle class."[18] American Marxist drama of the thirties uses each of these categories save the third, probably because the picaresque structure of the "bottom dog" novel was too episodic to lend itself to dramatic adaptation.

But proletarian literature was not so designated merely on the basis of its working-class subject matter. We may observe that Rideout's fourth category deals with the middle class. Throughout the early part of the decade the problem of defining "proletarian" as a literary term became the major subject of Marxist esthetic debate. Some critics supported a literal use of the word: proletarian literature designated those works by working-class authors which dealt with authentic areas of working-class experience. But others felt such a definition did not face the realities of the basic Marxist esthetic premise that art is a weapon in the class struggle. Just as the term "proletariat" came in the political lexicon to designate more than the working class —it transcended description, and assumed the connotation of "the wave of the future"—so proletarian literature had to be based on ideological awareness. The problem received considerable attention at the American Writers' Congress of 1935—not unnaturally, since the proletarian genre was then at its zenith. By and large, the speakers affirmed that proletarian art was not to be distinguished by its subject matter, but rather by its point of view: "The term 'proletarian' applied to art should refer to the key and vision in which the work is conceived, rather than to subject. It should be a qualitative, not quantitative, term."[19]

Such a definition had both loosening and restrictive consequences. Since "proletarian" was an evaluative, rather than a descriptive term, the Marxist writer was not confined to writing exclusively about the working class. His viewpoint, rather than his subject matter, qualified his work as "revolutionary." Nor need the viewpoint of the work be overtly militant. If the writer had made public commitment as either party member or fellow traveler, his work need not contain an overt revolutionary moral.

The concept of proletarian literature was, then, rather elastically applied, but it was never a purely descriptive term. For as Joshua Kunitz pointed out, it was not inconceivable that a novel be written about the proletariat by "someone from an inimical class with an inimical point of view."[20] Such a work, from a Marxist point of view, could not possibly express the "attitudes, experience and aspiration" of the working class; hence, it would *not* be a proletarian novel. But the dangers inherent in an ideological evaluation of art were soon manifest. Although some critics continually stressed the need for a concern with the technical problems of art, the more sectarian tended to evaluate literature almost solely on the grounds of political awareness. Art was, first and foremost, a class weapon, they asserted; the distinction between form and content was fallacious. "If a man has something to say, as all proletarian writers have," claimed Mike Gold, "he will learn to say it clearly in time."[21] Such a view, the less sectarian countered, grossly oversimplified the problems of art. Yes, they admitted, art *was* a weapon; but the better the art, the better the weapon.

After the inauguration of the Popular Front, the proletarian genre—and the esthetic debate which it engendered—disappeared, for although it was still acknowledged that art was a weapon, there was no longer agreement about what the weapon was to be directed against. The Marxists were less prone to assert their ideological differences with the noncommunist left, being more concerned with stressing the points of contact. Whereas in such pre-Popular Front proletarian plays as *Peace on Earth* and *Stevedore* the villain was inevitably the capitalist system, such doctrinaire aggressiveness might well have dissuaded New Deal liberals from joining in the anti-fascist crusade. The Class Struggle, no longer the dominant literary theme, was replaced by themes of anti-fascism and "Americanism." The communists now proclaimed themselves heirs to the American revolutionary tradition and pre-empted such native heroes as Tom Paine, Jefferson, Lincoln, and John Brown. Sklar's *Life and Death of an American* (1939) and Gold and Blankfort's *Battle Hymn* (1936), despite revolutionary implications, were both largely indistinguishable in theme from the work of such noncommunist anti-fascists as Rice and Sherwood. Themes of revolutionary Marxism were never revived; Marxist influence upon the drama steadily declined from 1936 onwards, until, in the period of the Nazi-Soviet Pact, the Marxist dramatic voice was completely silent.

There remains one other important characteristic of Depression drama which must be considered. As befits an age preoccupied with theories of collectivism, American drama of the 1930's was characterized by the dominance of theatrical groups. Few periods in our dramatic history have witnessed such intense theatrical activity under group auspices. Indeed, most of what has remained valuable in the dramatic legacy of the thirties was the result of the activities of such groups as the Group Theatre, Theatre Union, the Federal Theatre Project, and the Mercury Theatre. In addition to these professional groups, amateur theatres— mostly of left-wing persuasion—proliferated: Theatre of Action, Theatre Collective, Artef, Labor Stage, the New Theatre League made substantial theatrical contributions by producing such social playlets as *Waiting for Lefty, Bury the Dead, Hymn to the Rising Sun, Plant in the Sun,* and by offering opportunities to many young theatrical aritists. Elia Kazan's first directorial effort, for example, was *The Young Go First* for Theatre of Action (1935).

Even the established dramatist felt the need for a greater theatrical security than that available on Broadway. In the spring of 1938, the foremost non-Marxist dramatists of the age—Anderson, Behrman, Rice, Howard, and Sherwood— formed the Playwrights' Company for the express purpose of controlling the productions of their own plays. The organization subsequently produced, among other works, Sherwood's *Abe Lincoln in Illinois,* Rice's *American Landscape,* and Anderson's *Knickerbocker Holiday* and *Key Largo.* Although the Playwrights' Company cannot properly be termed a theatre, in that it did not recruit permanent theatrical personnel nor offer a specific program, it is significant that the playwrights involved felt the need to band together as a productional unit in order to minimize the hazards of Broadway commercialism.

The thirties may, then, be accurately characterized as an age in search of collective alternatives—both social and theatrical. All of the groups cited above were caught up in the social climate of the age; all included a sense of social obligation in their theatrical credos. Even the august Theatre Guild, which had relinquished the mantle of the theatrical *avant-garde* by the thirties, could not remain aloof from the issues of the age. It, too, climbed on the bandwagon of social drama, producing such plays as *Roar, China* (1930) by the Soviet dramatist Tretyakov, which attacked the commercial exploitation of China in the twenties; *Both Your Houses* (1933), Anderson's muckraking attack on politics; *They Shall Not Die* (1934), John Wexley's spirited defense of the Scottsboro boys; and Peters and Sklar's leftist revue, *Parade* (1935), which satirized the enemies of the proletariat in such verses as the following:

> Life could be so beautiful
> Life could be so grand for all
> If just a few didn't own everything
> And most of us nothing at all.[22]

That the respectable Theatre Guild would produce a revue by two of the decade's foremost Marxist dramatists offers some indication of the social atmosphere of the 1930's. Theatre groups—no less than the dramatists who comprised them—could not escape the social and political realities of their age. It is appropriate, then, that we begin our investigation of the dramatic implications of political commitment by examining the theatrical and social ideals of three major theatre groups of the decade, groups which, although all politically involved, reveal in the varied intensity of their respective commitments different facets of the general problem: Theatre Union attempted to create a professional, fully-committed political theatre; the Group Theatre, although it did not offer a specific ideological program, nevertheless was perennially concerned with social issues in an attempt to live up to its credo of founding a technique of the theatre on "life values"; and the Federal Theatre Project, essentially a product of social necessity, was, as a consequence, inevitably involved in the political issues of its age.

After these general considerations, we shall examine the specific political commitments of several important dramatists of the period. The playwrights have not been chosen solely on the basis of their subsequent reputations. It would be difficult by this criterion to justify, for example, the inclusion of Lawson and the exclusion of Hellman. Although I have indeed attempted to include most of the significant dramatists of the decade, I have not attempted to be all-inclusive. I have, rather, chosen those dramatists who best exemplify the problem under consideration. Thus Lawson is crucial to an understanding of the consequences of the Marxist commitment for the playwright; his affirmation of political faith contrasts significantly with Odets' loss of commitment. Sherwood has not been considered at length because his dramatic-political dilemma parallels, in many ways, that of S. N. Behrman. He too senses the insignificance of high comedy in a world of crisis, and his plays of the 1930's also reflect a new-found political awareness. Although his dramatic response is not precisely the same as that of Behrman (who strove at all costs to retain the genre in which he excelled), I feel that there are sufficient parallels in their respective commitments to obviate the necessity of extended treatment of Sherwood. Lillian Hellman represents a different case. In many ways she remains the hardiest dramatic survivor of the thirties, perhaps because, unlike Odets, she commanded a technique which could survive abrupt changes in the winds of doctrine. Doubtlessly her three plays of the decade reflect social concerns: *Days to Come* explicitly treats the theme of a strike, and *The Children's Hour* and *The Little Foxes* implicitly condemn the vindictiveness and rapacity of bourgeois society. Yet it is precisely because the corpus of her work in the thirties is small that I have not analyzed it at length. Although as a playwright pre-eminently concerned with the moral implications of drama Hellman is indeed relevant to our concerns, I have chosen rather to devote the limited space of this study to those dramatists who produced a considerable body of work in the 1930's or who were irrevocably involved with the political issues and forces of the age.

Part One

COMMITMENT AND THE
IDEA OF A THEATRE

THEATRE UNION: THEATRE IS A WEAPON

A revolutionary theatre without its most living element, the revolutionary public, is a contradiction which has no meaning.

ERWIN PISCATOR, "The Social Theatre"

CHAPTER THREE

THAT Theatre Union was primarily a class theatre is apparent from its initial manifesto:

We produce plays that deal boldly with the deep-going social conflicts, the economic, emotional, and cultural problems that confront the majority of the people. Our plays speak directly to this majority, whose lives usually are caricatured or ignored on the stage. We do not expect that these plays fall into the accepted social pattern. This is a new kind of professional theatre, based on the interests and hopes of the great mass of working people.[1]

The significant phrase is, of course, "the interests and hopes of the great mass of working people." Theatre Union—the first and only professional American Marxist theatre—was an overtly committed theatre; its *raison d'être* was to demonstrate the efficacy of the slogan: "Theatre is a weapon." "Theatre Union is based on a philosophy," Michael Blankfort, one of its members, asserted: "It has a 'touchstone.' "[2] And this "touchstone" was ideological; the group was less concerned with the creation of a theatrical style than with the presentation of plays which had at their core a coherent political point of view; its purpose was "to produce plays about the working class, written from the point of view of the working class,"[3] and to create a professional theatre supported primarily by working-class organizations. Theatre Union, in short, represented Marxism's most ambitious excursion into the mainstream of the American theatre.

That such a theatre should have emerged when it did is no accident. As the "first professional social theatre in

America,"[4] Theatre Union emerged as the impact of Marxism on American intellectual life reached its apogee in the mid-thirties. It is not surprising that Theatre Union's brief life (1933-37) should have coincided with the similarly brief reign of the proletarian novel. In fact, the intimacy of the group's relationship to its political commitment is revealed by the directness with which it reacted to contemporary social currents. It arose in response to specific social stimuli and disappeared when these stimuli were no longer operative.

Theatre Union had its inception in two interrelated phenomena of the early and mid-thirties: the growth of the amateur communist theatre—stimulated by the fact of the Depression—and the emergence of the Popular Front—during which period communists, socialists, and independent liberals found themselves in uneasy alliance. The first phenomenon provided the groundwork for the establishment of a professional "workers" theatre; and the second allowed the fledgling group to draw upon the professional talents of non-Marxist theatre personnel.

Despite such ambitious precursors of social theatre as the Workers' Drama League (1926) and the New Playwrights (1927),[5] there was little impetus toward the formation of radical theatre groups until the onset of the Depression. As social issues became of vital concern, amateur Marxist theatre groups—usually affiliated with social or labor organizations—sprang into prominence. Two groups became the spearhead of the movement, the German-speaking Prolet-Bühne, and the Workers' Laboratory Theatre of New York; and they specialized in a form of drama known as the "agit-prop," whose avowed purpose was, as its abbreviated name indicated, agitation and propaganda. This drama of didacticism and invective, held together by symbolic devices and rhythmic expression, was created for the specific purpose of serving its unorthodox theatrical environment:

labor meetings, rallies of the unemployed, etc. Although we shall analyze the agit-prop in greater detail in relationship to Odets' *Waiting for Lefty*, we may observe at this point that its primary weakness as an agitational device was that its magical repetition of slogans appealed essentially to the already converted. In its early stages, moreover, it was extremely crude both dramatically and theatrically (the performers were nonprofessionals) and separated entirely from the mainstream of American theatrical development.

Looking largely to European examples, the amateur radical groups who specialized in the agit-prop viewed the ideals and techniques of Broadway as inimical to political or theatrical virtue. As the Depression intensified, however, the movement flourished and by April, 1932, had grown to such an extent that a national festival and conference, the so-called Workers' Theatre Spartakiade and Conference, was convened to establish a central organization for the purpose of co-ordinating the activities of the various groups. The new organization, called the League of Workers' Theatres, inaugurated a number of theatrical activities, in addition to publishing its own journal, *Workers' Theatre*, and began to survey the radical theatre movement's new-found prosperity. It soon became apparent to the members of the League that if the radical theatre were to win adherents in an increasingly restive America, it would have to resort to greater professionalism; the agit-prop had its place, but it was, by its very nature, too limited to have wide appeal. As more intellectuals and theatre professionals found their way into the revolutionary movement, it was obvious that the principle of noncontamination by Broadway would have to be re-examined. Some of the die-hards still maintained the necessity of complete separation, but they were voices in the wilderness. *Workers' Theatre* affirmed the new attitude: "I think we must . . . examine the bourgeois theatre very closely, learn the methods it em-

ploys in its propaganda, learn and—as far as possible—
adopt the technique it uses to make its propaganda effective."[6] A new principle arose, that of "a theatre greater than
the labor movement but drawing its inspiration from the
latter and continuing the new social outlook on a broader
social scale."[7] In response to this trend, in September, 1933,
Workers' Theatre was rechristened *New Theatre*, and the
League of Workers' Theatres became the New Theatre
League. Eligibility for membership in the new group was
construed along the broad lines of the policy of the Popular
Front. The door was opened for the noncommunist professional who accepted the sole doctrinal commitment of opposition to "war, fascism and censorship," an invitation
many liberal theatre professionals accepted. *New Theatre*
proudly listed among its contributory editors Sidney
Howard, Lee Strasberg, and Hallie Flanagan. Since the
time was propitious for the radical theatre movement to
reach beyond its amateur status, the crude and sectarian
agit-prop theatre of the Prolet-Bühne and the WLT obviously would no longer suffice. Herbert Kline, the editor of
New Theatre, announced that "the day of the cliché and
mechanical statement has gone by for the workers' theatre."[8] The time had come for a departure from dramatized
poems, expressionistic satires, and mass recitations. Since
Marxism had won intellectual adherents and had begun to
influence the direction of American cultural life, a theatre
was obviously needed to reflect its new-found respecta-
bility.

In 1933 Theatre Union responded to this demand by creating a theatre which aimed at a level of esthetic excellence
hitherto impossible in the amateur radical theatre movement. Obviously, the agit-prop form was not conducive to
the development of major drama. Moreover, the very fact of
amateur status prevented the movement from sustaining
and developing theatrical talent. It was apparent that

Broadway was not going to provide patronage for revolutionary playwrights. There remained one answer: the establishment of a professional "working-class" theatre, which would cultivate its own class-conscious audience to support the kind of drama it felt must be produced. Such a theatre, proponents argued, would provide an outlet for revolutionary dramatists who were forced—by the absence of an alternative—to accept Broadway's terms. But, in the spirit of the Popular Front enunciated by the New Theatre League, Theatre Union did not construe "working-class" plays along strict, sectarian communist lines. The group aimed at creating the broadest-based Marxist theatre possible; not only was this consistent with the then current communist line, but it was a theatrical necessity if the group was to draw upon the reservoir of noncommunist Broadway talent. Time and again, the directors of Theatre Union were to assert its political inclusiveness and to disavow connection with any specific political doctrine, at least officially. In reply to a polemic by Lawson accusing the Union of insufficient specificity in its social criticism, Liston Oaks, a member of the executive board, asserted that "Theatre Union . . . is not an agit-prop theatre. It is a United Front theatre organized to produce plays that all honest militant workers and middle-class sympathizers can support."[9]

Its role as a United Front theatre continually presented Theatre Union with difficulties. On one hand, it was primarily organized for the purpose of presenting "working-class," that is, Marxist-oriented, plays which would lead inevitably to the assumption of a "progressive" political position; on the other, it was constrained by the necessity of Popular Front support to avoid a too-rigid affirmation of communist policy. Since political action is, of course, facilitated by specificity, as the communist critics of the Union continually affirmed, Theatre Union had to be ever-vigilant against the sin of "reformism." Oaks, in his rebuttal to Lawson, attempted to demonstrate that "political accuracy and ideological clarity does not necessitate specific organizational labels. . . . If liberals transfer the revolutionary content and implications of our plays into humanitarianism, that is not the fault of the playwright but the result of the confusion of liberal thinking."[10] Throughout its brief career Theatre Union moved precariously between its communist derivations and its United Front policy, a balancing act still possible in the heady political atmosphere of the mid-thirties.

Such, then, were the forces behind the formation of Theatre Union. How did it undertake to realize its ambitious attempt to create a professional "workers'" theatre? The directors of Theatre Union realized that the key to its survival lay in the creation of a new, atypical theatrical audience—an audience composed partially of militant intellectuals, but largely of the working class. A workers' theatre, they logically concluded, should be supported by the workers, a support Theatre Union attempted strenuously to provide. But the group was the victim of its own political semantics. We have observed that the words "worker" and "proletarian" connoted, in the Marxist lexicon, much more than belonging to the laboring force. More often than not, the proletarian novel or play was considered such not by virtue of its subject matter, but rather by virtue of its point of view. Thus from the outset Theatre Union was involved in a necessary contradiction. It attempted to create a theatre of protest which would express the "workers' point of view," i.e., a class-conscious Marxism, while, in actuality, this point of view was never that of any significant segment of the American working class. Theatre Union fought a perennial battle to achieve working-class support by organizing theatre parties, but despite sporadic success in its initial efforts, it was fighting a losing cause. It recognized, quite logically, that in order to survive it would have to depend upon an audience other than that of Broadway, and it made an all-out effort to enlist this support. Corps of Theatre Union council volunteers spoke nightly before labor groups, unions, and fraternal organizations;[11] its policy of low-priced seats (30¢ to $1.50) aimed at attracting a clientele that could not afford Broadway prices. Its efforts were not completely unrewarded. *Peace on Earth* would not have achieved its sixteen-week run without the support of theatre parties sponsored by such diverse organizations as the Communist party, the Socialist party, the Followers of Nature, the Jewelry Workers Club, the League of Women Voters, the Flatbush Culture Club, and the Bryn Mawr Alumni Association. Surely this was the Popular Front with a vengeance.[12]

But the unfortunate fact is that despite its efforts—despite continual assertions of a "dependable audience for plays dealing specifically with social questions"[13]—Theatre Union never did succeed in creating an audience for its plays which would ignore the "reactionary" verdicts of the Broadway critics. Labor and fraternal groups proved as susceptible to Broadway reviews as the bourgeoisie. Thus, *Stevedore*, which received a good press despite its "class" nature, had no trouble in finding an audience. However, subsequent plays fared so poorly that the ailing Union, which had been housed in Eva Le Gallienne's old Civic Repertory Theatre on 14th Street, in a last desperate effort decided to confront Broadway directly, and moved into the heart of the mid-town theatrical district for its final presentation—Lawson's *Marching Song*—a move which was dictated by the recognition that Theatre Union had failed in its attempt to create a dependable working-class audience. The inability to create a dependable audience lay at the heart of Theatre Union's failure. Without direct patronage, it succumbed to the commercial vagaries which it so consistently attacked. But although basic, this was not the sole

cause of Theatre Union's difficulties. As a political theatre
continually aware of its ideological function, it had to face
problems extrinsic to play production. For example, administration remained a permanent difficulty. Theatre Union,
committed to "collective, democratic" leadership, would
not permit authority to be centralized. All administrative
decisions had to come from a production committee, which
altered from one play to the next, depending upon who was
free at the time. Moreover, when emergency problems arose
during rehearsals, it was necessary to obtain the authority
of the entire executive board.[14] Thus Theatre Union's commitment to "collective" leadership compounded its administrative difficulties.

Political considerations similarly influenced the group's
attitude toward its acting company. Although the executive
board had started the theatre with professionals of varying
degrees of sympathy for what the plays stood for in order to
make a beginning,[15] it recognized the need and the advantage of a permanent group of actors—politically "aware" as
well as technically competent. Obviously, if the highest
production standards were to be achieved actors would
have to be hired on the primary basis of talent, not political
awareness. This presented difficulties, since a few of the
nonpolitical thespians balked at certain lines and bits of
business as "soapbox." The militant actors, however, soon
undertook the conversion of their recalcitrant companions.[16] Although it could not afford a permanent company,
Theatre Union made an effort to recast actors who had appeared in its previous productions—a significant gesture
towards the ideal of the permanent theatre. And in the season of 1935–36, seven actors were selected as the nucleus
of a potentially permanent company. But a large permanent
company was rejected on more than merely financial
grounds. Although the Union recognized the stylistic advantages of such an arrangement (as witnessed by the ex-

cellent productions of the Group), it feared that a large, closed acting company might result "in the dangerous tendency to choose plays to fit the acting company, rather than for their intrinsic merit as working-class drama."[17] The esthetic consideration had to take second place to the political consideration. Consequently, Theatre Union augmented its small permanent group of actors from previous casts, from Broadway, from other theatrical sources, and from its own studio.

The most difficult single problem that Theatre Union had to face because of its ideological commitment was the discovery of plays that were both politically aware and dramatically sound. When a theatre limits itself on subject matter as stringently as did Theatre Union, the script famine becomes even more acute than when the only considerations are box-office potential and personal taste. Thus, although the group was in continual search for suitable plays to present, so few were found that it had to have plays specifically composed by members of its immediate group (Maltz, Sklar, Peters).[18] This action brought forth criticism —in the late, faltering moments of the group's existence— that it was a closed corporation which discouraged new talent.[19] The problem of play selection was further complicated by the "collective" nature of the group's administration. When a script came into the office, the play-reading department, on deciding that it had possibilities, passed it on to the executive board of twelve men and women. If they found it acceptable, a meeting of the entire board was called, and the play was given a general reading. After several other readings a decision to produce the play or not to produce it had to be reached. Once the play was accepted, a playwriting committee was appointed to work with the author on script revision. Theatre Union held with no theories of the inviolability of the author's words. Frequently it demanded that changes be made, in the words of Michael Blankfort, "to fit the needs of its mass audience," i.e., for the sake of ideological correctness.[20] For example, *Stevedore* was revised three times. Peters had originally written it in 1930 under the title *Wharf Nigger*; but between that date and the Union's production of the play in 1934, he had found political enlightenment, and felt that the play dealt inadequately with the "real social forces" behind the racial conflict in the South. He and Sklar thus set about writing a new play which attempted to show that the Negro question "was not a racial issue at all, but an economic one."[21]

It is not surprising, then, that Theatre Union had difficulty in discovering adequate scripts. Many playwrights found themselves, in the words of Blankfort, "temperamentally incapable of collective work." They could not surmount the innumerable ideological roadblocks thrust in their path. For in addition to being passed on by the playwriting committee, the script had to receive (when the nature of the play called for it) the approval of a worker in the field with which the play dealt. Thus Negro and white longshoremen read *Stevedore*; Italian refugees read *Bitter Stream*. Finally the revised script was again read by the executive board, and, if definitely accepted, a production committee and director were appointed who, with the author, then decided upon a scenic designer and cast.[22] Since there had to be among all of these people a fundamental unanimity concerning what the play must say, a unanimity based upon the group's political "touchstone," it is no wonder that most of Theatre Union's scripts came from within the group itself.

What, then, was the dramatic contribution of Theatre Union? An investigation of the group's seven productions reveals that in each case the political touchstone remained paramount. Surveying the group's achievement at the time of the presentation of *Black Pit*, Margaret Larkin pride-fully noted the variety of the Union's productions. She observed, however, that despite diversity of style the plays all possessed a common aim: they all "laid bare the class forces surrounding each situation, pointing the way out."[23] "The way out" in each instance lay in the acceptance of Marxist social theory and a willingness to ally, in United Front, with all opponents of the capitalist system. All of the plays were either totally or partially proletarian in subject matter. *Stevedore, Black Pit,* and *Marching Song* stressed the class nature of industrial and racial strife; *Peace on Earth* attacked war as an instrument of capitalist expansion; and the Union's three foreign works—Wolf's *Sailors of Cattaro*, Brecht's *Mother*, and Silone's *Fontamara* (adapted by Victor Wolfson under the title *Bitter Stream*)—came from the pens of several of Europe's leading Marxist writers. (Silone had, as yet, not defected.) They stressed in turn the necessity of revolutionary preparation, the conversion of a proletarian to Marxism, and the oppression of the Italian peasantry by the Fascists.

Despite the Marxist bias in each of these plays, the lessons each contained were not always sufficiently explicit to satisfy the more sectarian communist critics. For this the Theatre Union's Popular Front role was partly responsible; it did not wish, after all, to alienate noncommunist support. Partly it resulted from a most rigid interpretation of the role of proletarian literature. Works which diverged from formula were often suspect, despite the attempts of the less sectarian critics to demonstrate that class-consciousness did not necessarily demand cliché.

The group's initial production, *Peace on Earth* (1933), for example, received the following chiding from William Gardener in the *New Masses*:

The theme and story of the play are not to be endorsed unreservedly. . . . There is too much emphasis on Professor Peter

Owens' individual sacrifice. Apparently the authors lacked confidence in their ability to achieve the desired dramatic and emotional effect by basing their emphasis more directly on the working class itself, through its organized representatives in the play.[24]

This dissent, however, was drowned in a chorus of praise from the left-wing press; for opposition to war was, after all, a cause to which most could wholeheartedly subscribe. But *Peace on Earth* is not concerned with generalized protest in the manner of *What Price Glory?*, *Johnny Johnson*, or *Idiot's Delight*. It is specific in its attribution of war to the logic of capitalism. Its antiwar theme is, in actuality, a device to assert the fact of another very real war, class war. The evils which Maltz and Sklar itemized are the evils which, according to Marxism, inevitably arise from an oppressive capitalism: the murder of militant strikers, the suppression of radical opinion, the alliance of religion and education with finance capital, the corruption and subservience of the police, the control of the media of communication by vested interests. The catalytic elements in the plot are two familiar standbys of the proletarian genre: the conflict between a group of defiant workers and their capitalist oppressors, and the conversion of an uncommitted individual to militancy and, ultimately, martyrdom. But the authors of *Peace on Earth* are less concerned with the solidarity of the striking longshoremen (after all, this is a United Front play) than with the conversion of Professor Owens to social awareness. At first happily ensconced in his ivory tower, he ultimately comes to recognize the meaning of the strikers' action. He confronts his educational superiors with the injustices he has observed and is censured for his radicalism. Finally, he interrupts a commencement exercise to protest the granting of honors to a trustee who, because of his financial interests, has encouraged violence against the militant strikers. In the tradition of many a proletarian hero

Owens is rewarded for his honesty with a frame-up and goes steadfastly to a martyr's death.

Peace on Earth is significant as a transitional work which touches on various themes which were to be more fully exploited in later proletarian drama. Stylistically, it reveals at times its agit-prop roots in the directness of its call to activism: the play's last lines are the slogan "Fight with us, fight against war." Despite the realism of specific scenes, its synoptic, staccato pace is reminiscent of much experimental drama of the 1920's. In fact, the last act of *Peace on Earth* abandons itself entirely to expressionism, a structural transition which mars the consistency of the work. Above all, however, *Peace on Earth* reveals Theatre Union's determination to woo the noncommunist left. The facts of class strife are circumscribed by the greater issue of war or peace. Maltz and Sklar attempted, not altogether unsuccessfully as reviews from the noncommunist left demonstrate, to link a condemnation of war to an acceptance of the Marxist interpretation of its causation. If leftists could not all agree on the skill of the production of *Peace on Earth*, they could at least agree with its fundamental thesis. They, too, were "agin' sin."

There were no doubts, however, of the success of the Union's second production, *Stevedore*; even the "bourgeois" critics praised it, although this verdict was not received without mixed reaction. After all, did not Broadway criticism of *Peace on Earth* reveal the effectiveness of its class analysis? Had not leftist critics continually affirmed that the condemnation of proletarian literature by the bourgeois critics was inevitable? Thus, the paradox of Theatre Union's theatrical position is revealed; although good Broadway reviews were a requisite to the filling of the more expensive seats in the house, the militants feared that the good reviews might compromise the effectiveness of the play's class criticism. The inevitable answer was that such praise had its roots in "mass pressure" which the Broadway critics did not dare to ignore.

In any case, *Stevedore*, with the blessing of Broadway, was Theatre Union's most successful production. Despite Lawson's charge that the play lacked specificity ("what union did [the strikers] . . . belong to?")[25] most radical critics were effusive in their praise. Mike Gold led the play's champions with characteristic enthusiasm: "When big, lovable, motherly Binnie who runs a lunchroom and bosses the husky stevedores with her spicy tongue, picks up an old gun and pops off one of the gangsters, the audience cheers. It cheers not only because a brute is dead, but because something has happened in the soul of a working-class mother."[26]

Perhaps there were those among the spectators of *Stevedore* who responded similarly to Binnie's spiritual enlightenment, but most responded to the simplicity of the play's melodramatic line. Peters and Sklar succeeded—where Maltz and Sklar had failed—in realizing their theme of class warfare structurally. In *Peace on Earth* the framing of Owens is gratuitously introduced in order to enforce the play's thesis; in *Stevedore* Lonnie's frame-up for the alleged rape of a white woman is intrinsic to the melodramatic plot. Thus, *Stevedore* moves forward with headlong directness to its violent conclusion in which Negro and white longshoremen fight side by side against the forces of reaction. Race prejudice is inexorably tied to economic factors: Lonnie is framed because he is the most militant of the Negro stevedores who support the fledgling union, and it comes as hardly a surprise that he should be offered as the traditional martyr to the proletarian cause. Indeed, *Stevedore* continually points the moral that race prejudice must disappear when Negro and white workers recognize their common class unity. In the words of the union song, "Black and white together / We shall not be moved." The Negro stevedores are joined in battle by their white comrades and

put the forces of evil to rout. It is as it should be in a melodrama; the cavalry always arrives in the nick of time. *Stevedore* succeeded because it appealed on the most primitive
dramatic level. In the words of Robert Benchley, in *The
New Yorker*, it was "a hell of a good show."[27]

Of all the plays which Theatre Union produced, the one
which aroused the greatest sectarian criticism was Maltz's
Black Pit (1935); for although it was proletarian in subject matter—it dealt with the life of the miners—and point
of view, it attempted something which ran dangerously
close to heresy, the sympathetic portrayal of a "scab"—a
man who betrays his class. In the black and white world of
class struggle such an undertaking was indeed hazardous,
and while radical critics recognized that Maltz portrayed
the horror and degradation of such an action, many felt he
might well have made a more positive statement. Joseph
North observed in the *New Masses*:

When the playwright sets out to tell his audience of workmen
that obloquy and limitless misery are the lot of the traitor, he
tells a tale more than twice told; . . . if through indirection the
tragedy of the stool pigeon would cast into bolder relief the
heroism of the rank and file (for that is the great reality) then
Maltz's emphasis could be understood.[28]

But despite its divergence from the formula of the proletarian play, *Black Pit* leaves no doubt as to its ideological
position. Joe Kovarsky, because of his defection, is anathe-
matized with a degree of fervor that is possible only in the
fully converted. No economic or personal difficulty can
justify the sell out; in the long run the worker's only salvation is to make common cause with his class. In the end,
rejected by those who loved and trusted him, Joe recognizes
the folly of his action: "What good get t'ings by be false to
odern [sic] miner? . . . Bett'r be starve, bett'r be live in hole
lak animal."[29] Maltz attempted to point his moral nega-

tively, but he pointed it clearly nevertheless. In place of melodrama he substituted a proletarian morality play: what does it profit a worker, he asked, if in gaining the world he loses his class?

It is a sad commentary upon the skill of American radical playwrights that the most significant, though not the most commercially successful, of the plays which Theatre Union produced came from the pens of Europeans. Friedrich Wolf's *Sailors of Cattaro* and Brecht's version of Gorki's *Mother* are undoubtedly the best of the group's seven plays. (Silone's *Fontamara* is certainly one of the great works of the decade—one of the very few genuine proletarian novels —but Victor Wolfson's adaptation, contemporary reviews indicate, unfortunately captured more of the letter than the spirit of the book.) Perhaps the European was more fundamentally involved in the radical experience than the American, who often seemed to come to his commitment more from an act of conscious will than from personal total involvement; certainly the American thirties produced no radical novels comparable to *Fontamara* or *La Condition humaine*, nor any playwright of the stature of O'Casey or Brecht.

Wolf's *Sailors of Cattaro*, for example, faces certain fundamental facts of the revolutionary experience and succeeds largely because it does not melodramatize. The class struggle is not viewed as a conflict between all-virtuous heroes and all-evil villains, but rather as a social fact which must be accepted and acted upon. The playwright does not exploit the emotive nature of the revolutionary situation. Although the sailors' grievances are duly listed, Wolf presents no scenes of wanton brutality, his concern being with the problem of revolutionary action manifest in the dramatic situation. The play is based upon the actual abortive revolt of the sailors of the Austrian navy in the bay of Cattaro, an inlet of the Adriatic sea, in the last year of the first

World War. Angered by their grievances and inspired by the expected support of the Viennese socialists, the crews of several battleships mutinied, demanding immediate overtures for world peace and democratic shipboard reforms. But the expected support from the mainland did not materialize, the revolt was quickly crushed, and the mutinous leaders executed.

Wolf is concerned less with the heroics of the Cattaro revolt than with the causes of its failure. He takes as his text Lenin's statement that "you can't play with revolution. Once it starts you've got to follow it through to the end."[30] Franz Rasch, Wolf's hero, is not the monolithic, all-virtuous protagonist of American proletarian drama. His militancy is indeed evident, and he fights to the end to prevent the sailors from accepting the captain's offer of clemency; but he is torn between his knowledge that autocratic action is demanded by the specific revolutionary situation and his reluctant willingness to act without the democratic consent of the Sailor's Council. This conflict is the key dramatic situation in the play, and it is not unequivocally resolved. Stonawski, the advocate of immediate action, observes that unless Rasch assumes direct command the revolt is in danger. But Franz refuses to compromise his democratic revolutionary ideals by assuming dictatorial control. Stonawski—and he is confirmed by the turn of events— counters with the traditional revolutionary excuse for the abrogation of democratic rule: there just isn't time. And yet he does not fully assent to the militant cry that "to debate is death," that Rasch is wrong. In the long run, Stonawski asserts, Franz is right, even if he has let "a sentimental sense of loyalty to the council overcome his loyalty to the fleet" (in other words, a too-intense dedication to democratic principles overcomes loyalty to the revolution). In the end despite his vacillation, Rasch emerges most heroically. He adamantly refuses to accept the captain's terms and exhorts the sailors to keep the revolutionary faith. His final statement in the face of defeat was the slogan with which the exiled Wolf was himself greeted when he arrived in Moscow: "Comrades, next time—better!" (p. 109)

Although the play was generally well received in the radical press, there were those who recognized the dangerous implications of Wolf's tactical equivocations. Burnshaw wrote in the *New Masses*, "Wolf . . . has failed to indicate the need for politically developed leadership, such as the Bolsheviks gave to the revolting sailors and soldiers of Czarist Russia. . . . The successful Bolsheviks . . . realized that in every revolutionary endeavor leadership must be delegated to politically clear individuals and groups guided by principles of the revolutionary vanguard."[31] But the superior quality of the *Sailors of Cattaro* was so manifest that even this objection was not too strenuously pursued.

Erwin Piscator pointed out that Wolf took his place with the "dramatic" contents of the drama, in opposition to Brecht's "epic" theatre: "By the dramatic principle we mean that treatment of the subject matter along lines of theatrical or dramatic movement which leads to its simplification, its crystallization, allowing freer stressing of political mood . . . than could the corresponding epic treatment."[32] But, he affirmed, "from time to time in political drama, the epic element has seemed more immediate, more indispensable, than the dramatic." And in its presentation of Brecht's *Mother* (1935), Theatre Union offered one of the first American epic theatre productions—albeit somewhat diluted.

Much has, of course, been written of late about Brecht's esthetics, indeed perhaps more than has been written about his work itself. Just how practical the concept of alienation —"Verfremdungseffekt"—has proven in theatrical terms is difficult to ascertain. Martin Esslin points out that it has yet to be proved that Brecht's theories have any validity apart

from his own works and productions, which they were intended to explain and justify.[33] And Brecht himself towards
the end of his career warned against a too-serious application of his esthetic: "My theories are altogether far more
naive than my way of expressing them might allow one to
suspect."[34] The difficulty is, of course, the dubious concept
that action has its roots in rational awareness, that a demonstration of fact—apart from emotional considerations—can
result in a fundamental change in human behavior. But let
us take Brecht's own counsel and not apply the concept of
alienation too literally; obviously action demands emotional
involvement. The question is one of primacy: emotion must
be grounded in knowledge if it is to be effective. One of the
best descriptions of Brecht's purpose is contained in one of
the earliest discussions of his work in English. Eva Gold-
beck wrote in 1935:

Whereas the old theatre tries to get below the level of the mind
and to use brute emotional force on our subconscious, the epic
theatre tries to make our own reason awaken and direct our emotions. The difference in emphasis and method is dictated by the
difference in purpose. The theatre of entertainment, though pro-
voking a show of excitement, really keeps us passive; the theatre
of education wants us to remain as calm and collected as possible in order to arouse us to ultimate action. . . . The drama has
become an object lesson.[35]

In short, the purpose of the work of art is not merely to show
the world as it is, but, by means of this demonstration, to
change it.

If we are still baffled by much of Brechtian theory after
twenty-five years of debate as to its applicability, imagine
the reaction of the producers of Theatre Union, bred in a
school of playwriting which demanded the maximum in
audience identification. The forms of the Brechtian theatre were not unfamiliar—its presentationalism seemed
grounded in European expressionism—but the spirit was

something else. How, for example, were actors striving for believability, by virtue of their recent initiation into the mysteries of what later was to be termed "the Method," to realize Brecht's idea that the actor must *not* identify himself with the character, but, rather, interpret him, both as actor and as critic? Consequently, the Theatre Union's production of *Mother* actually vitiated the intended epic effect by making the play, within the confines of its presentational form, as realistic as possible. In fact, Brecht himself went to New York towards the end of 1935 to attempt to forestall the conversion of his epic play to conventionality, to prevent the re-insertion of the naturalistic detail he had purposely omitted. He did not quite succeed, and the performance apparently vacillated between epic and naturalistic styles.[36]

Mother was born of the fullness of Brecht's Marxist commitment. It is, in fact, an expansion of the brief, didactic form of the *Lehrstück*, whose avowed purpose was the teaching, within an almost ritualistic simplicity, of certain specific social and communal lessons. The style (more so in the original German than in Peters' adaptation) is dry and matter-of-fact; its didactic elements are ever dominant. In keeping with epic techniques, lantern slides comment upon the action by means of photos of demonstrations, prisoners, the Czar, and working men; by informative statements such as "On May first the workers of Tversk demonstrate against the wage cut," or through revolutionary slogans such as "Class Struggle," or "Exploiter." Thus did Brecht attempt to demonstrate that individual action could no longer be understood in isolation from the historical and social forces which determine it.

In keeping with epic theory, *Mother* rejects the logically constructed well-made play. The drama of the conversion to Marxism of Pelage Vlasova is related in a series of independently constructed scenes which begin with the abortive revolution of 1905 and end with the revolution of 1917. Each situation is complete in itself: the mother distributing clandestine pamphlets by wrapping sandwiches in them, the mother educating the teacher in the ways of socialism, the mother beaten bloody in a sidewalk demonstration, etc. The total effect is thus achieved cumulatively through a series of montage-like images which approximate the technique of the cinema. The unifying element is the play's didacticism, its technique. In Brechtian theatre, play and production cannot be separated. Unlike American proletarian literature, in which didacticism often seems extrinsic to the work's essential form (the form, more often than not, being utterly conventional), neither Brechtian drama nor theory can be considered apart from its "message." The message *is* the play.

Theatre Union's last two productions, Victor Wolfson's *Bitter Stream* (an adaptation of *Fontamara*) and Lawson's *Marching Song*, took place in 1936 and 1937, respectively. Both were Marxist in ideology. *Marching Song*, which was intended to be the model of a proletarian play, dealt with the theme of class strife in terms of a sit-down strike in an automobile town. Overtly doctrinaire in ideology, it represented Lawson at his most polemical; we shall defer detailed consideration of *Marching Song* until a later chapter on Lawson's dramatic development. Since *Bitter Stream* was never published, we can only relate the judgment of its contemporaries. Reviews indicate that although it followed closely the plot of *Fontamara*, emphasizing the oppressive nature of fascism and Bernardo's conversion, most critics agreed that it failed to capture the scope and color of Silone's novel. Thus the record of Theatre Union productions confirms Blankfort's assertion that they had a political touchstone. Despite occasional sectarian criticism, beneath each play lay the Marxist substructure. The record of the group's dramatic achievement—particularly its native contribution—is unfortunately not impressive, but it does possess that most dubious of virtues, consistency.

The difficulties of Theatre Union were, of course, primarily financial. It is estimated that it sustained an annual deficit of over $15,000.[37] The leftist press offered several reasons for the group's lack of support. It was claimed that the Union had not done what it might have in creating a labor audience; the *Daily Worker* asked why the group had failed to bring its work to new audiences by using a mobile troupe for performances in union halls and settlement houses.[38] But by far the harshest criticism arose from the group's concern for the Broadway verdict, its "continual inner struggle between the desire to do plays which would be afraid of nothing and the knowledge that such productions would be lambasted by the critics and avoided by the moneyed patrons."[39]

The fact is that the brief heyday of proletarian literature had ended. By 1937 the great wave of indignation had abated; liberals who had taken a plague-on-both-your-houses attitude toward the major political parties found that they could, after all, find virtue in the Roosevelt administration. In fact, the Federal Theatre, in offering a low-priced (or free) theatre which did not have to worry about commercial exigencies, stole much of Theatre Union's thunder. The leftist theatre movement either collapsed or was absorbed by Broadway or other groups; *New Theatre*, as well as Theatre Union, folded in 1937. Moreover, the Popular Front was breaking up. True, it remained the official communist line until the end of the second World War (save, of course, for the period of the Nonaggression pact), but the New Deal captured many of the liberals, and the Trotsky purge trials alienated the socialists. It is not surprising, then, that the disbanding of Theatre Union should be shortly followed by recriminatory charges and countercharges, that

Mike Gold, for example, should accuse four members of the union's board of "Trotskyism."[40] The political honeymoon was over. The moment in American political and theatrical history which Theatre Union epitomized passed, and with it passed America's one and only professional revolutionary theatre.

4

THE GROUP THEATRE: THEATRE IS COLLECTIVE ART

The Group's inclusive philosophy adumbrated a cosmos; therefore the Group's function, even its duty, was to become a cosmos. It had to provide what society itself failed to provide.

HAROLD CLURMAN, *The Fervent Years*

CHAPTER FOUR

BECAUSE the Group Theatre was the theatre of *Waiting for Lefty* and *Awake and Sing!* it has generally been viewed as a product of the radical ferment of the thirties; inasmuch as the plays and policies of the Group were directed by this ferment the designation is not inaccurate. Indeed, in its time, the Group was invariably classed with the theatres of social protest. But, in another sense, this classification is incorrect. The Group was indeed the reflection of radical ferment, but it was not—as in the case of Theatre Union—a *product* of this ferment. In fact, the Group actually shared fewer common purposes with Theatre Union than with the art theatres of the twenties; after all, it was an offspring of the Theatre Guild. The Group's rallying cry was not "Theatre is a Weapon in the Class Struggle," but rather "Theatre is an Art which Reflects Life." It is in this broader sense that the Group was a social theatre; it owes its impetus not to the radical climate of the early thirties, but rather to the legacy of the new movement in theatre which had swept the playhouses of Russia, France, Germany—and to a lesser extent the playhouses of England and America— in the latter half of the nineteenth century and the first decades of the twentieth. The Group's forebears were not the revolutionary proponents of the agit-prop, but rather the great art theatres to which we owe the legacy of modern drama: the Moscow Art Theatre and its various studios in Russia, the Freie Bühne in Germany, the Théâtre Libre and the Vieux-Colombier in France, the Independent Theatre in England, and the Provincetown Players and the Theatre

Guild in the United States. Stanislavski and Copeau, not Marx and Engels, were the Group's patron saints.

The Group Theatre shared common aims and ideals with the great permanent theatres listed above; it inherited, and adapted to its own needs, three basic ideas of what a theatre should be: (1) The idea of Theatre as Art, (2) the idea of Theatre as a Collective, and (3) the idea of Theatre as Communion.

The tenets are mutually dependent. Although theatre was an art, it was also, to the founders of the Group, a necessarily collective art; thus esthetic questions of style and production could not be separated from the problems of a *group*. Clurman writes of the Group's beginning. "From consideration of acting and plays we were plunged into a chaos of life questions, with the desire and hope of making possible some new order and integration. From an experiment in the theatre we were in some way impelled to an experiment in living."[1] Since theatre was a necessarily collective art, it demanded a collective approach. The unity of theatrical production, Clurman pointed out, was not one that sprang out of an abstract sense of taste or craftsmanship, but, rather, out of a unity of feeling and thought and need among a group of people that had formed itself either consciously or unconsciously. Once this motivating force had resulted in the formation of a dedicated group, it was essential to do everything possible to affirm the group's collective nature. Thus the Group Theatre was considerably more than a play-producing unit. Its theatre artists—actors, playwrights, directors, designers—were integrated into most phases of the theatre's activity; the Group engaged in continual drives to interest new theatrical workers; it set up a number of projects to train its own members as leaders, teachers, and directors; above all, it protected its actors from the vagaries of the Broadway market by supporting a permanent acting company of from twenty to thirty performers for ten years.

But Theatre was viewed as more than a collective in the service of art. This belief the Group shared with the radical theatre movement: art did not exist for its own sake; the development of technical facility and collective purpose had to serve a goal beyond the artistic growth of the theatre's individual members. Theatre technique had to be founded on "life values." In the program to 1931– Clurman wrote: "In the end . . . the development of playwrights, actors, repertory and the rest are important only as they lead to the creation of a tradition of common values, an active consciousness of a common way of looking at and dealing with life. . . ."[2] Theatre was, then, a communion between artist and audience. Thus the Group was dedicated to producing plays which spoke in the authentic voice of its time. (Of all its plays only one—Piscator's adaptation of Dreiser's *An American Tragedy, The Case of Clyde Griffiths*—was not by a contemporary American playwright.) Actors were, after all, not merely artists; they were citizens of a community. It was the purpose of the Group to assert the artist's role as citizen not only within the theatrical collective itself, but also within the context of the artist's larger societal obligation. Ideas in the theatre did not exist in isolation; they had to be transmitted to an audience, "for it is the audience (seen as a 'community') that has given birth to its artists."[3]

Thus, the Group's dedication to plays which reflected contemporary social issues sprang from its conception of theatre as a social, as well as an artistic, institution. But this social role was not conceived in any revolutionary sense; theatre was communion, but it was not necessarily revolutionary communion. The Group Theatre did not attempt to cultivate, as did Theatre Union, a proletarian audience. Although it rejected Broadway values, it is significant that it worked within Broadway's commercial framework. The Group was committed to plays which concerned contemporary social problems, but it was not committed to any specific social solution. The Group's commitment was more *moral* than political; it felt compelled to raise and reflect social questions, rather than to offer a uniform solution. If the Group possessed one generic political assumption, it was that social problems were soluble; but beyond a general affirmation of the feasibility of political action, the directors of the Group affirmed no overt political commitment.

A good play for us is . . . one which . . . is the image or symbol of the living problems of our time. These problems are chiefly moral and social and our feeling is that they must be faced with an essentially affirmative attitude, that is, in the belief that to all of them there must be some answer, an answer that should be considered operative for at least the humanity of our times and place.[4]

But although the Group was not primarily a political theatre, it was impossible, considering the time of its existence, for it to remain free from the storm of political controversy which swirled around it. The life of the Group coincided with the life of the thirties, and it is inevitable that a theatre dedicated to "life values" should become necessarily embroiled in the turbulence of its decade. "Every wind of doctrine was reflected in some corresponding ripple in the flow of our lives," wrote Clurman,[5] and as the decade progressed the Group's lack of political specificity was to be challenged both by the orthodox Marxist press and its own small core of militants.

At the beginning of the Group's life, despite the onset of the Depression, Clurman reports that there was very little political discussion. Although the production of a Soviet play, *Red Rust*, was contemplated, the interest in it was more esthetic than political. Why—Clurman anticipates the objection—despite all the talk about the need of facing the times and of finding affirmative answers to the social problems of the day, did politics receive so little attention from himself, Strasberg and Cheryl Crawford, the Group's founders? He replied for himself that his training and inclination had been chiefly esthetic, and that he always demonstrated a reluctance to delve into problems while they remained outside the range of his experience.[6] In any case, none of the founders was primarily involved, in the aftermath of the Crash, with the recognition of the failure of capitalism; their major concern was the practical problem of organizing a theatre.

Clurman reports his initial contact with the radical theatre movement. Although the Marxists did not fully approve of the Group's initial production, *The House of Connelly* (they claimed Green sentimentalized the South), they were in sympathy with several of the "progressive tendencies" in the Group manifesto. Strasberg and Clurman were consequently invited to a symposium upon "Revolution and the Theatre" held by the John Reed Club of New York. Clurman did not anticipate either his introduction as a middle-of-the-roader (as compared with the Right of the Theatre Guild and the Left of the Workers' Theatre), or the barrage of epithets which followed his assertion that a play did not have to deal with obvious social themes in order to have social significance. Here for the first time he heard the slogan of the revolutionary theatre movement: "The theatre is a weapon." The experience, he relates, was "my first lesson in the temper of the thirties."[7]

It was by no means his last. Before the production of Lawson's *Success Story*, he noted a sudden preoccupation with social, economic and political matters among the actors of the company. And when the Group achieved financial success with the nonpolitical *Men in White*, dissatisfaction among Group actors became apparent. The *New Masses* reported that the cast fought hard to have lines inserted which would have allowed the play "to say something important about a hospital system which is kept alive by the whim of the wealthy."[8] The Group, some actors feared, was becoming too involved with psychological rather than social problems. Moreover, in contrast with Theatre Union's ticket ceiling of $1.50, the Group was still catering to the carriage trade at Broadway prices. A militant core sprang up within the acting company. (Odets reported to the House Un-American Activities Committee that of a total Group Theatre membership of 35 there were four or five, including himself, who were connected with the Communist party;[9] Kazan claimed a party membership of nine.)[10] But militant or not, all, in Clurman's words, "sought social knowledge." The perennial political debates on Roosevelt, NRA, communism, and fascism drowned out theatrical tabletalk. Controversy was in the air and the actors responded. "They seemed to hanker after barricade dramatics, a sense of being in the fight rather than on the side lines."[11]

Political objections to different plays were raised at various stages of the Group's career. Melvin Levy's *Gold Eagle Guy* failed, some actors claimed, to deal with contemporary social issues, an objection which caused Clurman to write a forty-page paper in which he pointed out that the Group's aim "was not and never had been to become a political theatre."[12] Despite Clurman's assertion that the theme of *Rocket to the Moon* was the inability of love to flourish in an acquisitive society, there were many who felt that Odets, in concerning himself with the amatory problems of a middle-class dentist, had betrayed his revolutionary roots. Similarly there were those who objected to Shaw's *Gentle People*, despite its obvious fascist parallels, on the grounds that the play might be thought cute, that the Group was indulging in quaint melodramatics rather than helping to change the world.[13]

In many cases, the group's self-criticism was more intense than that leveled at it by the Marxist press. Once the group had, in radical eyes, allied itself with the left by virtue of the early plays of Odets, Marxist criticism tended to be of a "corrective," rather than of a vituperative nature. After all, there was great prestige for the left in counting the Group among its supporters. Had not *Lefty* been produced by Group actors at a New Theatre League benefit? It was not unusual, therefore, to find the Marxists bending over backwards to affirm the revolutionary intentions of the Group's theatrical credo. Against the charge that the Group avoided proletarian themes, Norman Stevens wrote in *New Theatre*: "It is possible that the richest art of our time may developed out of the . . . attempt of the middle class to free themselves from the fears and phobias of the past and to take their place with the workers in the struggle for a better world."[14] The Group, in essence, was envisioned as a middle-class Theatre Union.

But the Group—despite its radical core—never allied itself fully with the radical theatre movement (though many of its artists participated independently in such groups as Theatre of Action and Theatre Collective). In fact, the directors of the Group found themselves in the crossfire between Left and Right, between the radicals who asserted that they were not going far enough left and the Broadway critics who often asserted that they went too far. Indeed, the Group's most overtly Marxist play (along with Odets' playlets), *The Case of Clyde Griffiths*, was severely castigated by the critics who resented its revolutionary didacticism, an attack which caused the Group directors to respond, this time to Broadway, that it did not— as a theatre—affirm any specific political doctrine, that it was not responsible for the political views of its playwrights.[15]

What *is* a social play? This was the question that was often lost sight of in the intensity of debate. The Marxists, although they often disagreed on particulars, could agree that social drama had to have at its base some fundamental Marxist criticism of capitalism; most Broadway critics, on the other hand, often merely equated the form with any dramatic didacticism. Although the Group was committed to plays which dealt with contemporary social issues, its personnel did not agree on the overtness of this criticism From the touchstone of Theatre Union, the record of Group plays reveals only five which suggest specific Marxist solutions; but if we accept as our criterion for social drama those plays which challenge basic social attitudes or institutions, which suggest social alternatives, either reformist or radical, or those plays which demand personal or collective action in response to specific social or political phenomena (e.g., the Depression, war, fascism), then the record of the Group's social drama is not inconsiderable. In fact only three or four of the Group's twenty-four plays do not meet the requirements of these criteria.

The Group produced five plays which suggest specific Marxist correctives: Odets' first four plays and Piscator's *Case of Clyde Griffiths*. Criticism of capitalism—often from an implied Marxist point of view—is manifest in the Siftons' *1931–*, in Lawson's Group plays, in Odets' later works, and in the exposé of the success myth in *Gold Eagle Guy* and *The Big Night*. Paul Green's two Group plays deal respectively with the death of the old Southern order and the absurdity of war. Robert Ardrey's two plays have for their themes "the enslavement of the individual by his job in a society in which the job for the individual is unconnected with a creative purpose"[16] and the necessity of facing the problems of the world. Irwin Shaw's *Gentle People* relates a fascist parable, and his *Retreat from Pleasure* and Odets' *Night Music* mirror the mood of young Americans in the period of the phony war. Nellie Childs' *Weep for the Virgins* deals with the theme of proletarian frustration. Even *Men in White* and *My Heart's in the Highlands*, although basically unconcerned with social problems, are contemporary in subject matter. It cannot be said of the Group that it evaded the issues of its day.

Much of the Group's reputation for being a radical theatre arose because of the phenomenon of Odets. The emergence of *Lefty* and its subsequent critical success on Broadway created the image of a theatre of militancy. But this image was, in fact, illusory. Surely the Group was proud that the foremost revolutionary talent of the day had emerged from within its own midst, but Odets' work was not produced because it was consciously revolutionary. Clurman rejected *The Silent Partner* not because of its proletarian subject matter, but because he felt that it needed more work. It was Odets' dramatic, not his revolutionary, voice that the Group cherished.[17] But there can be no denying that there was strong sentiment in the Group for the production of leftist plays. Although Clurman's standards were ultimately esthetic, one cannot imagine that the Group would have produced a politically conservative play. One wonders what reaction the Group personnel would have had if its theatre, rather than the Federal Theatre Project, had scheduled the production of *Murder in the Cathedral*.

Thus the Group spoke in several political voices, all, however, left of center. At the far left were Odets' militant playlets and his allegories of middle-class decay (all produced in 1935), and Piscator's adaptation of *An American Tragedy, The Case of Clyde Griffiths* (1936). Produced but a few months after Theatre Union's version of *Mother, Clyde Griffiths* similarly employed epic technique, and was just as heartily disliked by the critics (although the Group's physical production was more solidly praised).

The play, overtly presentational in style, follows the basic line of Dreiser's work; but Piscator, exploiting epic didacticism, loses no opportunity to make explicit in Marxist terms the social implications of Clyde's tragedy. As Piscator sees it, Clyde's downfall lies, like Joe Kovarsky's in *Black Pit,* in class betrayal. Clyde has his chance; when the union votes to strike against his uncle, he is temporarily with them. But when confronted by the elder Griffiths he reneges, and, in the Marxist catechism, falls from grace. But Piscator is less concerned with excoriating Clyde than with drawing from his fall the social lesson that evil is a product of institutions, not of individuals. In the last scene of the play—the trial— the Speaker enters consciously into the action (rather than serving merely as commentator) in order to affirm the play's thesis, counseling even against the adamancy of the Left's hatred of Clyde for his defection. For despite the fact that Clyde had left "the great army" of the proletariat to seek false goals, he is—no less than the exploited workers themselves—the victim of an oppressive social system. The District Attorney asserts that talk of social systems is irrelevant to the facts of the case (a judgment the reviewers enthusiastically shared), but the Speaker affirms its relevancy:

What is Clyde Griffiths without your poverty and your wealth? In him lies the longing that is in the hearts of everyone of us here for safety, comfort, beauty, happiness—and in his make up an indictment against a world that is not capable of giving sufficient to everyone. Who is responsible for this?[18]

Clyde's real crime was that he adhered too strictly to the capitalist ethic; on one side he saw the ragged poverty of the exploited poor; on the other, the luxury and power of the exploiting rich. Was he so guilty in desiring to leave the class which had nothing but degradation and misery to offer him? Hadn't he merely accepted the logic of the successful, that progress consists in the rise of the clever? Clyde's crime, from the point of view of capitalism, was that he overreached himself by committing murder. But once having committed himself to the desire to rise, had he any other alternative? The only distinction between Clyde's crime and capitalist exploitation was that he had done something that was officially unlawful. The play's moral is unequivocally stated. Mrs. Griffiths laments that Clyde "dies as a sacrifice to his restless, longing heart, but he will be forgiven!" The Speaker, however, denies her religious fatalism: "He dies as a sacrifice to society. And that will not be forgiven!" (p. 87). Of all the Group plays only *Lefty* ends on such a note of forthright radicalism.

In answer to the complaints of actors about the lack of socially-conscious scripts, Clurman had pointed out that the Group had produced the first Depression play in Claire and Paul Sifton's *1931–*. The play is particularly interesting because, while it points the way toward the proletarian drama of the mid-thirties, it retains umbilical connection with the expressionistic social drama championed by the New Playwrights, to which the Siftons had belonged. The drama of the New Playwrights—as reflected in such plays as Lawson's *Internationale*, Dos Passos' *Airways Inc.*, and the Siftons' *Belt*—presented apocalyptic visions of social protest based upon the chaos the authors feared capitalism *might* breed; in the context of the prosperous twenties their visions were necessarily prophetic. But in 1931 the Jazz Age had been interred, and the social apocalypse indeed seemed to be at hand. *1931–* is significant because, while it is conceived structurally in the semiexpressionistic style of the New Playwrights, thematically its social protest is based upon contemporary reality, not undefined prophesy. Structurally, the play consists of fourteen scenes which comprise one line of action—the plight of a modern everyman, Adam, in the grip of social and economic forces that threaten to destroy him—and, interspersed with this personal drama, ten interludes which occur as flashes between the scenes, and which comprise the drama of the group to which he belongs. The alternating rhythm of the scenes and interludes is progressively accelerated until the two lines finally converge, and the drama of the individual is seen in the light of the drama of his group.

The interludes are conceived cinematically as brief vignettes which progressively record the growing fact of class struggle in response to economic deprivation. At first the jobless are "silent and motionless as death, tense as a loaded gun,"[19] but slowly their desperation in the face of growing unemployment intensifies (Interlude II), then explodes into violence as they try to force a factory gate (Interlude IV); until, finally, genuine class strife results as the police attempt to break up the workers' protest (Interlude VIII); and the last interlude, with which the play concludes, ends on a note of proletarian solidarity in the face of police machine guns.

It would seem from the progress of these interludes that *1931–* is an uncompromisingly Marxist play. But the thesis of class awareness is not stressed in the play proper. It is true that Adam does join the militant marchers at the end of the play, but this "conversion," if so it may be characterized, occurs precipitately in the play's last seconds. Nowhere does Adam himself demonstrate any class consciousness, nor any of the other familiar attributes of the proletarian hero. The Siftons are primarily concerned with the horror of his situation, and the fact that it must be alleviated; they are more concerned with affirming that something must be done than in offering specific remedies. "Christ, why do they make us want what we can't afford," Adam cries to his girl, "why do they make us love and have kids . . . when we can't get the money to make them decent?" (p. 111); and this cry strikes the essential note of *1931–*. In short, the play is, in the Siftons' own words, "concerned with an individual in the tidal movement of a people caught in a situation which they can neither explain, escape nor exorcise."[20] It attempts to record the horror of this bewilderment, the horror bred by the recognition that the great economic machine had, in reality, broken down. The spectres on the bread lines challenged the American conscience: "I've got a right to live!" Adam cries, "I've got a right to work! Whaddeya say?" (p. 144).

One of the perennial themes of the Group plays—particularly in the early plays—was the emptiness of the myth of success. *Success Story* (1932), *The Big Night* (1933), *Gold Eagle Guy* (1934), *Golden Boy* (1937)—all had as their protagonist a man who sells out his better self in order to achieve financial gain. In the plays of Lawson, Odets and Dawn Powell the lesson was obvious: the capitalist ethic had—as in the case of Clyde Griffiths—proved corrupting. The social criticism, if not manifest, was at least implicit. In the case of Melvin Levy's *Gold Eagle Guy*, however, there were those within and without the Group who felt that the portrayal of the robber baron, Guy Button, was altogether too sympathetic. It was not that Levy had failed to show his protagonist's ruthlessness and avarice, but that he had, either consciously or otherwise, infused him with a tremendous vitality and zest for life which seemed, if not to justify his actions, at least to render them diabolically fascinating. Button's evil is of such a magnitude that, in the manner of the great Elizabethan villains like Barabas or de Flores, it seems to rise beyond any facile psychological or social motivation. I am, of course, not implying any invidious comparison; Levy's play hardly merits comparison with those of Marlowe or Middleton. I am, however, attempting to define, within the limitation of the play, why many objected to Levy's portrayal of Button. The latter, unlike Sol Ginsberg in *Success Story* or even Joe Bonaparte in *Golden Boy*, seemed less the product of social forces than the manipulator of them. His final destruction does not follow inevitably from the corruption of his character by zealous avarice, but is the result of an act of God: he is killed in the famed San Francisco earthquake. As one critic re-marked, Levy had created a character of such stature that it took a physical catastrophe to get rid of him. Button so dom-inates Levy's play that, despite his evil, he transcends hu-man limitations. No wonder that the Marxist critics chided that the play did not "resolve class issues," and that Levy (who, paradoxically, had himself chastised Lawson for the indecision of the latter's *Gentlewoman*) and the Group had strayed from their "serious and social purposes."[21]

But if *Gold Eagle Guy* did not "resolve class issues," it did at least present a figure who was clearly—despite his size—a class symbol, and on these grounds some defended the play's revolutionary intentions.[22] The fact of "class" was one that few American dramatists escaped in the thirties; man was primarily a social, not a psychological, animal. Thus Paul Green in his drama of southern decadence, *The House of Connelly* (1931), is less concerned with the forms of this decadence than with the juxtaposition of a healthy alternative. It was, as we have seen, not an uncommon de-vice in the drama of the period. Odets and the Marxist play-wrights posited the revolutionary alternative to middle-class decadence; Lawson (in *Gentlewoman*) and Rice (in *Between Two Worlds*) contrasted the sterility of the old order with the vitality of the new; even the ordered worlds of S. N. Behrman and Philip Barry admitted new social in-truders.

We might profitably contrast the south of *House of Connelly* with the south of Tennessee Williams. As Green paints the decay of the old order it seems to be, at first, in the manner of Williams: "Now the grace of hospitality is gone, the jovial host is gone, gone is the slave. The furniture is falling to pieces. . . . The dead Connellys in their frames wait for the end."[23] The living Connellys exist in a past world of Belle Reves and Blue Mountains; the old order is crumbling before the onslaughts of new social forces, and the Connelly clan, like the Sartoris, can only rail against the powerful upstarts who have perverted the values of the Old South.

So far so good. Now were Tennessee Williams proceeding with the play, the old aristocracy, however decadent, would still be preferable to the new forces of change. After all, is there not virtue in the posture of gallantry? Surely there could be no rapprochement between the old order and the new. And yet this is Green's theme: "Out of this death and darkness—into the light!" (p. 63). Will Connelly, the scion of the clan, recognizes that he cannot resuscitate a dead past, that the old, aristocratic order is gone forever. He finds in Patsy, the daughter of a tenant farmer, hope for the creation of a new future, and despite the cruelty of the choice (Patsy is bitterly resented by the older Connellys) he is convinced by her that it must be made. "That's the way it has to be, Will. To grow and live and be something in this world . . . you've got to push other things aside. The dead and the proud have to give way to us—to us the living" (p. 118).

The premise that resides at the heart of *House of Connelly* is that decadence is a fact of institutions and classes; in the work of Tennessee Williams corruption is existential. The first premise makes the concept of social action meaningful, the second declares all social gestures essentially irrelevant.

Green, in his second play for the Group, *Johnny Johnson* (1936), departs from his familiar regional environment, but he is again concerned with asserting a social thesis: in this case, the insanity of war. The method he employs—the juxtaposition of a supremely sane man against the organized absurdity of conventional institutions—has been employed more recently for purely comic effect in such military comedies as *No Time for Sergeants* and *At War with the Army*. But Green's purpose in *Johnny Johnson* is completely serious. As the play proceeds it becomes increasingly bitter in tone, until at last the laws of sanity apply only within the confines of an insane asylum. Why had Johnny been committed? Merely because he had acted upon the "mad" conviction that human beings were reasonable creatures, that mankind would not willfully destroy itself.

Green's ironic fable (which came out of the Group's "suggestion, stimulation, and actual assistance")[24] is not primarily concerned, as is *Peace on Earth*, with the causes of war; it is rather concerned with its ultimate absurdity and its devastating horror. In the name of country, religion, family, mankind forgets its common humanity and acts more viciously—because its actions are gratuitous—than the most vicious animal. Johnny's crime is that he demands a *reason* for fighting. In the play's first scene war is declared in the midst of the unveiling of a statue dedicated to Peace. All rush for arms, forgetting the pacifist slogans of the last moment. Only Johnny naively muses: "Why—I thought we were all for peace."[25] Finally he consents to fight when he is told that this war will end all wars, but he soon discovers, in the horror of the grime and dismembered bodies, that this reason is a lie. For the powers that control the destinies of the men who fight do not want peace. Johnny offers it to them, but the precious gift is denied; only a madman could believe that war could be ended by rational discussion, they conclude, and turn back to the abstract patterns on the planning board which represent the lifeblood of millions.

Johnny Johnson is a protest against the final absurdity of war; the paradox of Green's play resides in the question of whether, in a world governed by insanity, the forces of sanity must be eternally suspect. The leaders of the "civilized" world reject Johnny's pacifism as madness; the inmates of the asylum accept his leadership and unanimously create a League of World Republics. But Green does not end the play on a note of despair; Johnny, when released from the asylum, again sees the warclouds gathering, and again hears the familiar jingoism. Even when faced with the recurrence of mankind's perennial blight, Johnny does not lose his unconquerable optimism, his faith that sanity shall ultimately prevail: "Even so, Johnny Johnson is not hushed by the strange voice booming through the world. As he disappears down the long street that leads from the great city into the country and beyond, he begins whistling his song again—a little more clearly now, a little more bravely" (p. 190).

Paul Green's dramatic contribution to the Group canon raises wistful considerations of the dramatist he once was. As his career progressed the intense regionalism, which in the twenties and thirties was illumined by social and psychological insight, degenerated into the hollow formalities of spectacle. The playwright who had shown himself capable of *In Abraham's Bosom, House of Connelly, Hymn to the Rising Sun* and *Johnny Johnson* abdicated in favor of the scenarist for such confederate flag-waving extravaganzas as *Wilderness Road, The Founders,* and *The Confederacy*. Surely this record does not indicate that social concerns distorted Green's accomplishment; his recent total dedication to patriotic spectacle of the most obvious banality ("The Confederacy is now our Lost Cause, but the ideals we served are not lost." "Yes. Yes.") raises the unfortunate apprehension that, like the Confederacy, Paul Green's dramatic seriousness will not rise again.

We have observed that at the end of the thirties the threat of fascist belligerency jolted many liberals from a pacifist position into a realization of the possible necessity of force to combat it. It is not surprising then that two of the Group's plays for the year 1939—Irwin Shaw's *The Gentle People* and Robert Ardrey's *Thunder Rock*—should take for their themes the necessity for man to face the outbreak of social evil and act in order to eradicate it. Both plays face the issue obliquely—*The Gentle People* through the means of whimsical allegory, and *Thunder Rock* through the means of fantasy—but both leave no doubt as to their implications. Both Shaw and Ardrey significantly *accept* the phenomenon of social evil; they are not concerned with its causation. The problem they raise is: how can man accommodate himself to this evil? Both answer similarly: he cannot evade the necessity of action.

Shaw's play reveals the reversal of the liberal position on war. In 1936 Shaw had composed *Bury the Dead*, one of the most famous short plays of the decade, for a New Theatre benefit. In this pacifist piece, the soldiers senselessly killed in an exploiting war refuse to be buried despite the threats and cajoling of officers, politicians, family and friends. In ironic savagery it approached the intensity of Green's *Johnny Johnson*. However, in 1939 war did not appear so completely senseless. It was obvious to most liberals that Hitler could not be placated rationally, that a stand against him was inevitable. *The Gentle People* does not treat this theme directly; it deals in parable, and the difficulty with parable is that if it is too obvious it may lose all specificity and credibility on its primary level (e.g., Rice's *American Landscape*); and if it concentrates too intensely on the detail from which its allegorical implications are to arise, these implications may well be lost (Miller's *The Crucible*). There were those who professed to see in *The Gentle People* nothing beyond the whimsy of its Brooklyn environment, an obtuseness which astounded Clurman who saw the play clearly as an allegory concerning fascism and the common people.[26]

The parable which Shaw relates is simply stated. Two gentle Brooklyn fishermen are "shaken down" by a gangster who not only demands protection money but infatuates the young, headstrong daughter of one of the men. The gangster's creed is simple: the strong shall derive their suste-

nance from the weak. The superior man (or group) shall
enforce, by naked might, the law of the survival of the
fittest. But peace cannot be bought at such a price. Philip,
one of the gentle people, maintains that Goff, the gangster,
must be paid off because he obviously is a man who would
not be afraid to kill other men, and for a while indeed the
fishermen pay. But Goff will not be appeased; his demands
grow continually larger, and soon the men realize that they
must make a stand against him. The common man, eternally
persecuted, realizes that there must be an end to running.
"We're getting old. . . . We must take up a stand . . . before
we're pushed right off the earth."[27] They take their complaint against the blackmailer to court; but Goff is too
clever; the fishermen have insufficient proof. They are then
beaten by the gangster, and finally, they have no alternative
but to take the law into their own hands. There is only one
way to combat the evil that Goff represents; man must fight
it with its own weapons.

Finally . . . if you want peace and gentleness, you got to take
violence out of the hands of the people like Goff and you got to
take it in your own hands and use it like a club. Then, maybe,
on the other side of the violence, there will be peace and gentleness. All my life . . . I have believed in reason. I convince you,
you convince me. Can you convince airplanes with bombs and
men with guns in their pockets. [p. 149]

The answer is obvious, and Shaw's parable ends optimistically, considering the time of its composition, with the
triumph of his gentle people over the embodiment of
fascism.

    The dilemma which Robert Ardrey poses in *Thunder
Rock* is not that man is afraid to act, but that he fears the
ultimate futility of such action. His protagonist, Charleston,
has been engaged in the vital struggles of his time; but the
spectacle of misery which he has witnessed has destroyed

his faith in political solutions. To him, "Society itself is a lost cause."[28] Consequently Charleston retires to cultivate his garden; he removes himself from the society of men, and, in the ivory tower of a remote lighthouse, constructs a private strife-free world peopled with the ghosts of shipwrecked immigrants. But as the creatures of his fancy become progressively more defined, it becomes clear to Charleston that he has not in fact escaped the problem which plagued him, the significance of human effort. Each of the ghosts had fled from social forces which had seemed in their time insurmountable, each had despaired of ever achieving his goal, goals—such as the emancipation of women and the elimination of the horrors of childbirth—which had long since been realized. Kurtz, the ghost of a persecuted physician, points out the contemporary moral. All human problems have seemed in their time insoluble, but mankind has persevered, and in time solved them. Despite setbacks, Ardrey asserts, history records the ascending line of human progress. Each man has one question to ask himself: what can I do to accelerate the process? "Men may lose, but mankind never! Sooner or later, tomorrow or in a thousand years, mankind finds an answer. And we have only one power—to decide just this: will it be sooner? Or will it be later?" (p. 59). Ultimately, then, Charleston recognizes that man cannot absent himself from the issues of the day; he must commit himself. He cannot surrender to the forces which threaten civilization, no matter how horrible or invincible they may appear. Nor can he demand knowledge of the final outcome of the struggle. He must have faith in the lessons of history, that progress shall continue. "A man who fights for an ideal—a man who fights against poverty or ignorance or the rule of tyrants—he doesn't ask for assurance that he'll win. . . . All he asks for is assurance that he has a chance to win" (pp. 65-6).

If there is one basic affirmation which runs through the

corpus of the Group plays it is this faith in man's ability to ameliorate social evil. The method might vary, but the social gesture, whether radical or reformist, was obligatory. This faith the Group shared with its generation; indeed the Group represented the theatrical best that its generation had to offer. Whatever the final verdict as to the durability of American drama in the thirties, there is no doubt that much of this accomplishment was due to the efforts of the Group Theatre. Observe its dramatic contribution: it produced the first efforts of William Saroyan and Sidney Kingsley; it offered major works by such established playwrights as Lawson, Green, and Maxwell Anderson; its playwriting contest awarded public recognition for the first time to a young writer named Tennessee Williams (for *American Blues*); it encouraged the work of lesser writers like Irwin Shaw, Robert Ardrey and Melvin Levy; and it offered in the work of one of its own actors—Clifford Odets —the most characteristic dramatic voice of the decade. In sum, the record of American dramatic accomplishment in the thirties is very largely the record of the dramatic contribution of the Group Theatre. The Group is dead, but its tradition survives; at least it realized one article of its theatrical faith.

The Group failed because its ideals were inimical to the hard facts of commerce. It never succeeded in obtaining that which was almost an imperative for a theatre of its aims, a sustained subsidy from either public or private patronage. Indeed, it is astonishing that the Group survived as long as it did when one considers that in ten seasons it produced only two hits, *Men in White* and *Golden Boy*. That the dissolution of the Group occurred when it did cannot, as in the case of the Theatre Union, be tied too directly to changes in the winds of doctrine. It was always precariously balanced on the edge of commercial instability. "The Group Theatre was a failure," Clurman affirms, "because, as no individual can exist alone, *no group can exist alone.*"[29] But, in another sense, the philosophy which had sustained the Group could not survive the demands of impending global conflict. Through most of the Group plays ran "the hunger for a spiritually active world, a humanly meaningful and relevant art,"[30] and this social purpose was soon to be denied by political disenchantment and the exigencies of survival. In a sense, the Group, too, was dispossessed by history.

5

THE FEDERAL THEATRE: THEATRE IS MEN WORKING

CONGRESSMAN STARNES: Do you believe that the theatre is a weapon?

HALLIE FLANAGAN: I believe that the theatre is a great educational force. I think it is an entertainment. I think it is an excitement. I think it may be all things to all men.

Hearings of the House Committee
on Un-American Activities, 1938

CHAPTER FIVE

In the month of January, 1937, a terribly destructive flood struck the city of Cincinnati. All theatres, stores, and places of business were closed; the power plants of the electric light company and those of the water works were submerged, and except for the dim glow of candles and oil lamps, the city was plunged into darkness. During the trying days of the disaster a troupe of actors joined with other civic forces to meet the emergency. In fourteen days they played forty engagements to over 14,000 flood victims; traveling by car, they joined the caravan of trucks carrying food and medical aid to the sufferers, playing wherever they were needed. They were rowed across the swollen river to stranded colonies; they played in emergency shacks in the open, on overturned tables, by the light of lanterns, flashlights—even candles.[1]

During the very two weeks that these actors and entertainers were engaged upon their mission, a number of seemingly unrelated theatrical events were taking place throughout the country: New Yorkers were talking about Virgil Geddes' new play *Native Ground* and Orson Welles' dynamic adaptation of Marlowe's *Dr. Faustus;* they were traveling to a reconditioned theatre in Harlem to view two new plays presented by a Negro company; they and their children were applauding a puppet show entitled *The Big City,* and Gilbert and Sullivan's *Iolanthe;* Chicagoans were watching a new ballet by Katherine Dunham; Los Angeleans saw revivals of *Uncle Vanya* and *Redemption,* as well as a Yiddish version of Sinclair Lewis' *It Can't Happen*

Here; a new musical and a new Negro play were causing comment in Seattle; Paul Green's *House of Connelly* was revived in Indianapolis, as was Sidney Howard's *Ned Mc-Cobb's Daughter* in Cedarhurst, N.Y.; Bostonians witnessed the performance of an Italian play entitled *L'Avvocato defensore* in its native language. Omaha and Peoria offered revivals of stageworthy stock perennials.[2]

What possible connection could exist between these various productions and the improvised theatrics of the Ohio performers? The events were not so unrelated as first it might appear. All these theatrical activities—and a host of others too numerous to cite individually—were the work of the Federal Theatre Project, not only the most ambitious theatrical project ever undertaken by the Federal Government, but, surely, one of the largest co-ordinated theatrical experiments in the history of the world. To appreciate the vast extent of the project let us note that in New York City alone the Federal Theatre operated five major units—the Living Newspapers, the Popular Price Theatre, the Experimental Theatre, the Negro Theatre and the Try-Out Theatre—as well as a host of smaller, subsidiary units—a one-act play unit, a German unit, an Anglo-Jewish theatre, a Classical Repertory unit, a Poetic Drama unit, a vaudeville unit, a children's theatre, a puppet theatre, a Continental Repertory unit.[3] In one season New Yorkers saw over one hundred Federal Theatre productions, ranging from vaudeville and light comedy to W. H. Auden and T. S. Eliot.

The accomplishments of the Federal Theatre were not, as we have observed, limited to New York City, although the activities of the New York Regional Theatre naturally bulked largest. The improvised performances of the Ohio Theatre were no isolated phenomena. Across the entire United States, in thirty-five individual states, living theatre was brought back to the people; all in all, during the four seasons of its existence, the Federal Theatre produced over 1,200 individual productions in every section of the country, employing, at its peak, over 13,000 theatre personnel.[4] When one places this achievement against the eight major productions of the Theatre Union in a similar span or the Group's record of twenty-five productions in ten seasons, some measure of the fantastic scope of the Federal Theatre Project can be appreciated.

Nor were the Federal Theatre's activities exclusively productional. Among other services which the project offered were (1) the encouragement of local community drama and dramatic training; (2) the establishment of the National Service Bureau, which, among its many activities, read, wrote, and translated plays, sent synopses, scripts, and bibliographies to the field, and conducted theatre research; (3) the publishing of its own periodical, the *Federal Theatre Magazine*; (4) the creation of a Federal Theatre of the Air, which presented approximately two thousand programs a year, all released through regular commercial stations and networks;[5] (5) the development of psychodrama experimentation in various municipal hospitals;[6] (6) the establishment of playwriting contests in CCC camps and in colleges. Conceived and operated in this way, the Federal Theatre was much more than a play-producing organization; it had to meet, on all levels, the needs of the communities which it served and to which it offered a myriad of services.

The Federal Theatre arose from economic necessity, not esthetic theory; the noble experiment was based upon the fact of unemployment. In the spring of 1933, the most urgent problem that President Roosevelt had to face, once the banking crisis had eased, was the stark problem of relief. There were upwards of fifteen million unemployed and nearly six million persons on state and municipal charity rolls.[7] The problem of unemployment was particularly dif-

ficult for the artist, for art—within the context of breadlines
and soup kitchens—must have seemed the most dispensable
of commodities. It is estimated that 40,000 show folk were
destitute during the Depression, and their situation was
made even more desperate by the fact that they could not
turn to part-time employment in anticipation of the next
theatrical job—"temporary" jobs just did not exist. Thus the
theatre person, already the victim of technological unemployment created by the rise of the motion picture, not only
found job opportunities increasingly scarce (in the summer
of 1933 New York sustained only five productions), but was
denied the traditional economic alternatives.

To meet the relief needs of the unemployed, Congress
passed the first Relief Act on March 31, 1933, which, in
addition to providing relief for unemployed adults, set up
the Civilian Conservation Corps with the object of finding
jobs for unemployed youth. Six weeks later Congress established the FERA (Federal Emergency Relief Administration) for the purpose of granting federal funds to states
to assist in caring for the unemployed. On November 9,
1933, Congress established the CWA (Civil Works Administration) for the purpose of creating four million jobs for
men and women desperately in need. In all of these agen-
cies, the emphasis was upon immediate need, and theatre
people were among the recipients of this emergency aid.
The inadequacy of the initial, hasty, relief projects was
soon recognized, however, and on April 8, 1935, Congress
passed a bill authorizing a new approach—based upon the
experiences of FERA and CWA—to the problem of unemployment. The WPA (Works Progress Administration) rejected the concept of the dole; it attempted to remove the
stigma of relief by the implementation of three departures
from earlier methods: (1) only employables were to be
taken from the relief rolls of the states; (2) to these employables, work was to be offered *within their own skills and*

trades; (3) unemployables were to be returned to the care of the states.[8] Thus the preservation both of the skill and the self-respect of the worker was viewed as the corollary of the alleviation of economic want. It was deemed important not merely that the worker receive financial assistance, but that he work in the field for which he was trained. Since it had been learned upon investigation that thousands of unemployed artists were engaged in various relief activities for which they were basically unfit, it was decided to establish projects in order to provide proper work for the artists in their respective fields. Thus were created the major Federal Arts projects—in Art, Music, Writing, and Theatre.

But while the project had its origin in economic necessity, it was soon apparent that its director, Hallie Flanagan and her subordinates (chosen, it may be noted, largely from the ranks of the noncommercial theatre) conceived of their task as more than the administration of relief. "The arts projects were being set up to deal with physical hunger," wrote Mrs. Flanagan, "but was there not another form of hunger with which we could rightly be concerned, the hunger of millions of Americans for music, plays, pictures and books? Were not these aspects of hunger a part of the same equation which it was our job to solve?"[9] Thus, the directors of the Federal Theatre Project accepted the essential functional premise of the theatre's creation, but they were not satisfied with this premise. They wanted to create out of the fact of unemployment a theatre which would not only serve the entire nation in many ways, but which would be expressive of the attitudes and needs of the age. At the heart of the Federal Theatre lay an idea which co-ordinated its multifarious aspects, and which made it deserving of the title of a "Theatre": that art is an integral and necessary part of the social community. In a very real sense, then, the Federal Theatre reflected the social ferment which gave birth to the Theatre Union and molded the development of the Group Theatre. The essential requisite of art was conceived as the fulfillment of the social need which had brought it forth. Hallie Flanagan maintained that if the theatre were to be a vital social force, it could not afford to ignore the implications of social change. The theatre, in her view, had to grow up.[10]

The dual aims of the Federal Theatre—the satisfaction of immediate economic need and the creation of a vital contemporary theatre—were to some extent contradictory. For one set of aims—relief, popular appeal, commercial revival —was necessarily impermanent, while the other set—the training of actors, the improvement of public taste, the stimulation of the writing of meaningful contemporary plays— was permanent. If the conflict between providing relief and producing vital drama was manifest at the beginning and throughout the experimental stages, that conflict intensified when wholesale dismissals for economy forced a decision between relief cases and continuation of work by those best qualified to perform it. If the purpose of the project were solely relief, it would be logical for the competent to be discharged first, since they were most likely to find work elsewhere. But what theatre could survive on the basis of the dismissal of its most talented performers? The amazing fact is that the Federal Theatre was able to maintain the acting level of its productions despite these very basic difficulties.

The dilemma was reflected administratively; while Mrs. Flanagan and her assistants were striving to concentrate upon the permanent aspects of the theatre they were attempting to create, it was impossible wholly to extricate the Federal Theatre from the nation-wide WPA network. The WPA officials—usually businessmen pressed into civic duty —knew little of the exigencies of the theatrical profession and could not understand why the handling of the arts projects should differ in any particular from the handling of any other WPA project. Moreover, in the later stages of the project distrust of the Federal Theatre arose within the ranks of the WPA itself, a distrust which occasionally manifested itself in overt or covert censorship, and in the discontinuing of the *Federal Theatre Magazine,* which expressed the point of view of people on the project. With Harry Hopkins no longer in charge, the Federal Theatre found itself talking to increasingly unsympathetic ears. Thus the association of the Theatre Project with the WPA presented another series of obstacles to surmount. It is a tribute to the energy and indefatigability of Mrs. Flanagan and her co-workers that despite these difficulties the project was able to record a substantial achievement.

The Federal Theatre faced one other great liability: it was forbidden by law to advertise, and thus was denied the opportunity of both informing the public of its theatrical wares and of answering the attacks of its opponents. These attacks took two basic forms. On one hand, the Theatre—and the entire WPA project—was accused of "boondoggling" and shovel-leaning, of wasting the taxpayers' money. On the other—and this charge was ultimately instrumental in the denial of funds to the Federal Theatre—the Theatre Project was held to be a hotbed of radical activity, the plays it presented were described as "communist inspired." Significantly, few of the more virulent attacks upon the Federal Theatre came from the theatrical profession itself (except for a few old-guard producers like Brock Pemberton). Most came from the intransigent right, such as the Hearst press, which termed the project "an adjunct to the New York Leftist literary junta."[11] The fact is that because of its governmental support the Federal Theatre was particularly vulnerable to political attack. Moreover, by virtue of the WPA directive forbidding any coherent public relations

policy, the project was unable to respond publicly to its critics, with the familiar result that denials never caught up
with the accusations.[12]

As for the charge that the leadership of the project was
communist dominated, it was recognized by all responsible
critics that the accusation was manifestly absurd.[13] No more
substantial charge was ever leveled at Hallie Flanagan than
the fact of her "subversive" penchant for theatrical experimentation. In fact, she repeatedly pointed out to her subordinates on the project that she would not tolerate the use
of the Federal Theatre for the promulgation of any specific
political platform. She objected to—but characteristically
made no attempt to censor—certain of the political implications of the Living Newspaper's production of *Injunction
Granted.*When separate productions of Sinclair Lewis' *It
Can't Happen Here* were in rehearsal in twenty-five different cities, the following memorandum went out to all projects throughout the country:

> . . . avoid all controversial issues—political angles of any degree
> —special appeals—racial or group appeals—or interferences in
> any of these directions since Federal Theatre is interested only
> in presenting good theatre, neither adopting nor assuming any
> viewpoint beyond presenting a new and vital drama of our
> times, emerging from the social and economic forces of the
> day.[14]

Of course, it was to some extent naive to assume that such
a vital, contemporary drama as that desired by the directors
of the project could totally avoid assuming *any* political
viewpoint, and the Federal Theatre plays inevitably reveal
various social concerns and solutions. But the tenor of its
directive is clear: the directors of the Federal Theatre, like
the directors of the Group, aspired to a nonsectarian social
drama, a drama which affirmed the necessity of facing social issues, but which avoided a dogmatically consistent po-

litical position upon these issues. In the case of a government-supported theatre such a position was obviously a necessity. But the problem was further complicated by the scope of the Federal Theatre and its avowed principle of noncensorship (if the principle was not always scrupulously followed it was more the fault of nontheatrical WPA or governmental action than of censorship by the project directors themselves). Plays were chosen by the individual regions involved, subject to approval, rarely denied, by the Theatre's central directorate. Thus, unlike the Group, the Federal Theatre's plays were not chosen by its directors; although the National Service Bureau—the Theatre's official playreading unit—recommended plays to the various localities, the choice was generally left to the regional directors. Despite the fear that subsidized theatre might result in direct political control, the facts reveal otherwise. *Fortune* magazine spoke for many observers of the project when it noted: "The Arts Projects have been given a freedom no one would have thought possible in a government-run undertaking. And by and large that freedom has not been abused."[15]

Essentially, in the words of Hallie Flanagan, "the whole of Federal Theatre was greater than any of its parts just as it was greater than any personality connected with it."[16] That communists should have been counted among these parts of the theatre was, considering the radical ferment of the age and the inclusiveness of the project, inevitable. Since the five thousand people on the New York project were not selected with regard to any political or religious affiliations, it would have been impossible to exclude them. Political reliability had not as yet become the yardstick of theatrical excellence.

In general, the Marxist press supported the venture (it was—again let us reiterate—the era of the Popular Front), although it still found much to criticize in the operation of the project. Even if it could not approve the reformist nature of most of the Theatre's New York productions, it could at least support the concept of a theatre which was making a concentrated effort to fulfill a real social need; it consistently bent over backwards (in the manner of its attitude toward the Group) to minimize the ideological shortcomings of many Federal Theatre plays.[17] And inevitably the fact of this support in the pages of the *New Masses* and *New Theatre* was thrown back at the directors of the Federal project. The question rarely asked was: just what does the record of the Federal Theatre's dramatic accomplishments reveal? Had they looked at statistics, its opponents might have observed that less than ten per cent of the Federal Theatre productions dealt with such issues as government, politics, power, labor, etc.[18] They might also have noted a few of the project's substantial dramatic achievements: the organization of companies that presented cycles of plays by Shakespeare, Shaw, O'Neill; the presentation of a classical repertory that ranged from Aeschylus to Sheridan; the organization of units which presented European classics in their native tongues, the light-opera classics of Gilbert and Sullivan, regional plays by authors such as Paul Green, and plays and puppet shows for children. They might have noted such nonpolitical successes as the first American production of Eliot's *Murder in the Cathedral*, a Negro *Macbeth* set in Haiti (so successful that it went on tour), a "swing" *Mikado* which started a commercial trend, and Orson Welles' spectacular, sceneryless production of Marlowe's *Faustus* (which brought the then *enfant terrible* his first substantial renown); they might have observed the dramatic, rather than the exclusively political, implications of the exciting experimentalism of the Living Newspaper.

What, then, *did* the official critics of the Federal Theatre Project observe? Of a total list of 830 separate major titles, eighty-one were criticized as to content by witnesses before

Congressional committees, by members of the House and Senate on the floor of the House or Senate, during committee hearings, or in public statements for the press or radio. Of the eighty-one titles, only twenty-nine originated with Federal Theatre; the other fifty-two titles represent thirty-three standard or stock revivals, five plays that had never been produced by the project, seven plays that originated with local community drama groups, not with the project, one children's play, one Yiddish play, one Italian translation, two pieces of Americana, and two classics.[19] Since the range of Federal Theatre was so vast, consisting in large part of revivals, let us accept for purposes of evaluation a schematization based upon these officially criticized plays. Such a limitation has not been chosen arbitrarily. Inasmuch as they were cited for their specific political implications, these plays reveal most accurately the Federal Theatre's political commitment, despite the fact that they represent less than four per cent of the project's total production.[20] But let us not forget that although social plays constituted only a small percentage of its prolific record, the phenomenon of the Federal Theatre was itself indicative of a social atmosphere in which art and political commitment were intimately interrelated.

The drama criticized falls into several categories: (1) three plays by European authors: Ernst Toller, Bernard Shaw, and Friedrich Wolf; (2) new plays by American authors; (3) the work of the Living Newspaper; (4) other miscellaneous genres—a dance drama based upon Euripides' *Trojan Women*, a children's play, and a singularly unsuccessful musical. Of the three European plays only one, Wolf's *Professor Mamlock* (1937), pleased the left. Shaw's *On the Rocks* (1938), a parable on revolution which cited the need for a "man on horseback" to take those measures for the people's welfare which they are fearful of taking themselves, was soundly trounced in the leftist press: John

Cambridge attacked Shaw's "degenerative political creed," his advocacy of neofascism and his slander of the proletariat.[21] Similarly, Toller's *No More Peace* (1937)—a pacifist fantasy which placed evil within man rather than within institutions (a pessimism fulfilled by Toller's unfortunate suicide one year after the production of the play)—was criticized for its lack of a socially-conscious proletariat.[22] *Professor Mamlock*, however, was, in general, well received by liberals and the left. The play, which bitterly attacks Nazi racism, concerns itself with a loyal German Jew who, after steadfastly refusing to believe evil of the Nazi regime, finally comes to realize the bitter truth. Deprived of his honored position, deserted by his friends and his children, he is arrested by the Nazis; his last gesture—the fruit of his inner betrayal—is suicide. Although Mamlock's final awakening does assume political proportions, the focus of the play remains on the personal tragedy of the doctor's false faith; unlike the traditional Marxist play in which racial intolerance is viewed as the necessary corollary of economic exploitation, *Mamlock* recognizes the intense, individualized nature of Nazi hate; the fact of anti-Semitism is not necessarily tied to the logic of a dying capitalism.

Of the native American drama which was officially criticized only three or four plays (exclusive of the Living Newspaper) could be said to have predominantly political themes. By far the most celebrated of this group, by virtue of the fact that it received simultaneous production in twenty-one theatres in seventeen states (the productions, by the way, were individually conceived; they were not carbon copies of each other), was the adaptation by Sinclair Lewis and John Moffit of the former's anti-fascist novel, *It Can't Happen Here* (1936). Lewis' play is based upon the simple premise that "it," fascism, *can* happen here, but he characteristically weakens the case by presenting his indictment in the harsh colors of caricature rather than in the restrained tones of reality. Unlike George Orwell, for example, Lewis does not ground his negative utopia in the accumulated detail of the commonplace; he tends rather to scatter his shot in all directions, relying, in turn, upon devices borrowed from melodrama, romance, even expressionism. How, for example, can one accept the basic premise of the play—which is, after all, that the incredible is, in fact, only too possible—when the leader of the "Corpos" (the fascist group which takes over the United States) is presented in terms of overt, heavy-handed satire which belies all credibility? *It Can't Happen Here* is undoubtedly most effective when it concentrates upon the theme that it shares with many Marxist plays of the period: the conversion of a hitherto uncommitted liberal to a recognition of the necessity for action. But the conversion to militancy of Lewis' hero, Doremus Jessup, unlike that of Professor Owens in *Peace on Earth*, is *not* based upon the acceptance of any specific political premise. Jessup combats the Corpos for the simple reason that they represent a force of unmitigated evil that cannot be explained rationally. Ultimately, Lewis' reaction to fascism is one of revulsion, not analysis, an ideological deficiency of which the Marxists were not unaware, despite their praise for the play's anti-fascist stand.[23]

Barrie and Leona Stavis' *The Sun and I* (1937), also raised much controversy as to its specific political implications. Taking for its plot the story of Joseph in Egypt, it alternates between a rigid adherence to the details of the legend, and a flexible adaptation of the legend to reveal certain political ruminations. Structurally, the difficulty with the play is that the political implications do not arise out of the details of the legend per se. The dramatic coloration of the play arises from the traditional scenes, while its political theme—the fact that evil may often result from the attempts of reformers to do good—arises in scenes extrinsic to the play's essential development. Yet even this theme is not unequivocally stated. Joseph is portrayed as an idealistic rebel-reformer who finally comes to realize that power, even in the service of good, is inevitably corrupting; *The Sun and I* becomes a parable of the contradiction between revolutionary idealism and corrosive power. But the authors do not draw clear contemporary parallels; if, at times, the play seems to be an attack upon fascist philosophy, at other times its principal target seems to be the communists or even the New Deal. In any case, whatever the specific political opponent, the essential political implication of *The Sun and I* resides in the Pharaoh's statement that no political solution suffices at present: "Time is young yet. Some day a new Joseph will be born who will teach the people to put their faith in one another, and not in the deceptive powers of rulers, or in the false promises of priests."[24]

The Federal Theatre produced two plays which are at present chiefly of documentary interest for the fidelity with which they reveal the Depression malaise. Yet although neither *Chalk Dust* (1936) nor *Class of '29* (1936) is concerned primarily with political themes, both were officially criticized on political grounds. *Chalk Dust* by Harold Clark and Maxwell Nurnberg is an academic *Men in White* (written, however, without Kingsley's skill), which poses the inevitable conflict of love and duty within the confines of a municipal high school. Its social implications arise from the fact that one of its principal characters (though not the play's protagonist) is a crusading type who continually fights for social issues and consequently finds himself in opposition to the conservative authorities. He is, as a result, unjustly accused of amatory dalliance with the play's heroine and is ultimately transferred to another school. Told that a person with his ideas doesn't belong in the school system, he rejoins, "You're wrong . . . that's just where I do belong. You call me a trouble maker [because] I let the boys and girls talk about war and peace, strikes and share-croppers, communism, fascism and democracy. I intend to go right on making that kind of trouble . . . until your whole school system becomes a seething cauldron of American democracy."[25]

This is about the extent of *Chalk Dust*'s radicalism. In fact, the play is essentially a romance; it is less concerned with an exposure of the school system than with the romantic entanglements, the gossip and jealousies of the various teachers. Its principal interest for us lies in the fact that the authors felt the need to superimpose social significance upon a quite conventional love story; in a postscript to the play they revealed that the social thread was introduced *after* the composition of the play "to suggest the new and absorbing interest of young people in the welfare of America and its future." Could any statement be more reflective of the spirit of the time than the authors' contention that "a play that dealt merely with personal relationships no longer seemed to present a complete picture of the school life of today"?[26]

Class of '29 by Orrie Lashing and Milo Hastings also reveals the intrusion of social considerations into a situation that is basically concerned with personal relationships. The social theme is, however, more relevant than it is in *Chalk Dust*. The authors are concerned with the impact of the Depression upon a group of Harvard graduates of the class of '29. In each case their primary antagonist is the Depression itself, the necessity to find work and a way of life amid the economic difficulties which surround them. Although one of the characters is a communist and continually spouts Marxist doctrine, he is not the protagonist. The basic problem in *Class of '29* is posed in personal, not political terms: how to retain integrity and self-respect though unemployed. If this dilemma seems at times hyperstated, it is perhaps because we can no longer appreciate the reality of the social situation which invoked it. Ken, one of the young men, tells his girl:

If it were a choice between you and a job I'd take the job. . . . I wouldn't need Martin to turn me into a Communist. All I'd have to do would be to knock out the partition in the middle of my brain and let the left side mingle with the right.[27]

The chief significance of this play consists in its evocation of the mood of the Depression. The very title registers an ironic comment on the bright promise of the twenties which turned to dust on Black Thursday. It records certain basic characteristics of the generation of the thirties: the intrusion of economic reality into one's personal relationships; the belief that human problems are fundamentally social; the search, therefore, for social alternatives (in particular, the concern with the Marxist alternative); above all, the humanitarian concern for the anguish born of economic breakdown. The play's essential virtue rests not in dramatic excellence nor political significance, but rather in the authenticity with which it records a moment in history.

If any play produced by the Federal Theatre were above the imputation of political radicalism it would seem to be E. P. Conkle's *Prologue to Glory* (1938). Conkle's drama of the Salem days of Abraham Lincoln touches on few political questions; it is not even involved with the problem of slavery. Sherwood's *Abe Lincoln in Illinois* is a much more political play in its treatment of the theme (in Sherwood's own words) "of a man of peace who had to face the issue of appeasement or war."[28] Conkle, however, ends his play with young Lincoln's decision to become a lawyer; his major concern is with the heroic stuff of the legend of the young railsplitter who wins the affection and respect of the community, and the ill-fated love of Ann Rutledge. In fact, Abe's decision to remain in politics, after the initial defeat, is based not upon any political consideration, but rather on the romantic premise that this was the course that Ann would have wanted him to follow. At one point in his unsuccessful initial campaign, Abe advocates "'internal improvements, a lower rate of usury, and a better system of education"[29]—hardly a radical political platform. The Marxist press complained that Conkle had written about the wrong period in Abe's life; the real issues of slavery and secession were avoided.[30] And yet, to Hallie Flanagan's total bewilderment—*Prologue to Glory* was cited as a subversive play. Representative J. Parnell Thomas particularly objected to the scene in which Lincoln debated on the subject "Resolved: that bees are more valuable than ants," and won the day by suggesting that more important issues should be placed before the forum. "It seems to me that the subjects for debate before the forum ought to be alive—subjects for action, useful in living" (p. 46). "That," Mr. Thomas complained, "is communist talk. . . . The play, *Prologue to Glory* deals with Lincoln in his youth and portrays him battling with the politicians. This is simply a propaganda play to prove that all politicians are crooked."[31] Since in 1949 Representative J. Parnell Thomas—Chairman of the House Un-American Activities Committee from 1946–49—went to jail for defrauding the government,[32] we may observe the subjectivity of critical judgment.

William Du Bois' *Haiti* (1938) does indeed deal with the subject of revolution, but not as the conflict of social classes. The play—produced by the New York Negro unit—is rather involved with the racial nature of the conflict, with the successful attempt of the oppressed black Haitians to throw off the colonial shackles of their French overlords. The issue of race is central in the play; the plot concerns the dilemma of a mulatto woman brought up as white who must decide whether to align herself with the black or the white communities. Ultimately, after much soul-searching, she decides to aid the slave revolt and accept the world of her father's black forbears, a choice surely applauded by the predominantly Negro audiences for whom the play was performed. But Du Bois does not stress the social implications of his heroine's choice. *Haiti* is less a problem play than a rousing good adventure yarn dominated by the machinery of romance—amatory intrigue, hairbreadth escapes, sliding panels, and secret lockets.

It is paradoxical that of all the Federal Theatre plays the one with the most obvious Marxist implications should be a children's play, *The Revolt of the Beavers* (1936) by Oscar Saul and Louis Lantz. Whether the play's allegorical theme, the revolt of the oppressed beavers against their exploiting chief, penetrated the nonideological minds of its nonadult spectators is a moot, but by now unresolvable, point.

The Revolt of the Beavers shows us, among other things, that in the thirties even the world of childhood fancy had turned grim; the play is significant not because it uses a childlike parable to pose a political moral for adults (in the manner of *Animal Farm*), but because its political moral gives rise to its elements of fancy. The seriousness behind the fancy is immediately established: "Well, if I had a real wishing stone," the nine-year-old hero states, "I would never be sad—'cause first I would wish for a big piece of chocolate—and then I would wish my father got a job."[33] In fact, the play contains, in miniature, the prototypes of proletarian drama. The Beaver-Professor is satirized for his equivocation: "My favorite instrument is the fife / But I'm also fond of the fiddle / I sit on the Left and I sit on the Right / But my favorite spot is the middle" (Act I. Sc. ii. p. 5). Ultimately, however, in the best proletarian tradition, he is awakened to militancy and joins the other beavers in their revolt against the wicked chief and his goons. With the aid of Zippo guns, sling shots, and bean shooters stolen from the chief's arsenal, the revolutionists kick out their exploiters and establish a truly democratic Beaverland: "There's bark for every beaver / Who swings a cleaver / Or pulls a lever / There's not a barkless beaver / In all of Beaverland" (III. i. p. 14). The allegory is not ambiguous, but one wonders, again, to what extent its unsophisticated spectators were roused to political action by the play's example.

Curiously, one finds on the list of criticized plays no mention of two works by avowedly revolutionary playwrights. In the case of George Sklar's *Life and Death of an American*, the oversight may be explained by the fact that this play— the last production of the New York Federal Theatre—was not produced until 1939. But *Battle Hymn* by Mike Gold and Michael Blankfort was performed early in the project's existence (1936) and contains unmistakably revolutionary sentiments. The legend of John Brown serves the authors as a parable of the inadequacy of pacifist resistance to tyranny, and as a lesson in revolutionary tactics. Brown, at first, is portrayed as a man of deeply pacifist convictions who is forced into a position of militancy by the oppression and brutality of the slave system. True, the revolutionary implications are couched in the Americanism so consistent with the Communist Party's United Front policy of the time (the platform of 1936 stated that "The CPUSA continues the tradition of 1776, of the birth of our country"),[34] but the play's contemporary political significance is continually affirmed: "For each his turn, and for each his generation, performing each his task."[35] When Oliver Brown tells his brother that "You're either for slavery or against it" (p. 29), he is asserting the leftist battle cry of the thirties: which side are you on? Perhaps it is too much to expect consistency of the political mind, or perhaps the explanation for the omission of *Battle Hymn* rests in the simple fact that criticism of the project was seldom based on any well-informed evaluation of the Federal Theatre's actual dramatic record.

By far the heaviest barrage of criticism was leveled at

those plays produced by the Living Newspaper unit of the Federal Theatre Project; considering the basic concept behind the form—the theatrical treatment of serious contemporary social problems—such criticism was inevitable. The Living Newspaper was the product of the dual aspects of the project, economic necessity and social purpose. The immediate cause for the adoption of the form was the necessity of dealing with a problem peculiar to the project, a surplus of manpower. Unlike almost every other theatrical group the Federal Theatre had the problem of using the thousands of actors and technicians on the relief rolls; even if twenty plays were in rehearsal in one city simultaneously, with an average of thirty in each cast, only a fraction of the personnel would be employed. At the very moment that the directors of the project were pondering this dilemma, the Newspaper Guild of New York City was looking for a way to absorb some of its own unemployed in the Federal Theatre.[36] Out of this dual necessity arose the decision to produce dramatizations of the news with living actors, light, music, and movement. Such a form was ideally suited to the needs of this project: first, it solved the problem of the use of personnel; second, its emphasis on production allowed the directors to minimize the deficiencies of some of the acting talent available; third, it appealed to the project's spirit of dramatic experimentation by creating a unique theatrical form; and, fourth, it served the project's social ideal of speaking articulately upon contemporary social problems.

From a technical point of view the form of the Living Newspaper was not a complete innovation. As several commentators pointed out, precursors of the form were to be found in the agit-prop and the epic theatre, in the cinematic documentary, in the political cabarets of the Parisian and Berlin cellar theatres, in the al fresco varieties put together by Chu Teh's propaganda division in Red China.[37] But these examples were not before the directors of the Living Newspaper when they were molding a workable style; the exigencies of each individual production continually modified the shape that the form assumed. Several critics pointed out the affinities of the Living Newspaper to the then current film documentary series, the March of Time, but, as several of the directors noted, the Living Newspaper differed not only in the presentation of a different social point of view but in its approach to current news. The March of Time was essentially concerned with the dramatization of a news event; because of its social purpose and productional exigencies (governmental delay caused the directors to fear that news items of the moment might be dated before actual production) the Living Newspaper was invariably concerned with the dramatization of a *problem*, composed in greater or lesser extent of many news events, "all bearing on the one subject and interlarded with typical but nonfactual representations of the effect of these news events on the people to whom the problem is of great importance."[38] In essence, the Living Newspaper viewed its function as primarily editorial.

The form of the Living Newspaper varied from play to play. In *Ethiopia*, the Loudspeaker—The Voice of the Living Newspaper—served in the role of narrator, "a kind of nonparticipating date line which introduced the various scenes."[39] But in *One Third of a Nation*, the Loudspeaker served as *raisonneur*, inquiring, cajoling, polemicizing, pointing the moral of the dramatic action. In the "pure" form evolved in *Triple-A Ploughed Under, Power,* and *One Third of a Nation* historical characters spoke only direct quotations, and "creative" scenes were introduced to point up the effect of the given situation upon the average man. In *Spirochete*, however, the dramatist took greater license, and constructed imaginative scenes involving historical personages. In general, the technique of direct quotation was followed, with the quoted dialogue broken up only for dramatic effect.

The Living Newspaper was particularly successful in translating abstract concepts into concrete visual action, and in making its editorial point through the use of theatrical device. In *Power* the complexities of a holding company are reduced to the simple act of a man creating pyramids of different colored boxes; in *One Third of a Nation* the fact of slum congestion is transmitted through the farcical device of a great number of persons crowding onto a small rug. Satire was expressed theatrically by various devices: a capitalist consulting himself by rapidly running from one side of a desk to the other, to indicate the monopolistic power of the holding company; actors equipped with puppet-like strings to designate the control of the Louisiana legislature by Huey Long.

The Living Newspaper attempted to create the theatrical equivalent of the film documentary, another characteristic genre of the period; in the former case, however, the material of art was not the juxtaposed celluloid images of reality, but rather the formal verbal recreation of this reality through fact and comment theatrically expressed. Light, music, staging—these were the formal media through which the Living Newspaper worked. The durability of the form from an esthetic point of view rests not in the various plays which were presented, for these, being living *newspapers,* were intended to serve only an immediate function; the form's durability rests in its theatrical principle, in the *conception* of news theatrically expressed. The validity of the form remains. Why not contemporary Living Newspapers on Castro, or the African situation or nuclear disarmament?

The Living Newspaper's first production, *Ethiopia,* was never publicly performed. The State Department, hearing that the play severely criticized the Mussolini regime, exerted pressure, and a ruling was handed down from Washington forbidding the dramatic representation on any Federal Theatre stage of any living foreign ruler. Although the directors explained that only direct quotations were being used, the fear of international embarrassment caused the cancellation of the production—and the resignation of the then regional director of New York City, Elmer Rice. Yet Rice's resignation, and the furor that the issue of censorship raised, had beneficial effects. The project was assured that on any American subject it would have complete freedom of expression. And the subsequent record of the Living Newspaper testifies that this principle was, in general, maintained.

Considering the freedom afforded the staff of the Living Newspaper, it is not surprising that four of the five New York "editions" were officially criticized. Significantly, the one which escaped censure, *Highlights of 1935*, was by common agreement of critics and project workers the weakest example of the genre. Since dramatic interest and continuity could not be sustained by plot or protagonist, the lack of a coherent subject or editorial thread caused *1935* to appear diffuse and meandering; its series of dramatic re-creations of events of the past year was unified solely by chronological proximity. On the other hand, the four other New York editions demonstrated that an audience could be held by traditionally undramatic material. *Triple-A Ploughed Under* (1936) and *Injunction Granted* (1936) dealt with two of the problem areas of the economy—agriculture and labor; *Power* (1937) and *One Third of a Nation* (1938) were concerned with problems arising from the power utilities and the housing situation. All shared a strong reformist bias; all were sharply critical of the practices of private enterprise; all cited the need for specific governmental action; all criticized to a greater or lesser degree certain aspects of the administration's social programs—but none advocated any revolutionary alternative.

Triple-A Ploughed Under is basically a documentary record of the farmer's economic plight, albeit with a strong note of protest. In a series of quotations and recreated vignettes, the play traces the farm problem from the first World War to the Agricultural Adjustment Act, ending on a note of hope that some remedy will shortly be forthcoming from Washington. *Injunction Granted*, however, is more editorially selective in its recounting of the development of unionization and history of labor strife; indeed it goes back to the seventeenth century in order to record the history of working class exploitation: Bacon's rebellion, the Haymarket riots, the Pullman strike, the Danbury Hatters, the U.S. Steel strike, the Gastonia strike; in each case the resistance of vested interests to the workers' demands is observed. But despite the acceptance of the class nature of industrial struggle, despite capital's use of the injunction to thwart the unionization of labor, it is significant that *Injunction Granted* presents the history of labor relations in the United States as a progressive development, culminating in the triumph of John L. Lewis and the CIO. The Marxist analysis of class conflict is accepted, but the revolutionary moral is rejected. Although the play is sharply critical—much more so than *Triple-A*—of governmental policy, of the NRA, of General Johnson, and of the anti-labor attitude of the courts, its ultimate plea is for increased unionization.

If John L. Lewis and the emergent CIO are the heroes of *Injunction Granted*, George W. Norris and the TVA are the heroes of *Power*. Again the staff of the Living Newspaper makes a strong indictment of private enterprise—in this case, the target is the public utility; and, again, a strong plea is entered for direct governmental intervention to correct social abuses. But despite the fact that the play strongly suggests the necessity for the nationalization of power, despite its assertion that monopolistic control of power has already denied the premise of free competition, the Marxist press did not find its thesis strong enough. (The ideological deficiencies of *Triple-A* and *Injunction Granted* had already been noted.) Charles Dexter pointed out that Arent —the "editor" of *Power*—had missed the real social point, the fallacy of reform. The play did not point out the "shortcuts to true government ownership of power through political action by the plain people, the farmers and workers of America."[40] If the Living Newspaper went too far in the direction of radicalism in the eyes of its conservative critics, it did not go nearly far enough for the Marxists.

One Third of a Nation, in the simplicity of its dramatic line and in the ingenuity of its theatricalism, was by far the most effective of the Living Newspapers. It shared the basic elements of *Triple-A* and *Power*: the presentation of the history of a social problem (in this case, housing), the emphasis upon the inadequacy of free enterprise to deal with the problem, the support, therefore, of governmental intervention, and the final admonition that existing action was not sufficient. Its success (it played for an entire season in New York) may be attributed to the direct relevancy of its subject to the lives of its spectators, to its spectacular production (an entire tenement was engulfed by flames nightly on the stage of the Adelphi), and to the maturation of the Living Newspaper form itself. The play utilized the most successful elements of its predecessors: notably, it carried over from *Power* the use of an Everyman whose enlightenment becomes the task of the play. The relationship between the little man, bewildered by the fact of his own inadequate housing, and the Loudspeaker thus becomes that of student and teacher; and the disparate elements of the play are unified by the progress of this relationship.

It is a significant fact that the Living Newspaper continually stressed the need for intervention in those areas of the economy in which the New Deal had formulated specific social programs. The premise of *One Third*, like those of the other Living Newspapers, was essentially reformist. Nathan Straus is quoted within a favorable context: "There is no reform within my memory that has not been attacked as an invasion of private rights and as contrary to economic laws."[41] The wife of the play's Everyman echoes a familiar New Deal complaint when she protests limitations on housing legislation for purposes of economy. The plea that ends *One Third* is similar to the final complaint of the starving farmers in *Triple-A:* the principle of social reform is fine but it has not been translated into effective action. What is the social answer? Articulate protest:

You know what we're going to do? We're going to holler. And we're going to keep on hollering until they admit in Washington it's just as important to keep a man alive as it is to kill him! . . . Can you hear me—you in Washington or Albany or wherever you are! Give me a decent place to live in! Give me a home! A home! [p. 120]

There can be no doubt that the enemies made by the Living Newspaper were powerful ones, instrumental in the final closing of the project. Had the Federal Theatre played it safe and avoided all political controversy, it might have received a more sympathetic hearing from the distributors of the nation's funds; but it would also have abrogated one of Mrs. Flanagan's basic concerns, that "our plays . . . concern themselves with conditions back of the conditions described by President Roosevelt."[42] It is curious that while Congressional critics were complaining of the Federal Theatre's political preoccupations, several professional drama critics, who could hardly be accused of radicalism, criticized the project for not concerning itself more exclusively with contemporary social issues. Burns Mantle, for example, wrote of the production of *Faustus*: "It seems to me that the people's theatre would be better employed, considering the greatest good, in producing plays of timely significance."[43] This, by the way, from the drama critic of the New York *Daily News*.

The Federal Theatre did not die a natural death; it was killed by Act of Congress on June 30, 1939. The ostensible reason for the denial of funds to the Arts projects was economy, but this reason is belied by several facts: all the Arts projects used less than three-fourths of one per cent of the total WPA appropriation, and the appropriation *was not cut one cent* by the termination of the Federal Theatre; the money was simply distributed among other WPA projects.[44] Furthermore, there was no opposition from the theatrical profession itself. Letters and telegrams poured into Washington from the greatest names in the American theatre, as well as from the major theatrical unions, urging the continuation of the project, and New York's drama critics sent a joint letter to Congress maintaining that "the theatre project in New York . . . has been on the whole an institution of great value to the life of the community."[45] The project was ended primarily for political reasons, because enemies of the administration saw in the issue of communism within the project a means of embarrassing the New Deal. And the administration itself, fighting hard for its social program, could not risk the sacrifice of much of this program by demanding the continuation of the Arts projects. That the accusations against the project were largely unfounded was not important to its critics; they were not concerned with the record, and, in fact, resolutely refused to accept the theatre's invitation to attend performances of its plays.[46] The following exchange between Representative Starnes of the Dies Committee and Hallie Flanagan, who had petitioned repeatedly to be allowed to answer the charges brought against the project, clearly reveals the caliber of the attack:

Congressman Starnes: (quoting from Hallie Flanagan's book, *A Theatre is Born*) "the workers' theatres ... intend to remake a social structure without the help of money and this ambition alone invests their undertaking with a certain Marlowesque madness."
> You are quoting from this Marlowe. Is he a Communist?

Hallie Flanagan: I am very sorry. I was quoting from Christopher Marlowe.

Starnes: Tell us who Marlowe is, so we can get the proper reference, because that is all we want to do.

H.F.: Put in the record that he was the greatest dramatist in the period of Shakespeare, immediately preceding Shakespeare.

Starnes: Put that in the record, because the charge has been made that this article of yours is entirely Communistic, and we want to help you. Of course we had what some people call Communists back in the days of the Greek theatre. I believe Mr. Euripides was guilty of teaching class-consciousness also, wasn't he?

H.F.: I believe that was alleged against all of the Greek dramatists.

Starnes: So we cannot say when it began.[47]

Implicit in this exchange is another reason for the demise of the project. Art, in puritan eyes, is eternally suspect, eternally an instrument of the devil. Congressman Dies was shocked by the "vulgarity and profanity" that had been pointed out to him in several of the project's productions.[48] Representative Everett Dirksen called the work of the Federal Theatre "salacious tripe."[49] That taxpayers' money was being utilized for the propagation of radicalism and blasphemy was obviously not to be endured. Nor were Southern Congressmen happy about the nondiscriminatory policy of the project, the creation of Negro units in many large cities, and the antiracist themes of several project plays.

In short, normalcy was returning. As the decade came to its close, as the economy improved, the social forces which converged to create the Federal Theatre were dissipated. As the relief aspect of the project diminished there were those who proposed its continuity on a permanent basis. A Federal Arts Bill was introduced for the creation of a Department of Science, Art, and Literature.[50] But the ideal was short-lived; the belief that the government had a responsibility towards the arts was, with the Federal Theatre itself, plowed under.

The theatrical loss was immeasurably greater than the dramatic. The record of original Federal Theatre drama, as we have seen, is not very impressive. The project's main dramatic contribution was the Living Newspaper, a genre which was necessarily ephemeral. There seems to have been little incentive for major dramatists to write for the project, perhaps because of their fear of bureaucratic control and because commercial outlets were sufficient to absorb their energies. The project's main contribution was theatrical, not dramatic—in the principle rather than in the results of government-sponsored drama. Perhaps the Federal Theatre was unable to reconcile its commitment to the principle of economic relief with its commitment to a viable, socially-conscious theatre. Perhaps the two commitments were essentially irreconcilable. The significant fact, however, is that for a brief moment in American theatrical history there were many who felt they were not.

Part Two

COMMITMENT AND
THE PLAYWRIGHT

THE ROAD TO MARXIST COMMIT-
MENT: JOHN HOWARD LAWSON

"If you want to engage yourself," writes a young imbecile, "what are you waiting for? Join the Communist Party."

JEAN-PAUL SARTRE, *What Is Literature?*

An artist who takes his place with the working class begins to outgrow the split personality, because his life and work are integrated. His creative activity is logical and objective. He is no longer concerned with timeless achievement, because he has real work to do in the real world.

JOHN HOWARD LAWSON, "Art is a Weapon"

CHAPTER SIX

In *A Part of Our Time,* an attempt by a member of the
Depression generation to exorcise the ghost of his radicalism, Murray Kempton relates an incident in which John
Howard Lawson was being introduced at a May Day rally
in 1951. A young communist turned to the crowd and in-
toned into the microphone, "And now I want to introduce
a great anti-fascist, a great fighter for peace, a man you all
know." He then stopped, turned to his superior, and without bothering to put his hand over the microphone, asked
for all to hear, "What did you say his name was?"[1]

The price of fame—and notoriety—is dear, and if the
name of John Howard Lawson has faded even among the
remnants of American radicalism, it has all but disappeared
from the consciousness of the current generation of play-
goers. And yet Lawson once filled an honorable page in the
history of American drama; he was at one time considered
by Harold Clurman the hope of the Group Theatre,[2] and
Joseph Wood Krutch, among others, was "thrilled by the
passionate beauty of his *Processional.*"[3] *Roger Bloomer* was
indeed the first native expressionistic play, and *Processional*
employed jazz organically within a theatrical context almost thirty-five years before Jack Gelber's *The Connection.*
As an exponent in the twenties of a new experimental social
theatre, Lawson was involved in the formation of the Workers' Drama League and the New Playwrights, precursors
of the social theatre of the thirties; and as the dean of the
revolutionary movement in the theatre he wrote one of the
most militant proletarian dramas of the thirties.

And yet if the name of Lawson has any currency it is in quite another context from that of experimentalist or social dramatist. The image of Lawson retained—already somewhat dimly—by our generation is that of an unfriendly witness. It is the image of a man angrily refusing to answer questions from the House Committee on Un-American Activities concerning his communist affiliations, the image of a man who with nine other recalcitrant screen writers served a term in jail for contempt of Congress because of the intransigence of this refusal.

But the very role of unfriendly witness has significance for us in that it indicates the intensity of Lawson's political commitment. Unlike others of his generation—Cowley, Dos Passos, Wilson—Lawson did not relinquish his Marxist commitment; he was the one that stayed. For us, however, the interest in Lawson lies not in his steadfastness, but rather in the consequences of his road to commitment in terms of his role as dramatist.

For in the work of John Howard Lawson the conflicting demands of artist and ideologist are manifest. From his earliest plays onward, one senses this ambivalence; the necessity of social commitment hovers uneasily over the work of the Jazz Age experimentalist. The shadow of Karl Marx falls among the gallery of Freudian portraits. Both "bourgeois" and Marxist critics were at one in applying to Lawson's work that cruelest of epithets, confused. And most certainly there is a legitimacy in their verdict. But this confusion was not merely the result of technical inadequacy; the confusion manifest in Lawson's work lay at the very root of his personal, as well as his esthetic, dilemma. For if Lawson was at one with the Jazz Age condemnation of the "booboisie," he diverged in the intensity of his need to substitute positive values for the negative ones rejected; in fact, to commit himself. As the Jazz Age came to an end, he was no longer sustained by his earlier experimentation, and yet he found himself unable either to terminate his indecision or to give it coherent esthetic form. With the catalyst of the Depression, however, Lawson found himself—as one of many of his generation—faced at last with what seemed to him the possibility of choice.

Thus Lawson's experience is crucial to our investigation of the implications of commitment for the dramatist. Lawson, perhaps because of the fact that his talent was never of the highest rank, was particularly susceptible to the forces and movements of the decades in which he lived and worked. He was never possessed by the personal, all-conquering vision of an O'Neill, which rendered its possessor seemingly impervious to the vagaries of social conflict and enabled him to account only to the bitter demands of his individual, tragic microcosm. Lawson represents the man who was always conscious of his role in society, of his debt to it, and also of its encroachments upon his individual conscience. He reflects the dilemma of the Lost Generation in an age in which one could not afford to be lost. Lawson, as many of his generation, had to come to terms with the Great Depression; he is important for our purposes because he represents the defeat of the values of the old generation by the values of the new. And yet we are also interested in Lawson as an individual playwright, a man of considerable talent, whose dramatic promise was never fulfilled. In the last analysis, for all its analogues, his road to commitment was his own.

Lawson was a charter member of the Lost Generation; he served the traditional apprenticeship: in 1917 he joined the volunteer American ambulance service with the French Army, and later with the Italian Army on the Italian front. In this service he was associated with men whose reputations have not suffered his eclipse: John Dos Passos, Ernest Hemingway and E. E. Cummings. He acknowledged his debt to this experience in 1956: "This European experience was the root and beginning of the cultural development of my generation."[4] And *Roger Bloomer,* his first major play (he had had two plays produced in the summer of 1916), was started before his return to the United States in 1920. Of all Lawson's plays it is perhaps most definitively of its age, reflecting two trends explicit in the literature of the twenties: the tremendous impact of European experiment upon the American consciousness, and the young American's rejection of business morality and his tortured search for spiritual maturity.

Expressionism reflected both the impact of Freudian psychology upon art and the breakdown of traditional standards—in morality and esthetics—in the aftermath of the Great War. It made its postwar debut in the United States through such films as *The Cabinet of Dr. Caligari* (1920), and such theatrical productions as Kaiser's *From Morn to Midnight* (produced by the Theatre Guild in 1922). *Roger Bloomer* (1923), produced but a few days before our most durable example of American expressionism, Rice's *The Adding Machine,* used the essential characteristics of the form derived from these European examples: type characters (in the play, a Ragged Man, a Street Walker, a Judge, etc.); abstract characters, who represent not a class or type, but rather *aspects* of character or the personification of social or psychological forces (the Grotesques, who represent in Roger's dream the objectification of the Freudian death wish); telegraphic dialogue and telescopic characterization, whereby people who play similar roles in the protagonist's life are often made up to appear identical (the Judge and the College Examiner); antinaturalism and the reinstatement of the soliloquy and the aside; kaleidoscopic dramaturgy, whereby scenes are conceived cinematically; and, as a consequence, décor, which, through its sparseness and distortion, enhances both this fluidity and the nightmare quality of the entire effect. In short, the essence of expressionism lies in the conception of the monodramatic; all technical devices, all characters and situations combine to reveal the psychological workings of the mind of the hero, or as the case may be, the antihero.

Roger Bloomer displays all the characteristics of the expressionistic genre. If these devices are not original with Lawson, it is still no small distinction to have been among the very first Americans to employ them in an indigenous context. For *Roger Bloomer,* within its expressionist form, reflects the adolescent yearning for maturity which is at the heart of much of American writing. If, in comparison with the work of our expatriate experimentalists such as Pound and Eliot, it seems at times almost unbearably naive in its rejection of bourgeois values and its absolute awe in the hallowed presence of Sex, it is nonetheless extremely American precisely because of these limitations. The world that Roger rejects is Winesburg, Ohio, as well as Excelsior, Iowa; his groping toward maturity is one of the basic metaphors of American literary experience.

Roger Bloomer's odyssey is the familiar one of every fresh-faced adolescent who arrives in the metropolis with the hope of finding the self-realization impossible in the stultifying atmosphere of his home town. Having failed his college entrance examinations because of the authoritarian bullying of his examiner, Roger had cried that he was "able to refuse" the values of his culture. Significantly this refusal is based less upon hostility to oppressive authority than on the threat to the young man's virility. It is the sexual quest which continually illumines his rebellion. In a scene with Eugene, the defender of American ideals, Roger acknowledges his sexual inexperience, but sexuality represents to him more than physical release; he is obsessed with the female principle as the one meaningful fact in the universe; he must possess it: "I want the impossible, I want to change things, I want women's souls—and I'll never be satisfied

with less. I swear. . . . Never!"[5] He finds himself alone, but
it is not the loneliness of the political rebel in conflict with
authority, but the loneliness of the adolescent imprisoned
by his passion. Roger finds the incarnation of the female
principle in the person of Louise, a young girl who is similarly discontented but attempts to escape the horror of her
existence by living most strenuously by the ethic of acquisitiveness. "There's one thing that beats out Hate," she cries,
"sets you above tiredness—money!" (p. 251). But behind
her facade of toughness lies an instinctive tenderness which
draws her to Roger; and the young couple, alone in a hostile
world, cling together for protection.

However, the relationship cannot be fulfilled; Louise is
possessed by a fear of sex which prevents her from fully
loving Roger, and as a final sacrifice, to free Roger from the
prison of her passionless domination, she commits suicide.
And Roger, in jail pending investigation of the cause of
death, by means of a nightmare of pursuit which coalesces
and unifies the disparate elements of his mind, finally
achieves his long-sought-for maturity. In the three strophes
of the dream—the first full scale Freudian dream in American drama—"all the figures of the play, representing the
conventions and proprieties, surround Roger threaten-
ingly," engage in a "mocking orgy of Sex and Obscenity"
behind which lurks the Freudian death wish, and are finally
dispelled by Louise, the Life Force, "the dream that will
not die," who rises to protect Roger and set him free from
the bondage of sex. "I've given you yourself, take it. . . .
Laughter is not enough, denial is not enough. . . . In yourself you must find the secret" (p. 295). And as her image
fades into the darkness the attendant unlocks Roger's cell
and sends him into the world outside.

The search for maturity which lies at the heart of *Roger
Bloomer*, while primarily a personal quest, also reflects
Lawson's condemnation of the values of a society in which

Roger has no place. In this condemnation of materialism
Lawson is not at odds with his generation. However, what
characterizes his work, even in his first play, is the intensity
of this condemnation, and the awareness, albeit implied
in *Roger Bloomer,* that personal salvation is not enough,
that there is something radically wrong with the fabric of
society which the resolution of sexual difficulties will not
alter. Roger is afflicted by more than personal anguish; he is
constrained by the Babbittry represented by his father and
Eugene, by the values of acquisitiveness which help destroy
his love affair with Louise. Even at the moment of his
greatest introspection, Lawson felt compelled to fragment
his vision; as Roger wanders the streets of New York, home-
less and penniless, he has eyes for more than his own despair:

In the grey pit of the streets pass the gray millions—and all these
that pass are hungry . . . starving men and women. . . . What
doom will come on this place, what doom, oh, hungry city? . . .
Death will come in a whirlwind breaking your sky towers—and
the hungry will shout for joy! . . . I am yours, oh, city of slaves
. . . I am one of the millions, servants of death and time, hungry,
moaning for bread! [pp. 257-58]

Roger senses that the turmoil is both within and outside
himself. He is tortured by the universal torment of adoles-
cence, a torture independent of class, and yet he senses that
his anxiety has more than personal roots. Already at the
outset Lawson's dilemma is delineated. For *Roger Bloomer*
fails as a play precisely because Roger's personal anguish
is in only a small sense activated by the oppressions of his
society. The fault lies not in his being a member of an exploited class, or even in the possession of false values, like
Mr. Zero, the antihero of Rice's *Adding Machine.* His
values are good, and his search for realization would occur
in any social system. Woman, Sex, the Life Force—this is

what frees Roger from his adolescent bondage, and it is in no way dependent, in the context of this play, upon the follies of capitalist morality. Lawson's focus is thus obscured: on one hand, salvation lies in the search for self-realization; on the other, in the reformation of society. "I feel a doom all over the world," laments Mrs. Bloomer apocalyptically, "people breaking things . . . carelessly . . . churches falling down!" (p. 260). The old order is crumbling—this intuition lies beneath the surface of the play. And Roger, at the moment of his sexual liberation, is chosen heir to the new order: "Away! Away, ghosts of yesterday," chants the dream-image of Louise, "for the young are coming marching, marching; far off, listen, the tread of marching people singing a new song . . ." (pp. 294-95). And in 1937, John Howard Lawson wrote a revolutionary play called *Marching Song*.

Processional (1925), Lawson's second play, deservedly his most famous, possesses an authentic originality; for in this play Lawson attempted to use the stock devices and figures of American vaudeville and the drive and power of the then recently discovered indigenous music, jazz, as the means through which he could create a panorama of American life. He called his play a "jazz symphony of American life," and attempted to employ several expressionistic devices in a native context:

I have endeavored to create a method which shall express the American scene in native idiom, a method as far removed from the older realism as from the facile mood of Expressionism. It is apparent that this new technique is essentially vaudevillesque in character—a development, a moulding to my own uses, of the rich vitality of the two-a-day and the musical extravaganza.[6]

Although several expressionistic devices are still in evidence (the Man in the Silk Hat, for example, is in the tradition of abstract satire; the Klan scene, among others, uses taut, telegraphic expressionistic dialogue), *Processional* is conceived panoramically rather than monodramatically. Lawson is not concerned with the individual's struggle against the stultifying forces of modern society, but rather with the depiction of the joys and the bitterness—above all, the *vitality*—of American life through the means of the exuberant popular form of vaudeville.

To achieve his end he employs a group of jazz-playing miners who represent the spectrum of vaudeville comic stereotypes. They include Rastus Jolly, an easily intimidated Negro prototype of Stepin Fetchit; Dago Joe, "a sleek, greasy Italian" with an accordion; and Alexander Gore, the perennially dumb hayseed. To this gallery of stereotypes add Isaac Cohen, the money-conscious Jewish storekeeper, and Phillpots, a George M. Cohan "stop-the-presses" version of a newspaperman, and Lawson's gallery of grotesques of the American environment is completed.

But while Lawson's technique is formally experimental, his subject matter concerns a situation which was to be dear to the succeeding generation; the plot of *Processioal* concerns a bitter strike, and the play possesses many elements which were to constitute the structure of the proletarian novel and drama. For example, class lines are rigidly drawn; unlike *Roger Bloomer, Processional* hinges upon the fact of class strife. Among the characters is a Polish communist who continually intones the coming of the workers' revolution; and the hero, Dynamite Jim, is in what is to become the tradition of the proletarian hero. Rebellious, proud, contemptuous of capitalist authority, he enacts the traditional martyrdom: he is blinded by the forces of reaction. The representatives of capitalism—the Man in the Silk Hat, the Sheriff, the leaders of the KKK—are not merely figures of satiric contempt; they represent a conspiratorial force directed against the workers. All this would seem to second Murray Kempton's contention that

"Lawson's was always a consciously revolutionary voice; and *Processional* was a class war piece."[7] But just how conscious was Lawson's revolutionary voice? Although *Processional* contains the elements of class strife that were to distinguish proletarian literature of the thirties, it is significant that Lawson handles them humorously. *Processional* is hardly a play of bitter social protest. More often than not, Lawson exploits the comic possibilities of his vaudeville machinery and the racial stereotypes of Negro, Jew, and Italian. For example, after the Klan scene, both Cohen and Rastus are unmasked in Klan uniforms. The sight of an Uncle Tom Negro in a Klan outfit could hardly have brought joy to the more radical of the play's viewers. Moreover, Psinski, the communist, is for all his revolutionary mouthings essentially a comic figure, at times admirable, but finally almost ridiculous. Thus, while Lawson senses the underlying class struggle manifest in American life, his voice at that time was hardly consciously revolutionary. The strike is not won by the organized demands of militant workers, but rather through the generosity of capital, because the powers that be sense the publicity value of stopping the hostility. As Phillpots says to Psinski: "The laugh is always on you" (p. 212).

That Lawson recognized the revolutionary deficiencies of *Processional* is reflected by the changes that he made in the script when the Federal Theatre revived the play in 1937. Although *Variety* reported that few revisions had been made in the script, an examination of the revised version shows this to be untrue. For one thing, Lawson, presenting the play to a Depression audience and as an active member of a revolutionary party, could hardly allow the racial stereotypes to remain. This is most manifest in the complete revamping of the character of Rastus Jolly, the Negro minstrel. He is now called Joe Green, and where he had previously been characterized as "one lonesome nigger . . .

with a heart full of care an' desecration" (p. 58), forced by Dynamite Jim to assist in the latter's escape from jail, he is now almost a militant Negro worker, assisting Jim voluntarily. Psinski does not undergo so striking a metamorphosis, but all elements of ridiculousness are expunged from his character, and he emerges almost wholly admirable.

There can be no doubt of Lawson's intentions: *Processional* (1937) must conform to the demands of proletarian drama, even at the expense of the play's vaudevillesque metaphor. The objectivity which enabled Lawson to invest even his sympathetic characters with elements of ridiculousness has been abandoned in the face of his commitment. And yet the leftist press remained unsatisfied by Lawson's revision. The *New Masses*, calling the revival "a disheartening and discouraging mess," particularly objected to Lawson's racial stereotypes, which, it claimed, were "caricatures and libels."[8] The Marxist critic sensed that there was something in *Processional* which could have been expunged only by a complete overhaul of the play, that the key to the play lies in the love of Jim and Sadie (the conventional hero and heroine), that the forces of social conflict do not hold the center of the stage but form, instead, the backdrop for a drama of love and redemption. As in *Roger Bloomer*, Lawson alternates between social awareness and psychological determinism. It is a woman's voice that is the "kind of a song that's behind change and politics" (a line cut from the revised version); man, the rebel, is forever dwarfed by the Eternal Woman. Even in the revised version, the last line of the play is given to Sadie, singing gently to her unborn child: "I'm agonna raise my kid, sing to him soft. . . ."

Lawson's intellectual confusion was projected disastrously upon the form and substance of his next produced play, *Nirvana* (1926). This work, described by one commentator as a "brash, headless, groggy debauch of catch phrases and inflated situations,"[9] was an ambitious failure and may have been a chastening experience; for Lawson's next play, *Loud Speaker* (1927), is primarily a farce. It is, however, a farce with a difference. First of all, its technique is experimental. Lawson has, in fact, combined various kinds of experimentalism within the conventions of farce, and, on the whole, he has done so remarkably successfully. From constructivism he has appropriated his stage, from expressionism he has borrowed such devices as the long, revelatory monologue and satiric stereotypes, and from his own *Processional* he has continued the use of jazz as leitmotif and racial, vaudevillesque caricature (e.g., the Harlem delegation which breaks into a jazz dance). The conventions of farce are observed, therefore, within the confines of experimentalism.

Secondly, the purpose of *Loud Speaker* is not solely to amuse, but also to comment seriously upon the very premises of life in Boom-Age America. Lawson follows Coolidge's counsel to "look well to the hearthstone, therein all hope for America lies" (the epigraph to the printed version)—and finds there futility, mendacity, pomposity, and ignorance. The ills that afflict the American home, moreover, are symptomatic of the ills which afflict society at large; if there is one major theme in *Loud Speaker,* it is the deceitful manipulation of the public by the politician in alliance with the mass media. The play is, in fact, undiluted Menckenism. "If X is money and Y is bunk," claims a politician, "the answer to X plus Y is the great American public" (p. 32). And to confirm this cynical contention, Lawson allows one of his characters his "moment of truth"; Collins, a candidate for governor, is forced because of a family crisis to reveal himself to a radio audience as the fraud he is.

The newspapers are blah . . . the Government is blah, you folks are fed on pap that wouldn't deceive an infant in diapers. . . . Are you listening, you gang out there . . . to hear me slobber about honesty and good government! . . . I'm a man standing here now with truth coming out of my mouth instead of drool, but for the first time in my life I'm a man! [p. 139]

But of course, the irony is that this speech is the most endearing form of American hokum, and Collins is elected precisely because he has touched the great American sentiment for public confession. It is a criticism not without justification in our own day.

Politicians, newspapermen, broadcasters, society women trying and discarding new religions, society girls on the make—all these reflect the iconoclastic Menckenism which pervades *Loud Speaker*. But, again, Lawson cannot accept the radical implications of his violent criticisms of society. Indeed, the one radical in the play is a yellow journalist who has made his peace with the false values of his society. But if Lawson as yet sees no specific political solution for the evils of capitalism which he has satirized, he again senses that change is in the wind and that it is inexorable. Characteristically, it is a woman, Mrs. Collins, who, like Mrs. Bloomer and Old Maggie (in *Processional*) before her, senses Lawson's familiar apocalyptic vision. "I feel a darkness coming over me and out of the darkness a voice. . . . The birth of Silence is coming, the kaleidoscope of the Future" (pp. 176-77). And Johnny, the Jazz Age radical, despite his personal disillusionment, gives voice to Lawson's persistent yearning for political commitment: "This will go on for twenty years, and then we'll discover a new religion which is neither new nor religious" (p. 184). For Lawson this new nonreligious religion was indeed to be Marxism, and the song of the future which he hears, now dimly, now more distinctly, in the twenties, is the "Internationale."

The Internationale (1928) is Lawson's farewell to experimentalism, a potpourri of expressionistic, vaudevillesque devices in the context of a play which is part farce, part musical, part melodrama, and part prophetic poem. The elements in the play are in a continual state of imbal-

ance: expressionism vies with realism, seriousness with
farce, symbolism with mystery melodrama, and if the
esthetic result is largely to be deplored, it is significant in
that its very confusion articulates the crisis of Lawson's
social ambivalence. For in *The Internationale*, Lawson
comes at last to a recognition of the power of communist
ideology, and while he has not as yet chosen sides, he at least
attempts to define his political dilemma.

The play fulfills Lawson's earlier apocalyptic visions; it
attempts to prophesy the coming of class war brought about
by imperialist capitalism's attempt to obtain the oil resources of the Far East. But this social vision is cast in terms
of a plot which, more often than not, reduces these implications to the intrigues of melodrama; and one has, for much
of the action, the feeling that somehow one has blundered
into a theatre where *The Green Goddess* is playing. There
is also throughout the play a continuing thread of Freudian-
ism that is at times almost in complete opposition to the
revolutionary thesis upon which much of the plot hinges.

The revolution which was dimly perceived in Lawson's
earlier plays has, at last, in *The Internationale*, arrived, and
the moment of political choice seems at hand: "At your door
crowds are singing, soldiers are dragging machine guns. . . .
Which side, then, which side?" But when the revolution arrives, when the red flags are flying in Union Square, all is
for nought. The workers' revolution is suppressed by the
capitalists in alliance with the fascists; but Lawson does *not*
draw political lessons from this suppression. David, the
erstwhile communist, tells his girl friend that he has learned
one thing from all the bloodshed and violence: "Revolution!
I didn't know what it meant, I'm not sure now: but I see
your eyes!"[10] In short, he surrenders himself to his love for
Alise, the Soviet girl, who finally rejects her militancy to
love him as well. Thus, just when it appears as if Marx were
conquering Freud, we find that this is not the case. At the

moment of the workers' revolution, Lawson had tried to render the triumph of Marxian over Freudian principles symbolically.

Chorus: . . . We are the field waiting for the plow.
Alise: The plow is a sword!
Gussie: Open to the sword, take me, shining sword. . . . Plow
    sword . . . Plow!
    [Alise rises, all the others still kneeling.
    She holds up a sword with a ragged red flag
    tied to it.]
Chorus: Tell us how . . . Tell us how. . . .
Alise: It is now . . . Now! [pp. 226-27]

The symbolic transference of the sexual sword into the revolutionary sword might well have been a coherent metaphor with which to order the disparate elements of *The Internationale*. But Lawson's dilemma is that he cannot as yet fully assent to this transference. Consequently his intellectual ambivalence sends the play down confusing corridors, and it is difficult to emerge from the maze with any sense of artistic coherence. Ideologically the play intensifies explicitly the attack upon capitalism reflected in the earlier plays, but behind the revolutionary mask lies the face of futility. We note a number of contradictions: on one hand, the ambivalence toward communism as a specific solution to social ills; and on the other, the ambivalence concerning the ultimate efficacy of political action. In the first case, Lawson's communist characters, including his hero, are more sympathetic than their capitalist counterparts. But how is one to explain the equal condemnation of Aretini, the fascist, and Rubeloff, the communist? If the war is indeed a class war in which the imperialists and the exploited are sharply delineated, how can one explain the sympathetic treatment of one of the instigating capitalists? It is clear that Lawson had not clearly thought out the implications of his political sniping. He seemed to be shooting at every moving thing in the vicinity.

But behind this confused, revolutionary iconoclasm, despite the attempt to dethrone Freud, it is clear that in the end it is the Woman Principle—manifested previously in Louise and Sadie—that triumphs over political zeal. Alise, the once zealous revolutionary, exchanges her political principles for David's love. The Freudian serpent conquers the Marxian sword: all of us, revolutionist or not, "have a mutual friend whose name is despair" (p. 82). The last line of the play perhaps most plaintively summarizes both Lawson's need for belief, and his sense of not having put all the pieces of the puzzle together coherently: "How do I get home? Christ, for the love o' pity, where do I go home?" (p. 276).

If Lawson had not fully defined his political position in the late twenties, there can be no doubt, as we have demonstrated, of his social awareness. When, in *The Internationale*, he invokes the ghosts of Sacco and Vanzetti as harbingers of revolution ("suddenly the ghosts of America's martyrs, Sacco and Vanzetti . . . blacken the sky over New York!" [p. 211]), he was citing a cause in which he had been passionately involved. He had joined the Citizen's National Committee for Sacco and Vanzetti, an emergency organization the purpose of which was to bring pressure upon the Federal Government to open the files of the Department of Justice for evidence bearing on the case. Along with a number of other writers—Dos Passos, Michael Gold, Ruth Hale, Grace Lumpkin, Edna St. Vincent Millay, Dorothy Parker, Katherine Anne Porter, and Lola Ridge—he went out on a picket line in Boston and was arrested.[11] This experience was Lawson's first taste of direct political action, and he later acknowledged that "my participation in the last days of struggle to save Sacco-Vanzetti played an important part in my artistic and political development."[12]

Lawson's social awareness, combined with the very real need of the playwright to find a theatre hospitable to his art, involved him first in the formation of the Workers' Drama League in the spring of 1926 (with Mike Gold, Ida Rauh, and Jasper Deeter); and then, in February, 1927, in the formation of the New Playwrights (with Gold, Francis Faragoh, Emjo Basshe, and John Dos Passos). The group reflected the very difficulties manifest in Lawson's plays; according to Clurman, they "wanted something but it wasn't very clear what. . . . Their productions were undisciplined, amateurish, lyrical, frivolous."[13] Lawson acknowledged the group's weakness, but claimed later that "in spite of . . . its aesthetic manifestoes and vacillating policies, it was an important forerunner of the more mature social theatre of the 1930's."[14]

Thus, Lawson did not come to his political commitment without previous apprenticeship. It is significant, however, that unlike many of his circle—among them Dos Passos, Cowley, Grace Lumpkin—he did not sign the *Culture and the Crisis* pamphlet, in which a number of prominent intellectuals urged other professional workers to vote the Communist ticket in the 1932 election. In fact, Clurman reports that in the early days of the Depression Lawson "from time to time . . . vented opinions that led us to believe that though he was definitely of progressive, even radical opinion, he was violently opposed to official communist doctrine."[15]

Success Story (1932), Lawson's first play of the Depression years, reveals, first of all, his abandonment of experimentalism. The style of the play is realistic, a form surely more congenial to the method of the Group Theatre which produced it, than the lyrical expressionism which characterized his previous work. The Experimental Age was dead, and economic reality seemed to demand of all writers a stern apprenticeship to the facts of life. Lawson's attack on capitalist ethics gathers new meaning in a society in which "when you see those breadlines on Broadway, it shows how insecure everything is."[16] The prime target is the ethic of acquisitiveness which decrees that everything has a price, that profit and power are the only gods. Lawson's protagonist, Sol Ginsburg, the tough Jewish kid whose rise to the top of the business world is the "success story" with which the play is concerned, is possessed by a demon which drives him to destroy even those who love him. As a product of the slums of the Lower East Side, he learned at an early age that "there's no future without money," and he is determined to obtain it at all costs. Until freed from poverty there can be no room in his life for love, pity, or any of the normal human decencies.

But despite his avarice, Sol Ginsburg, like his later counterpart Budd Schulberg's Sammy Glick, is a man of great potential for good. Had his energy, drive, and intelligence been channelled in a positive direction, Sol might have cut quite a different figure. Lawson continually affirms that in his zeal, his energy, and his dedication to his false God, Sol is, in reality, a revolutionary *manqué*. "You're a revolutionist," one of the characters tells Sol, "never content, pursuing a vision, you want to change the whole world in the image of your ego" (p. 183).

In fact, Sol had been a political radical in his youth, and throughout the play he continually attempts to escape the guilt born of political disavowal. He castigates the poverty-stricken radicals at every opportunity: "I'm sick to death of radical meetings and sour-faced people and cheap gab" (p. 40). But when the chips are down and Sol, like all men, has to face what he has become, he recognizes that he had a choice, that he might have lived according to a very different ethic. He reveals this to Sarah by means of a parable:

Sol: This fellow Christ took me up to a high mountain and showed me the earth . . . and He said, "Do you want the earth, Solomon Ginsburg, or do you want to join me in a cellar,

sweating and plotting with a few close friends?" Well, I made my choice and somewhere Christ is in a cellar laughing at me right now. . . .
Sarah: You mean the people in cellars are stronger than you are?
Sol: Stronger than all Hell because they know what they want . . . maybe when I get a billion I'll hand it to the Communist Party. [p. 230]

But Sol's choice has been made and he cannot remake himself in a new image. For a moment he almost convinces Sarah that he has changed, that he has found in her, and not in the success that he has achieved, something to believe in, "something to hold on to" (p. 235). But this change of heart is short-lived; Sarah realizes that the ethic that Sol has lived by has created a monster that cheapens everything it touches, and, in the melodramatic conclusion to the play, shoots him rather than allow him to keep on destroying. Then, as he dies Sol clearly recognizes the viciousness and futility of his life: "I bin dead a long time" (p. 242).

There is a very real dynamism in the character of Sol Ginsburg which vitalizes the play, in spite of such defects as the gratuitousness of his death, occasional scenes of almost embarrassing theatricality, and dialogue which at moments suggests the more overripe metaphors of Odets: "You stick me with a knife right in the pride" (p. 128). But, more significantly, Lawson has specified the target of his social criticism, and not dissipated his creative energies by exploding simultaneously in all directions. There can be no doubt in the reader's mind that Sol made the wrong choice, that the values by which he lived were immoral, that he would have lived a more meaningful life had he not forsaken his youthful radical ideals. And yet, despite the explicitness of Lawson's criticism, the play was deplored in the Marxist press. Sol's disavowed radicalism, for example, seemed to Mike Gold "to have been only the mask for an overwhelming craving for money and bourgeois success."[17]

But if the Marxist critics deplored aspects of *Success Story*, they could find almost nothing to recommend in Lawson's next play, *The Pure in Heart*, which he had started in 1928. Why was Lawson "willing to finish and produce such a pretentious and muddled play in 1934?" asked the *New Masses*.[18] Indeed, Lawson had the unpleasant experience of satisfying neither the Marxist nor the Broadway critics, and of enduring two Broadway flops in one week, for *The Pure in Heart* and *Gentlewoman*, produced within two days of each other (March 20 and 22, 1934), both received bad notices. This double rejection seems to have been crucial to Lawson's ideological and artistic development, for it is not long after this experience that he arrives, once and for all, at his political commitment.

The adverse criticisms of *The Pure in Heart* were, however, quite apart from ideological considerations, most deserved. The play cannot be dismissed as sheer hack work, for there is some evidence of Lawson's ultimate seriousness, but the melodramatist does triumph over the craftsman. While Lawson's social criticism is still trenchant, it is mired in a plot that contains many of the tried and true clichés of the Hollywood scenario. The tale of Annabel Sparks, the stage-struck girl who comes to the Big Town and conquers Broadway, is in the best *Morning Glory* tradition; and her love for the gangster-hero, Larry—a love doomed less by the pressures of society than by the exigencies of melodrama —was to become one of the dominant clichés of the genre of the sentimental gangster film, in which the hero—usually portrayed by James Cagney, Henry Fonda or John Garfield —is more sinned against than sinning. The plot is replete with melodramatic contrivance: fortuitous backers, love scenes of monumental conventionality, violent gun-play, and gratuitous death—indeed, Lawson seems to have ransacked the Hollywood bag of tricks.

About all that redeems Annabel's "success story" is that,

like Sol's, it is hardly conventional, for Lawson explicitly rejects the values which she has accepted, as does Annabel herself at her "moment of truth." The world of the theatre is viewed in all its sterility and unreality as the microcosm of the larger world of which it is a part; and its inhabitants are doomed by false values to a life of absurdity and make-believe. For the theatre is a cynical business in which "the biggest commodity in the world—dreams, forgetfulness" is sold, and the cynicism of the theatre is merely the reflection of the values of a society in which profit is the only morality, in which all positive values are negated. In such a world all actions are equally meaningful, and equally futile. *The Pure in Heart* is, then, Lawson's farewell to the futility of the Jazz Age; the cynical philanderer, Goshen, realizes that his world is crumbling. Looking at New York, spread out below his penthouse window, he asks what is behind the glare of lights that symbolizes our civilization: "Crazy people all hopped up with crazy ideas, selling bad stock, passing bad checks, chasing money, chasing glory, millionaires with their brain-addled girls . . . looking for dreams . . . found in bad movies . . . a crazy show on a glaring stage. Every time I look at that skyline I want to die!"[19]

The obvious difficulty with the play, however, is that its melodramatic structure is unable to sustain the weight of Lawson's social criticism. The elements of realistic motivation and social insight are indeed present, but they seem almost gratuitous; they cannot survive the triteness of the plot, and the reality of social dislocation plays only a small part in *The Pure in Heart*. Lawson not only uses the theatrical metaphor; he succumbs to it, and the very theatricality of the machinery of the play dissipates the seriousness of his criticism. Annabel, for all her vitality, emerges as a stock heroine—the girl who retains her inner core of purity despite the corruption of her flesh—in short, that familiar figure, the whore with the heart of gold; and in the character of the gangster-hero Larry, Lawson has smothered the real core of personality in a stereotype.

One can understand why the Marxists considered the play ideologically retrogressive; despite the intrusion of the world of the Depression—an intrusion which smacks of rewriting—the world of *The Pure in Heart* is indeed that of the Jazz Age and, unlike *Success Story*, does not attempt to come to terms with issues raised by the economic crisis. It remained for *Gentlewoman* to make this attempt anew.

There can be no doubt of the solid anchoring of *Gentlewoman* in an age of crisis. Not only breadlines, but the Soviet Union, the Scottsboro case, stevedore strikes, the imminence of war, famine, industrial crises are matters of concern and conversation for the characters of the play. Lawson's vision is no longer prophetic; change is not imminent; it is here: "everything's changing . . . corporations crumble and die."[20] Social questions are no longer academic. As Dr. Golden, the psychiatrist, puts it:

The real question is whether our culture is equal to the tasks which face it. . . . Can we remake the world? Can we create a decent standard of living? Can we preserve peace? [p.126]

Lawson frames his answer in a play which avoids the melodramatics of *The Pure in Heart*. He has objectified the crisis of choice incumbent upon the individual living in the thirties in the dual personages of the gentlewoman and her proletarian lover; for in them the struggle between the old order and the new is expressed in personal terms. But although Lawson senses that the answers to Dr. Golden's queries are uniformly "No," he cannot as yet make a full-scale revolutionary commitment. He is too much of the bourgeois world to reject it out of hand. Thus the relationship between Gwyn and Rudy reflects Lawson's social inde-

cision: on the one hand, he recognizes that capitalism is
decadent, and yet, on the other, he realizes that he is a
product of this society, that in rejecting it he is rejecting
himself.

Lawson's criticisms of capitalism are no longer the
iconoclastic gestures of the Jazz Age rebel; the bourgeois
ethic is not only evil, it is unsuccessful. Gwyn's husband had
lived by Sol's rule that "ethics is one thing . . . business another" (p. 161), but still could not survive the Crash. Yet
while bourgeois society is portrayed as corrupt, licentious
and decadent, it is significant that Gwyn, the gentlewoman,
the embodiment of this dying class, is a woman of great
emotional depth and integrity—all in all, one of Lawson's
finest dramatic creations. Lawson's ambivalence toward his
own bourgeois status is most keenly expressed in her portrayal. Although she is unable to convince herself that
politics is important, she is disturbed by the emptiness
which both surrounds and is within her; and in the person
of Rudy, Gwyn thinks she has found the prophet to lead
her from the wilderness of despair. In surrendering herself
to his love, she attempts to reject her bourgeois past and
create a new life based upon positive values. But she comes
to realize that for her the transformation has come too late.
She deliberately becomes pregnant to hold Rudy, but finally
recognizes that he must be free to pursue his own destiny in
his own way. For Rudy fulfillment lies "in the streets and
on the docks and in the fields" where "people are carrying
burdens in the night and in the heat of the sun" (p. 203).
It is a world that Gwyn wants desperately to enter, but she
realizes that the sum total of her previous existence unfits
her for proletarian living. Ultimately she sacrifices herself—
her love for Rudy—by keeping the secret of her pregnancy
and sending him out to participate in the struggle free of
the restriction of his love for her. She, with the class she

represents, is condemned. The future, however, will be different:

Our children won't play at life in boudoirs and offices: they'll face something different whether they like it or not. . . . We're not fit for the future, we're little people, we comfort ourselves with little fears, we walk in a funeral procession—towards a red horizon; we can't see the cities burning and the marching armies—there's blood in the sky. [p. 220]

The revolutionary implications of this speech are manifest; and yet, despite his vision of the wave of the future, Lawson's attitude toward revolutionary commitment is still indecisive. It is not only that his major character is bourgeois, not working class, but that his radical representative is himself tortured with doubts. Despite his proletarian background and his instinctive radicalism, Rudy is not quite sure of his position: "Maybe I'm just a bourgeois slob. . . . I bluster a lot, I used to be sure of myself . . . now I'm not clear about anything . . ." (pp. 184-85). Beneath the surface of this bluster there is an underlying insufficiency which turns Gwyn's prophet into a tin god. One wonders finally if her sacrifice has been worth it; the bourgeois gentlewoman, in the last analysis, emerges as more credible and admirable than her proletarian lover. Thus the relationship between Gwyn and Rudy reflects various facets of Lawson's indecision: the need to reject the old order without the ability to accept fully the new; the recognition that the world which produced the avarice of Sol Ginsburg also produced the nobility of Gwyn Ballantine; and, finally, the playwright's apprehension that like his gentlewoman, he may be too late for the brave new world he knows is coming.

The Pure in Heart ran seven performances; *Gentlewoman* lasted twelve. This dual rejection launched Lawson on a vitriolic attack upon the Broadway critics; he published the plays in a volume entitled *With a Reckless Preface,* and

proceeded, once and for all, to wash his hands of Broadway. Like many an angry playwright before and after him,
Lawson excoriated the dismissers of his art as men "whose
incompetence . . . seriously hampers the normal activity of
the theatre."[21] But Lawson did not limit himself to personal
abuse; he attempted to demonstrate that the unhealthiness
of the Broadway stage was fundamentally a *social* phenomenon, that the commercial theatre could not tolerate
seriousness because it was obliged to express "the despair
and weakness . . . of the middle-class mind" which supported it. Therefore, Lawson adamantly refused to accept
Broadway's terms, and decided to direct his creative
energies in an alternative direction: "The only answer is to
turn resolutely to the building of the revolutionary theatre."[22]

But despite the Marxist basis of this attack and evaluation, despite Lawson's assertion that the characters in
Gentlewoman found "a new balance and reason for their
lives in communism," the attitude of the Marxist critics was
no less hostile to the implications of Lawson's efforts than
that of the bourgeois critics he had reviled. In the *New
Masses* of April 10, 1934, Mike Gold launched an attack
upon Lawson's work under the title "A Bourgeois Hamlet of
our Time," which was to be crucial in Lawson's political
development. Gold claimed that Lawson's plays were
vitiated by an ideological confusion which belied the social
promise of *Processional*:

The world has changed enormously, but this author has learned
nothing. He is still lost like Hamlet, in his inner conflict. Through
all his plays wander a troop of ghosts disguised in the costumes
of living men and women and repeating the same monotonous
questions: "Where do I belong in the warring world of two
classes?"[23]

In view of Lawson's statements concerning the class basis
of American theatre and society, in view of his social in-

sight, partially revealed in his plays, Gold felt compelled
to ask: "What have you learned in these ten years?" And he
answered the question himself: " 'Nothing. I am still a bewildered wanderer lost between two worlds indulging myself in the same adolescent self-pity as in my first plays.' "[24]

The intensity of an attack from such an unexpected quar-
ter brought an immediate reply from Lawson. But where he
had previously been defiant in his replies to his Broadway
critics, he was in answer to Gold contrite and humble. In
the very following issue of the *New Masses* Lawson sub-
mitted a reply which from the outset tried not so much to
contest Gold's criticisms—he acknowledges "the truth of 70
per cent of Mike's attack"—as to explain the reasons for his
deficiencies and offer hope for change. He admits that his
"work to date is utterly unsatisfactory in its political orientation," but claims in defense that it is very difficult for a
person of bourgeois background to achieve a genuine acceptance of proletarian ideals. Moreover, he denies the
charge that his preoccupation with capitalist decay necessarily implies that he is involved in this decay; he maintains
that his work *does* demonstrate an orderly development toward revolutionary consciousness.

After the childish high spirits of *Processional*, I turned to a confused religious escape in *Nirvana*; that was the inevitable step
considering my background and intellectual processes. *The Internationale* was a serious attempt to portray a world revolution,
but my lack of a theoretical background betrayed me into many
inexcusable errors and a general air of anarchistic sentimentality. . . . I believe *Gentlewoman*, in spite of faults, shows a considerable ideological advance. . . . It is a play about a dying
bourgeois class . . . on Marxian lines.[25]

In short, Lawson rebukes Gold only for not offering constructive criticism that could help him attain ideological
clarity. There is, he affirms, no need to fear that he is drift-
ing toward "any sort of liberal betrayal of the working

class," for he intends to demonstrate clearly his new-found ideological awareness: "Where do I belong? . . . I intend to make my answer with due consideration and with as much clarity and vigor as I possess."[26]

Harold Clurman confirms Lawson's humility in the face of Marxist criticism. Clurman, as co-founder of the Group Theatre, which had produced *Success Story* and *Gentlewoman,* and as a fervent believer in Lawson's talent, accompanied the latter to a radical literary club. Lawson had accepted an invitation to speak to the members on the meaning of his plays. But before he could take the floor he was subjected to a bombardment of indictments, the burden of which was that though undeniably a writer of talent he was ideologically confused.

When Lawson rose to speak [reports Clurman] I was shocked to find him not only humble but apologetic. He talked like a man with a troubled conscience, a man confessing his sin, and in some way seeking absolution. He wanted his present critics to like him; he wanted to live up to their expectations, fulfill their requirements. He knew his plays were faulty; he was seeking in his heart and mind for the cause and remedy.[27]

Thus, in 1934, began what Lawson later termed "an intensive reevaluation of my work as an artist,"[28] a reevaluation made meaningful for him in light of the significant fact that he joined the Communist party.[29] It was no longer any question of "which side are you on?" Lawson was committed; he belonged.

It had been suggested to him by his new comrades that what he needed for both ideological and esthetic clarity was greater contact with the working classes. Lawson readily admitted this, and soon went on a trip to cover the Scottsboro case for the *Daily Worker* and the *New Masses.* He was arrested almost immediately by the police in Birmingham, Alabama, and returned at once to New York to write about the "small but powerful groups of politicians in

Georgia and Alabama [who are] . . . proceeding to Hitlerize
those states in defiance of the majority of white and Negro
citizens."[30]

Thus Lawson's career as an activist began. During the
next decade and a half he was to involve himself in most of
the Marxist and Popular Front causes and organizations of
his day,[31] and the intense political involvement of this period of commitment reveals him in several roles in relationship to the drama. As dramatic theorist he calls for and
oversees the production of revolutionary drama, and attempts a formal analysis of dramatic technique in Marxian
terms; as dramatist he writes a proletarian play, *Marching
Song*; and as screen writer (apart from his organizational
and supervisory duties), he writes a film on the Spanish
Civil War, *Blockade*, which was to become the subject of
intense controversy. Let us consider each of these roles in
turn.

Lawson announced his commitment formally in the
pages of *New Theatre*, the official organ of left-wing theatre, in an article entitled "Towards a Revolutionary Theatre," and most significantly subtitled "The Artist Must Take
Sides." The tone of self-depreciation is still present, but it is
balanced by the fervor of new faith. Above all, Lawson's
premises are now completely Marxist; he calls for the theatrical artist to renounce the tawdriness and futility of the
bourgeois theatre and work towards the creation of a completely independent revolutionary theatre, a theatre which
would reflect the realities of class warfare.[32] Once having
begun, Lawson warmed to the role of social and dramatic
critic; throughout his many pronouncements of the decade,
he continually excoriated the values of Broadway drama.
He attacked the Theatre Guild as too conservative for the
present period of change[33] and the Pulitzer Prize awards
as a defense of the social and theatrical status quo. And as
he felt more secure in his critical position, he offered "cor-

rective" criticism to the left itself. He attacked *New Theatre* "for not giving us the Marxian attack or the proletarian vitality which we (workers in all branches of the theatre trying to solve the difficulties of a revolutionary approach) need so desperately";[34] and he took Theatre Union to task because its productions were not sufficiently specific in their social criticism. The effectiveness of art, he pointed out, "depends on the ability to grapple, in strictly dramatic terms, with the detailed reality of economics and politics." The artist cannot avoid partisanship; he must face the problems which the working class itself faces. As for himself, Lawson has completely exorcised his past indecision: "I do not hesitate to say that it is my aim to present the communist position, and to do so in the most specific manner."[35] Thus, in his newly acquired role as dean of the revolutionary theatre, Lawson found himself by virtue of his past reputation in a position to criticize some of its methods. It was a new role for Lawson, that of the dispenser rather than the recipient of criticism, and one cannot escape the feeling that it was a role that he thoroughly enjoyed. In speeches before left-wing theatre groups, in the pages of the Marxist press, his critical voice became increasingly frequent and increasingly shrill. As the decade progressed, the ideologist in Lawson emerged ever stronger, and his new role became progressively defined as dramatic guardian of the revolutionary faith.

But Lawson's criticisms were not entirely negative. He recognized that much of Marxist criticism was ineffective because it did not concern itself with the problem of technique; he strongly felt that "the greatest need of current dramatic criticism is a comparative method of analysis, by which art can be judged in relation to cultural trends and social pressure."[36] It was precisely this kind of method that he attempted to provide in the *Theory and Technique of Playwriting* (1936). It is significant that Lawson should

begin such an undertaking at the expense of his artistic energies, for he insisted upon completing the work rather
than finishing the play for which the Group Theatre had
given him an advance.[37]

Having been purged ideologically by his commitment,
Lawson endeavored in his work to clarify himself estheti-
cally by carefully analyzing dramatic history and technique
in the light of Marxism. It is an ambitious work, simultaneously, in the words of Barrett Clark, "a preachment, a criticism of life, a practical treatise and a plea."[38] It tries not
only to demonstrate the underlying historical connections
between the drama, criticism, and philosophy of a given
period, but also to demonstrate the more difficult thesis
that the laws of dramatic construction inevitably express
social purpose. Lawson's dramatic analyses attempt to answer the larger social question of what contemporary lessons are to be learned from the dramatic experience of the
past. He considers not only the historical determinants of
dramatic art, but also those distinguishing elements present
in all great art which transcend their historical determination. In a paper delivered at the 1935 American Writers'
Congress entitled "Technique and the Drama," and written
at a time when Lawson was actively engaged in research
for his work, he summarized briefly, but, I feel, without
violence, the thesis of his impending work:

There are three basic principles of play construction: conflict,
action, unity. The application of these principles is complex, and
requires careful definition and analysis . . . (a) Conflict and
action involve the exercise of the conscious will toward a goal;
(b) this involves social judgments and social purpose; (c) it
may then be assumed that the dramatist's conception of social
meaning and purpose will determine the exact form of the conflict; (d) then construction is not merely a pitcher into which
the social content is poured, but is the core of the social content itself.[39]

In short, Lawson affirms that "the distinction between form and content is a metaphysical distinction, which has no meaning in terms of life or art."[40] Modern drama is largely deficient technically because it is deficient ideologically; great art always came to terms with the reality of social issues in its period. The essence of great drama has always been social conflict—persons against persons, or individuals against groups, or groups against social or natural forces— in which the conscious will, exerted for the accomplishment of specific social aims, is sufficiently strong to bring the conflict to a point of crisis.

If in the light of these convictions—the equation of ideological and technical coherence—Lawson undertook, in his *Theory and Technique,* and in his criticisms in the Marxist press, to document the failings of bourgeois drama, in *Marching Song* (1937) he endeavored to demonstrate how sound ideology can produce sound art. In this play, the story of a sit-down strike in an automobile town, Lawson attempted to write the model of the revolutionary drama, a play which would illustrate conclusively the decisiveness born of ideological clarity. It is, in fact, Lawson's esthetic testament of faith. He had demonstrated in his many actions and statements the firmness of his new-found revolutionary commitment; it remained to demonstrate the validity of the thesis propounded in his *Theory and Technique of Playwriting.* Lawson would show that not only had he purged himself of political indecision, but of dramatic confusion as well.

Marching Song conforms structurally to the tripartite formula of overt proletarian literature: (1) the proletarian hero (or heroes—the mass is often the protagonist in proletarian literature) is, by pressure of economic exploitation, mired in defeatism and hostility; (2) the revolutionary situation—invariably a strike—arises, and the hero is not sure of his allegiance; he is fearful of (a) losing the little he has, (b) associating with "reds"; (3) the hero throws in his lot with the militant revolutionary faction and marches on to victory or heroic defeat.

In order to affirm its revolutionary implications, proletarian fiction and drama often resorted to the most obvious devices of melodrama. Thus *Marching Song* presents as overt a series of melodramatic villains as ever graced the pages of popular fiction. The gangsters brought in to break the strike are a uniformly sadistic and bloodthirsty crew, sketched in the colors of the comic strip, and, in contrast, the proletarian heroes are, of course, staunchly heroic. The battle lines are clearly drawn; the melodramatic structure serves as the means of social protest. Lawson does not commit the error of generality for which he had taken Theatre Union to task. He specifically praises the militancy of the union, the Electrical Workers, and does not miss a chance to insert contemporary references and comment. He makes the appropriate remarks on such subjects as the Scottsboro boys, women's rights, and all varieties of prejudice: against foreigners, Italians, Jews, Irish, and, most particularly, Negroes.

There is no individual protagonist in *Marching Song*; following in the tradition of many proletarian novels and plays, Lawson's real hero is the collective group of workers who achieve militancy as the play runs its course. These include Bill Anderson, the union organizer, who characteristically is offered as a sacrificial martyr to the revolutionary cause—he is tortured to death by company thugs; Hank and Mary McGilliguddy, the courageous workers who play a large part in the union activities (Hank in fact, succeeds in turning off the power, an action which, at the end of the play, presages the workers' triumph); Lucky, the Negro brought in to scab who remains to become a stalwart of the revolutionary cause and offers the final, defiant peroration;

and Pete, the indecisive but honest worker, who finally is converted to the union's cause.

It is clear that Lawson's dramatic voice is now stridently revolutionary, that class warfare is his basic esthetic metaphor; and in such a war, Lawson affirms, the working class must unite against its common enemy; once united it cannot help but triumph; and to confirm this fervent belief, the play ends on the note of solidarity inherent in the words of the miner's song which, as the marching song of the title, explicitly points the revolutionary moral: "Step by step the longest march / Can be won, can be won; / Single stones will form an arch / One by one, one by one. . . ."[41]

A play such as *Marching Song* is involved with the religious issues of salvation and damnation in terms of a specific orthodoxy, and thus demands a certain communion between author and audience. Much of its effect is built upon anticipation, the knowledge that some, like Pete and Lucky, are assured of salvation, and that others, like the gangster villains, are ultimately assured of damnation. The very predictability of structure serves the work's ritualistic function; the call to arms and the marching song itself are the play's sacraments. Therefore, it is only as a political communicant that one can appreciate *Marching Song*, and the press in its evaluation of the play split quite logically along ideological lines. The Marxist press was uniform in its praise (the *Daily Worker* headlined Nathaniel Buchwald's review "*Marching Song* Finest Labor Play—Lawson's Drama the Most Eloquent and Poetic Dramatization of the Class Struggle In Our Time");[42] and the Broadway critics were just as unanimous in their condemnation. Had Lawson displayed a real sense of the working class, the reactions to *Marching Song* might have been less ideologically predictable. But Lawson's difficulty (shared by many who attempted proletarian novels or plays) was that he was bourgeois, and not at home in the proletarian milieu. His working-class characters smack of contrivance, of the will-ful projection of certain qualities which the political mind *feels* should be characteristic of workers. For example, can one imagine (in the context of a naturalistic play) the fol-lowing language in the mouth of an uneducated worker? "I'd tear her flesh till she'd bleed, kiss the blood away. I had no more shame than a stallion trumpeting my strength" (p. 35).

Obviously *Marching Song* was written out of the intel-lectual conviction of what a revolutionary play should be; it had no roots in Lawson's emotional experience. As with much of middle-class "proletarian" literature, it fails to sub-stantiate Lawson's dramatic thesis that sound ideology in-evitably produces sound art. Clurman felt the same way; he had been offered the play for the Group Theatre, but re-jected it because he found it "cold, artificial . . . lacking in spontaneity." Lawson angrily countered this rejection with the query, "Don't you think proletarian plays should be written at this time?" To which Clurman replied: "Perhaps. But not by you."[43]

Marching Song was Lawson's last published or produced play. He was obviously happier in the role of polemicist and critic than that of playwright. But there is one other crea-tive role in which Lawson was engaged during the thirties and the forties, that of screen writer; and it is in that role that he achieved his greatest notoriety. His career in Holly-wood began earlier than is generally supposed; although he did not engage himself primarily as a screen writer until 1938, he was, in fact, one of the first playwrights brought to the film industry after the introduction of sound and the sudden need for dialogue, in 1928. It is significant that at no time during his career as screen writer did he (unlike Odets) subject Hollywood to the merciless attack which he leveled at Broadway. It was only in 1954, after his release from prison for contempt of Congress and his dismissal by the Hollywood studios, that he saw in the film capital the same capitalistic rapaciousness reflected on Broadway. In fact, as early as 1932, Lawson attacked those writers who, after achieving some literary or theatrical success, go to Hollywood for a few months and then "hasten back to New York with a lot of amusing stories and a vow never to return to the flesh pots—a vow which is broken as soon as a new contract is offered."[44]

Although the problem of the communist screenwriter concerned the House Un-American Activities Committee on the grounds of the "subversive" character of their screenplays, it concerns us from quite the opposite point of view; the question we must ask is how could the Marxist screenwriter content himself with the sugar-coated pap and hack melodrama which he turned out?[45] Lawson's credits are better than some, but of his sixteen major films (which include *Algiers, Earthbound, They Shall Have Music, Sahara,* and *Counterattack*), only one, *Blockade*, in any way touched a controversial political issue, and this, as we shall see, was hardly revolutionary. Murray Kempton's explanation is bitterly critical:

We are told now that this was a time when the communists influenced Hollywood's most passionate creative minds; if this is true, we may wonder why so few of them felt any impulse to take time off and form independent companies to produce films of deeper social content and involvement than the stuff they were fabricating for the big studios. The answer must be that they did not really care and were not fundamentally ashamed of what they were doing.[46]

Perhaps Lawson was not ashamed of what he was doing, but we cannot maintain in face of the evidence that he did not *care* to further the revolutionary cause. Perhaps the answer lies in a compromise which he felt impelled to make, in the feeling that he could serve the Marxist cause better in his role as critic, theorist, organizer—as, in fact, leader of the Hollywood radical colony—than in his role as artist. For Mike Gold had written in his challenge to Lawson in 1934, "When a man has achieved a set of principles, when he knows firmly he believes in them, he can, like the Soviet diplomats, make compromises, box office or otherwise."[47] Lawson had achieved his set of principles; he was permitted his artistic compromise.

Lawson had one chance, however, to make a vital comment on a controversial political subject. In 1938 Walter Wanger engaged him to revamp a script that Clifford Odets had written on the subject of the Spanish Civil War. Lawson responded with an original story based upon the same characters called *Blockade*. It was this film which the Un-American Activities Committee cited in 1949 as particularly subversive in its content.

Inasmuch as Lawson's position on the Spanish Civil War had been typically uncompromising in its support of the Loyalists (a not uncommon partisanship, one might add), his film was eagerly awaited by radical and liberal circles. Granville Hicks writes: "I remember how excited we were . . . over advanced reports on *Blockade*, which, we were told, was going to strike a great blow for the Loyalist cause in Spain. But when the picture was released, it did not even indicate on which side the hero was fighting."[48] The Marxist press was, indeed, puzzled. The *New Masses* reviewer wrote: "The picture is, of course, without the direct reference to the Spanish situation that would make it complete and unmistakably clear. . . ."[49] In a study of film content, Dorothy Jones writes:

Since the film contained no symbols or terminology being used by the Communists, it cannot be said to have been Communist propaganda. Actually the primary theme of this movie was antiwar, a viewpoint widely endorsed at the time not only by liberals, but by conservative isolationists, who reviewed the picture favorably.[50]

Obviously, Lawson's dicta about specificity did not apply to his screenplays. An examination of the script reveals it to fall not even in the category of serious antiwar protest which includes such memorable films as *La grande Illusion* or *All Quiet on the Western Front*. *Blockade* is first and foremost an espionage melodrama; what "social consciousness" it contains is gratuitously grafted upon the main body of the film in speeches of generalized protest. For example, Norma, the heroine, defects to the (presumably) Loyalist side "because I've seen the eyes of the women—I've seen the children dying—it's not their war—I've seen the truth —I can't go on."[51] But what *is* the truth? It is never specified. Who indeed *is* behind the war? Lawson does not—or cannot—answer. Thus the real issues involved in the Spanish Civil War are evaded, and the villains, Vallejo and Gallinet, are portrayed in terms of conventional melodrama. They are not even "proletarian" villains; they represent nothing beyond their own intrinsic evil. Perhaps Lawson felt that he could get away with nothing better than generalized antiwar protest, but his melodramatics blunt the edge even of that; *Blockade* is "controversial" in subject matter, nothing else.

The bulk of his work in Hollywood adds nothing to Lawson's reputation as dramatist. He found financial sustenance as a member of the movie colony and satisfaction in his role as critic and polemicist. However, he returned to New York in 1940 to offer Clurman a new play, *Parlor Magic,* in which, according to Clurman, he "took some of the subjective turbulence and divided conscience of his earlier work and tried to order this material with a rational, correctly contemporary (that is, progressive) point of view. The whole thing failed to come off."[52] Lawson was bitterly disappointed by Clurman's rejection, returned to Hollywood, reconsidered the script, and decided that it contained too many stories. Although he subsequently revised it, *Parlor Magic* has never been produced or published.

The dramatist in Lawson was dead; the polemicist remained. He resumed his role as dramatic guardian of ideological correctness, chastening Budd Schulberg (ironically, in the light of his own *Success Story*) for the "negative" savagery of *What Makes Sammy Run?*, and Albert Maltz for his apostacy in criticizing Marxist critical orthodoxy;[53] after his term in jail the polemicist in Lawson was further strengthened. He finally finished his long study of American and European history—"the search for the real meaning of our traditions"[54]—which he had begun back in 1934. In *The Hidden Heritage* (1950) Lawson "tried to find the roots of culture in the life of the people, . . . in their battle against exploitation and oppression. . . . Culture must be studied as a weapon in the struggle of classes."[55]

The weapon remains. Lawson's last published book was entitled *Film in the Battle of Ideas* (1953). Political stridency is its dominant characteristic; Lawson even takes himself to task for maintaining in his revised edition of *Theory and Technique* (1949) that there could be no permanent interference with the development of the American motion picture as a "people's art." He scornfully notes that no Marxist critic had chastised his unwarranted optimism: "I am not one of those who hold that 'the integrity of the artist' is best served by ignoring mistakes."[56] The voice of the artist is indeed silent; we hear only the chastening tones of the commissar. And in a new introduction to the paper-back reissue of *Theory and Technique of Playwriting*, Lawson shrilly condemns the "negativism" of contemporary drama: "Today the world is being transformed by heroes whose name is legion. The drama of our time is being enacted by these millions who refuse to accept the 'absurdity' of existence, who live, and if necessary die, to give life meaning."[57]

Can we draw any moral from the experience of John Howard Lawson's road to commitment? Insofar as we are concerned with the dramatist and not the man, I think we can. For the unfortunate fact is that the esthetic legacy of Lawson's commitment has been largely silence; *Marching Song* remains the sum total of his committed drama. Clurman's assessment of Lawson is astute:

Lawson was now [i.e., in 1940] probably a much more practical, useful citizen than he had been from 1925 to 1935; he was no longer working as an artist. Had he "bottle-necked" himself through a too-strict discipline of moral self-scrutiny, a self-imposed censorship calculated to make the old wine of his emotions pour properly into the new bottles of his social sense? Had he tamed his unruly imagination and inner drives with the self-inflicted rod of a stiff ideology?[58]

The record would seem to answer Clurman's questions affirmatively. Although Lawson's talent was never major, the bulk of his work does possess a driving vitality and a passionate integrity which command respect. His personal tragedy as a dramatist was that his very real talent lay precisely in the intensity of his emotional conflict, in the documentation of the struggle between man's inner drives and his social conscience. It is this conflict which makes his early plays, for all their manifest deficiencies, significant. After his commitment, he feels intellectually compelled to write "correctly," an action disastrous for him as a playwright because his virtues were never intellectual to begin with. He makes one attempt to write what he believes *should* be a significant drama, but comes to realize, perhaps for the reasons Clurman suggests above, that he had best use his energies in other roles. The "bourgeois Hamlet of our time" left the stage and never returned.

7

THE ROAD FROM MARXIST COMMITMENT: CLIFFORD ODETS

The artist never gives the thing or the person; he gives only the trend represented by the thing or the person.

CLIFFORD ODETS, "Genesis of a Play"

CHAPTER SEVEN

EVERY AGE destroys the idols of its predecessor. Literary idols are particularly vulnerable, for that quality which allows an artist to speak in the authentic voice of his age will also tie him inexorably to it; and the new generation, retrospectively viewing the furor of his emergence, will wonder what all the fuss was about. Such has already been the fate of Clifford Odets, the Golden Boy of Depression drama, the texture of whose work is intricately interwoven with the dislocated strands of American life in the 1930's. Odets was the angry young man of his day, and in this very anger he represented the anguish of a new generation forced to come to terms with the most fundamental social and political questions. When in one tremendous burst Odets' voice was heard on the American stage, a wave of recognition went out to meet it. It was more than the young man's radicalism which endeared him to his generation. Articulating the dilemma of a society frustrated by economic breakdown, he offered above all a fervent faith in the possibilities of a new world in which all mankind could awake and sing, a world in which "happiness isn't printed on dollar bills."

Clifford Odets scrawled his name across the page marked 1935 in American dramatic history. In the course of that year he had five plays produced, four of them on Broadway: *Waiting for Lefty, Till the Day I Die, Awake and Sing!*, and *Paradise Lost*. His short monologue, *I Can't Sleep*, was produced at a union benefit, and the aforementioned *Lefty* began a theatrical career that was to carry it, not only from one end of the United States to the other, but all over the world.

The name of Odets became the number one topic of literary conversation, and the hitherto unknown and struggling young actor became one of the foremost celebrities of the day. The *Literary Digest* described his emergence:

In less than ninety days, toiling with the unrest of his times as a central theme, a young actor in the New York theatre . . . has become the most exciting spokesman the world of workers yet has produced, and he has become perhaps the most articulate dramatist available in the theatre.[1]

For once the Broadway and Marxist critics were unanimous in their praise. Richard Watts wrote in the *Herald Tribune*, "It is pretty clear by now that Mr. Odets' talent for dramatic writing is the most exciting thing to appear in the American drama since the flaming emergence of O'Neill. . . ."[2] And the Marxist critics, despite specific reservations, found much to cheer about in the fact that the new young dramatist had emerged from their own ranks, for Odets' initial discovery was indeed the result of his radical affiliations. *Lefty* had been written in response to a contest by the left-wing New Theatre League which was looking for one-act plays on a revolutionary theme which might be easily produced. The play was written at fever heat in three days and nights, won the contest, and was produced at one of the New Theatre League's Sunday night benefit performances by members of the Group Theatre (to which Odets belonged). The performance on January 5, 1935, was one of the electrifying moments in American theatre. Harold Clurman relates its initial impact:

The first scene of *Lefty* had not played two minutes when a shock of delighted recognition struck the audience like a tidal wave. Deep laughter, hot assent, a kind of joyous fervor seemed to sweep the audience toward the stage. The actors no longer performed; they were being carried along as if by an exultancy of communication such as I had never witnessed in the theatre before. Audience and actors had become one. . . . When the audience at the end of the play responded to the militant question from the stage: "Well, what's the answer?" with a spontaneous roar of "Strike! Strike!" it was something more than a tribute to the play's effectiveness, more even than a testimony of the audience's hunger for constructive social action. It was the birth cry of the '30s. Our youth had found its voice.[3]

Odets had succeeded where other revolutionary dramatists before him had failed. He had written a militant "agit-prop" drama which succeeded in appealing to unaffiliated liberals as well as to convinced Marxists, and he had done so by humanizing a form of drama whose avowed purpose, as we have observed, was to present political doctrine directly to the audience by means of broadly theatrical playlets. The following titles indicate the thematic simplicity of the agit-prop: *Work or Wages, Unemployment, The Miners are Striking, Vote Communist.* To achieve overtly didactic ends, a variety of dramaturgical devices were employed, many of them stemming from the theatrical experimentation of the twenties: choral recitation, episodic structure, satiric caricature, theatrical stylization.

To understand the manner in which Odets utilized the basic form of the agit-prop, let us examine two representative samples of the genre. *Newsboy,* produced in 1933 by the WLT and probably the most effective of the earlier agit-props, affirms as its thesis that the capitalist press dwells upon murder, rape, and violence in order to keep the proletariat's mind off the real social issues. The crowd on the stage, representing a cross section of workers, has been worked up into a jingoist frenzy by the Newsboy's shouts of violence: "We need another war—war will end depression . . . war is natural." A Black Man, symbolizing revolutionary militancy, shouts back at the Newsboy, "how long you goin' to stand there . . . yellin' . . . that workers should be murdered and strikes outlawed? . . . Come into the light,

Newsboy, come into the light!"[4] The symbols of capitalist manipulation are trotted on to the stage: Hearst, Huey Long, Father Coughlin, voicing warlike and antiproletarian sentiments. Finally, however, a second newsboy appears shouting revolutionary wares: "Fight against war and fascism. Learn the truth about the munitions racket." The crowd gathers around and reads the "truth," that eight and one-half million were killed in the last war; that ten million will probably die in the next war. The truth has set them free of capitalist lies, and they display copies of *Fight*, the organ of the American League Against War and Fascism, to the audience. And the Black Man, finding them converted, now turns to the audience: "Get yourself a trumpet, buddy, a big red trumpet, and climb to the top of the Empire State building and blare out the news . . . it's time to fight war. It's time to fight fascism" (p. 5).

Although it contained in embryo most of the elements of the conversion drama, *Newsboy* dealt with abstractions rather than with actual human beings who could command an empathic response. As an appeal to "come into the light, comrade," its agitational deficiency was that it spoke only to those who were already "comrades." It did, however, appeal for specific action, support of the magazine *Fight*. This kind of appeal to direct action on a specific issue is perhaps best exemplified by a play by Art Smith and Elia Kazan called *Dimitroff*, which was presented at a Sunday night New Theatre League benefit as a companion piece to *Lefty*. The avowed purpose here is not conversion but action by the already converted to free the imprisoned German Communist party leaders. As the introductory note to the play stated, "the story of this play is not primarily the story of Dimitroff. The hero of the production should be *mass pressure*. The production play . . . should lead directly into the present mass struggle to force the release of Thaelmann and Torgler."[5]

The choral antiphony with which *Lefty* concludes was not original with Odets. It was a common device in the agit-prop play. At the end of *Dimitroff*, instead of a curtain call, Dimitroff comes out in front of the curtain and speaks to the audience: "We have been saved by the world pressure of the revolutionary masses. But Torgler is still in prison and Thaelmann is held in chains. We must not falter now. *We must fight fascism with undiminished strength and courage. We must free our comrades! Free all class war prisoners!!!*"

> Audience: Free all class war prisoners!!
> Dimitroff: Free Torgler!!
> Audience: Free Torgler!!
> Dimitroff: Free Thaelmann!!
> Audience: Free Thaelmann!! [p. 24]

It is apparent that *Waiting for Lefty* is essentially in the agit-prop tradition. Its purpose is overtly didactic in its affirmation of communist doctrine; it is episodic in structure, cartoon-like in its character delineation, directly presentational in technique, and replete with slogans and political comment. Yet while its conclusion is strikingly similar to that of *Dimitroff* in its merging of actor and audience, in its militant cry to action, we may observe that Odets' plea to strike is essentially a device. The answer and response of actor and audience is not designed to achieve an immediate goal as in the case of Kazan and Smith's play, but is rather a symbolic call to arms, a demonstration of unity and achieved class consciousness. *Lefty's* success lay in the fact that it appealed to the unconverted as well as to the committed; it swept all of a liberal persuasion into militant participation, at least in the theatre, by virtue of the precision with which Odets enunciated the Depression malaise. Odets' achievement lay in his ability to humanize the agit-prop without forgoing its theatricality and didacticism. He succeeded not only in presenting the conversion to militancy of a series of taxi-cab workers, but in forcing the audience to see in the plight of these characters a reflection of their own social predicament. Several Marxist critics, among them John Howard Lawson, objected to the designation of *Lefty* as a proletarian play because "the militant strike committee [is] made up largely of declassed members of the middle class. One cannot reasonably call these people 'stormbirds of the working class.' "[6] But *Lefty's* strength as a conversion drama lay precisely in the fact that Odets' appeal was directed essentially to the class to which he belonged. Of the principal characters only two, Joe and Sid, are proletarians; the others represent various members of the declassed bourgeoisie: a lab assistant who refuses to become an informer, an actor who can't find work on the Broadway market, an interne who is fired because of the anti-Semitism of his superiors. All are forced into activism by social circumstances. "Don't call me red," shouts Joe. "You know what we are? The black and blue boys! We been kicked around so long we're black and blue from head to toes!"[7] But Joe had not always been as adamant as he is now. He had been goaded to militancy by his wife's threat to leave him unless he organized and fought for his rights: "Get those hack boys together! . . . Stand up like men and fight for the crying kids and wives. Goddamnit! I'm tired of slavery and sleepless nights" (p. 12).

Joe's social awakening is but one in the series of conversions that constitute *Waiting for Lefty*. Each episode presents the road to commitment of each of the several characters against the backdrop of various capitalist evils: labor spying, informing, anti-Semitism, economic aggression, etc. One by one the dramas of conversion are enacted: the interne finds that Jewish and Gentile capitalists are cut from the same cloth; the lab assistant recognizes that the logic of capitalism demands war; the workers, Sid and Joe, realize that the cards are stacked against the proletariat; and the young actor, turned down by a producer who cares more for his pet dog than for human beings, is taken in hand by a radical stenographer who undertakes his ideological enlightenment:

One dollar buys ten loaves of bread, Mister. Or one dollar buys nine loaves of bread and one copy of the Communist Manifesto. Learn while you eat. . . . Read while you run. . . . From Genesis to Revelation . . . the meek shall not inherit the earth! The MILITANT! Come out in the light, Comrade![8]

All roads lead to Agate's final peroration, his cry for alliance with the proletariat: "It's war! Working class, unite and fight! Tear down the slaughter house of our old lives!" (p. 30). The basic metaphor of the play is, of course, the futility of waiting for something that will never come, the hope that somehow conditions may be alleviated by other than direct action. Fatt, the personification of the capitalist system, had counseled the workers to put their faith in "the man in the White House" in his attempt to dissuade them from striking; but half-way measures are doomed to failure. Salvation must be earned; Lefty never comes because he has been murdered—the ritual martyrdom of proletarian literature —and the act of waiting must be replaced by militancy.

Hello America! Hello! We're Stormbirds of the Working Class. Workers of the world . . . our bones and blood! And when we die they'll know what we did to make a new world! Christ, cut us up to little pieces. We'll die for what is right! Put fruit trees where our ashes are! [p. 31]

The impact of *Waiting for Lefty* is irrevocably dependent upon its contemporaneity. In the thirties the play was a formidable weapon. Within weeks after its initial production it became the public property of the left, and groups were organized all over the country to perform it. Odets later doubted if he had earned a thousand dollars out of the play: "People just did it. . . . It has been done all over the world . . . and I have not received five cents of royalties. . . . It was at one time a kind of light machine gun that you wheeled in to use whenever there was any kind of strike trouble."[9] A storm of censorship accompanied its production in many different cities. In Boston, the actors were arrested for language that was "extremely blasphemous"; in Philadelphia, the theatre in which the play was to be produced was suddenly called "unsafe," and the performance was canceled.[10] Will Geer produced the play in Hollywood despite threats and was severely beaten by hoodlums; and in general, the stridency of conservative criticism revealed that Odets' "machine gun" was not far off target.

The instantaneous success of *Lefty* at the New Theatre League Sunday performances caused the Group Theatre to present the play as one of its scheduled productions. In moving to Broadway, however, a new companion piece was needed to fill out the bill, since *Dimitroff* would hardly have succeeded uptown, and Odets wrote a play based upon contemporary life in Nazi Germany called *Till the Day I Die*. Based upon a letter in the *New Masses*, the plot concerns Ernst Taussig, a German communist captured by the Nazis in a raid and subjected by them to torture in an effort to force him to inform upon his associates. Although he is never completely broken, Taussig is made to appear a traitor to his comrades. Blacklisted by his former friends, fearful of compromising the revolutionary cause, Ernst commits suicide.

Lawson objected that "the sustained conflict, the conscious will of man pitted against terrible odds is omitted. We see [Taussig] . . . only *before* and *after*. The crucial stage, in which his will is tested and broken, occurs between scenes five and seven."[11] The significant fact is that the audience is never really sure whether or not Taussig *was* broken by the Nazis or whether or not he retained his integrity to the end. At the beginning of the play he is a convinced revolutionary fervently viewing the classless future. Has he indeed changed when he is released from his initial Nazi captivity? It does not seem so. To Tilly's query as to whether or not he was afraid Ernst answered, "A man who knows that the world contains millions of brothers and sisters can't be afraid. . . . In the cell there—I know I stayed alive because I knew my comrades were with me in the same pain and chaos."[12]

All the evidence of the play supports Ernst's contention that he kept the revolutionary faith, that he had been forced to accompany storm troopers on their round-ups of radicals, that he was forcibly brought into court at political trials, that, in short, it was planned to make him appear to be an informer. Nowhere is it implied that Taussig was actually broken. The important fact is that the issue of his innocence or guilt is not the crucial dramatic question which the play posits. It is rather involved with the problem of political loyalty; the play affirms the revolutionary contention that the individual is less important than the cause to which he is dedicated. In the best scene in the play—best because it smacks of the authentic logic of political debate—the local cell excommunicates Taussig because his comrades cannot afford to take the chance that he may be guilty; he cannot be trusted, whether he is innocent or not. Love and fraternal affection must bow before the iron exigencies of the revolutionary situation, since in a warring world "it is brother against brother." Just as the labor spy in *Waiting for Lefty* is exposed by his brother, Ernst Taussig is disavowed by his brother Carl:

Many a comrade has found with deep realization that he has no home, no brother—even no mothers or fathers! What must we do here? . . . We must expose this one brother wherever he is met. Whosoever looks in his face is to point the finger. Children will jeer at him in the darkest streets of his life! Yes, the brother, the erstwhile comrade cast out! There is no brother, no family, no deeper mother than the working class. [p. 146]

Ernst recognizes that there is but one action left him, and he asks his brother to administer the *coup de grâce*. He knows that he must be cast away, that the individual is unimportant in the greater struggle, that his realization will come through the work of his comrades: "the day is coming, and I'll be in the final result" (p. 153). Unlike the traditional martyrs of Marxist literature, whose deaths serve as the catalysts for the awakening of others, Ernst believes that he is the phoenix that will arise from the ashes of his necessary death. Thus the play ends, not with the conversion of the previously uncommitted, but with the affirmation by the committed that their existence is contained in the collective of which they are a part.

When he was writing *Waiting for Lefty* and *Till the Day I Die*, Odets expressed himself in typically Marxist tones, maintaining that the function of art was primarily propagandistic. "It may be said that anything which one writes on 'the side' of the large majority of people is propaganda. But today the truth followed to its logical conclusion is inevitably revolutionary."[13] It is not surprising, then, that the author of such a statement should be, in fact, a member of the Communist party, having been recruited by the small core of communists within the Group Theatre. Years later, in the familiar purgative drama of the fifties, Odets related to the House Un-American Activities Committee the circumstances of his enrollment:

In a time of great social unrest many people found themselves reaching out for new ideas, new ways of solving depressions or making a better living, fighting for one's rights. . . . These were . . . horrendous days . . . there was a great deal of talk about amelioration of conditions, about how should one live. . . . One read literature; there were a lot of . . . pamphlets. . . . I read them along with a lot of other people, and finally joined the

Communist party in the belief, in the honest and real belief, that this was some way out of the dilemma in which we found ourselves.[14]

Odets testified that he remained in the party "from toward the end of 1934 to the middle of '35, covering maybe anywhere from six to eight months."[15] It is not our purpose here to scrutinize the motivations which resulted in Odets' disavowal. We are concerned primarily with the dramatist, not the individual; we may observe, however, that Odets' act of disaffiliation in 1935 is in no way clearly obvious from either his public statements or his dramatic work. As the counsel for the Un-American Activities Committee embarrassingly pointed out, Odets continued to affiliate with left-wing groups throughout the Depression and war years. Perhaps the answer lies in the intellectual climate of the mid-thirties, the era of the Popular Front. Unless one was, as an intellectual, directly involved with the vagaries and variations of social doctrine (e.g., Edmund Wilson, Sidney Hook), it was quite possible to drift away from overt commitment without the painful process of making a clean break.

Thus Odets' Marxist commitment was very different from that of John Howard Lawson. The latter came to his political beliefs, as we have seen, after a long period of conflict and indecision; once he made his commitment, Lawson became a political man, his role as artist receding behind the ideological facade. Odets, however, did not arrive at his radicalism after a long period of intellectual debate. He was, in a sense, born to it; radicalism was in the air his generation breathed. Since his commitment was never primarily intellectual, he never formally rejected it in the manner of the intellectuals who, having made themselves political men, one day awake with horror to a sense of betrayal and find it necessary to destroy their radical roots.

We cannot, therefore, discover any crucial moment of

commitment or disaffiliation in the life and work of Clifford Odets. For whatever reasons he left the party, there can be no denying the pervasive influence of Marxism upon the great bulk of his work. Surely Odets' temperament, particularly after his sudden access to fame and his defection to Hollywood, was unsuited to political obligation. He was too concerned with his own problems ever to assent fully to the role of party member. But since his commitment to Marxism was essentially more emotional than intellectual, he retained, throughout the Depression, an umbilical connection with the radical movement. It is interesting that despite Odets' statement to the Un-American Activities Committee that he left the Party in 1935 because "it came to the point of where I thought . . . I can't respect these people on a so-called cultural basis"[16] Odets was still talking in terms of the social "usefulness" of art in the preface to his *Six Plays* (1939). He stated his esthetic aim as follows: "Much of my concern during the past years has been with fashioning a play immediately and dynamically useful and yet as psychologically profound as my present years and experience will permit." This is the artist's great problem "since we are living in a time when new art works should shoot bullets. . . ."[17]

Odets' aggressive Marxism of the mid-decade is reflected in a short monologue, *I Can't Sleep*, written for performance at a benefit for the Marine Workers Industrial Union in 1935. It, too, is a party play in that it overtly considers the greatest of revolutionary sins, heresy. It is reminiscent of the Grand Inquisitor sequence in *The Brothers Karamazov*, in which the silence of Christ forces the Inquisitor into self-revelation. Odets' hero—played originally by Morris Carnovsky—rejects a beggar's appeal for charity, and finds himself imprisoned in a cell of guilt constructed by the disavowed radicalism of his youth. He initially answers the beggar's unpitying stare with belligerence—

"Listen, don't be so smart. When a man offers you money, take it!"—but soon he turns from aggressive self-justification to personal revelation. He tells of his inability to communicate with his wife, of the gulf of misunderstanding which separates him from his children, of all the bitter frustrations which afflict him, symbolized by the ever-present fact of his insomnia. Consumed by loneliness, he yearns to cry "Brother" to his fellow man but is constrained by the fear of appearing a fool.

And slowly the last layer of artifice is pulled away and the true cause of the man's depression is revealed: "I spoke last week to a red in the shop. Why should I mix in with politics? With all my other troubles I need yet a broken head? I can't make up my mind—what should I do? . . . Join up, join up. But for what? For trouble?"[18] This question reaches the heart of the man's dilemma, and in a torrent of words he reveals the source of his guilt, the renunciation of his working-class roots, his acceptance, against his better nature, of the capitalist ethic:

Last week I watched the May Day . . . I watched how the comrades marched with red flags and music. . . . I went down in the subway I shouldn't hear the music. . . . The blood of the mother and brother is breaking open my head. I hear them cry, "You forgot, you forgot!" They don't let me sleep. All night I hear the music of the comrades. Hungry men I hear. All night the broken-hearted children. Look at me—no place to hide, no place to run away. Look in my face, comrade. Look at me, look, look, look!!! [p. 9]

Like many others of revolutionary conviction, Odets had his brief moment of political glory. He went on an ill-fated mission to Cuba as head of a delegation whose avowed mission was "to investigate the situation of the Cuban people under the military dictatorship and to bring greetings to the Cuban people, to tell them the American people are their friends and will help them."[19] The Cuban police, however, took a dim view of the proposed commission, promptly arrested Odets and his companions, and put them upon the swiftest available return boat. Despite his intention to "make a fight about" the indignities to a group "whose sole purpose was to lend encouragement to Cuban intellectuals and college students" who were the subject of "fierce repression,"[20] Odets never renewed his personal warfare with the Cuban government. The Cuban episode remained his one formal effort in the arena of political activity.

The source of much of Odets' strength as a "proletarian" playwright lay precisely in the fact that he did not force himself to write about the proletariat. Unlike other middle-class writers of Marxist persuasion, he had the esthetic sense to write about areas of his direct experience. In his early days in the Group he started several plays, one in particular on the subject of his much-beloved Beethoven. A diary entry of the time reveals his dissatisfaction with these early attempts: "Now I see again in myself flight, always flight. Here I am writing the Beethoven play, which when it is finished may not be about Beethoven. Why not write something about the Greenberg family, something I know better, something that is closer to me?"[21]

The resultant play, initially entitled *I Got the Blues*, was started in a cold-water flat on West 57th Street, New York City, and finished at Warrensburg, New York, during the rehearsals of *Men in White*. It was finally produced by the Group, after the success of the subsequently written *Lefty*, under the title of *Awake and Sing!* In it the Greenberg family emerged as the Berger family of the Bronx, and Odets revealed himself not only as a young writer of intense revolutionary fervor, but as a skillful recorder of the pungent detail of Jewish lower middle-class life.

The basic image *of Awake and Sing!* is resurrection, the emergence of life from death. For the life of the Berger family in Depression-age America is spiritual death, dehumanized by a thousand irritants, frustrated by the exigencies of economic breakdown. Yet precisely because the sources of the Bergers' difficulties are primarily social, *Awake and Sing!* is an essentially optimistic play; dangers are without, not within, and they may be combatted. The fundamental activity of the Bergers—"a struggle for life amidst petty conditions"[22]—is a noble one; nor is it meaningless. Significantly Odets changed the title of the play from *I Got the Blues*—a statement of the Depression malaise—to *Awake and Sing!*—and the imperative commanded by the exclamation point is no accident. "Awake and sing, ye that dwell in the dust," he is crying, the American blues can be eliminated. But the play is not a direct call to militancy; its strength rests in the depiction of the social dislocation of the middle class and the skill with which this dislocation is personalized in the several characters.

At the core of all of the characters in the play, even the capitalist Uncle Morty, lies the possibility of what they might have become. Bessie, the matriarch, is driven to cruel action by the very intensity of her desire to protect her family, to prevent its decay at all costs. If she breaks up Ralph's romance, if she forces Hennie to marry a man she does not love, it is always from the single motivation that is the core of Bessie's being, the family must be preserved. The intensity of Bessie's maternalism is reinforced by the abdication of her husband, Myron, from the role of head of the family. Unable to cope with the present, he lives by the dream of the windfall, the horse player's fervent hunch that the big killing is just around the corner. Thus he is perennially entering contests with the faith that "someone's got to win. The government isn't gonna allow everything to be a fake" (p. 87).

But Moe Axelrod knows that "there ain't no prizes," that everything around him is fake. In a world in which everything is a racket, he is determined not to be a victim; like Sol Ginsburg he is convinced that in life there are only two kinds of people, the exploited and the exploiting, and he is determined not to be found in the former category. But Moe's bitterness is, in actuality, a protective veneer. Hating the futility of a world in which he gave his leg for a phony cause, he has "learned his lesson"; he will not be soft. It soon becomes apparent that Moe has been more sinned against than sinning. "Was my life so happy?" he shouts at Hennie, "Chris', my old man was a bum. I supported the whole damn family. . . . I went to war; got chopped down like a bed bug; . . . What the hell do you think, anyone's got it better than you?" (p. 98). Moe's plea to Hennie is to live —to run away with him before both are totally crushed: "There's one life to live! Live it!" (p. 99).

Awake and Sing! is not merely a catalogue of frustration. In the portrayal of old Jacob, the radical of the family, Odets provides the play with its explicit social commentary without violating the demands of character. Throughout the early action Jacob serves as a kind of chorus, drawing the Marxist moral from the statements and activities of the other characters. When his somber social analyses are laughed at by his family, particularly by his business-man son, Morty, he responds: "Laugh, laugh . . . tomorrow not" (p. 72). It is in the hope of achieving this tomorrow in the person of Ralph, the young son of the Berger household, that Jacob commits the sacrifice of leaping to his death so that Ralph might have his insurance money as a means to escape the strangle hold of the family and society. When Ralph learns of the old man's sacrifice he vows that it will not have been in vain. Jacob's legacy is not money, which Ralph in fact rejects, but social awareness. To his mother's justification of life in America, he retorts, "It don't make sense. If life made you this way, then it's wrong." Bessie answers, "So go out and change the world if you don't like it," and Ralph affirms, "I will! And why? 'Cause life's different in my head. Gimme the earth in two hands. I'm strong" (p. 95). Jacob's books, his ideas, are Ralph's real inheritance, and he has become infused with the old man's revolutionary fervor:

Get teams together all over. Spit on your hands and get to work. And with enough teams together maybe we'll get steam in the warehouse so our fingers don't freeze off. Maybe we'll fix it so life won't be printed on dollar bills. [p. 97]

And the play ends on the note of resurrection. "The night he died," states Ralph about Jacob, "I saw it like a thunderbolt! I saw he was dead and I was born! I swear to God, I'm one week old! I want the whole city to hear it—fresh blood, arms. We got 'em. We're glad we're living" (p. 101).

Thus, despite the effectiveness of realistic detail, it is apparent that *Awake and Sing!* still retains strong agit-prop roots. But instead of appealing directly for revolutionary action, it attempts to demonstrate the thesis of revolutionary awareness in the relationship between Jacob and Ralph against the family background of middle-class decay. Its success is dependent upon this conjunction of thesis and detail. Odets never was a genre painter; his strokes are broad, his dialogue heightened. What he succeeded in delineating were the specific images of social dislocation. The importance of the Marxist premise from a dramatic point of view does not lie in its specific truth or falsity; it serves rather as a dramatic metaphor which orders the disparate elements of the play, which relates the images of frustration and dislocation to a guiding thematic concept. The spine of the play is the conviction that the world of the Bergers must be changed if human potentiality is to be realized. For Odets at that time this faith was affirmed by

Marxism; far from marring the play, the Marxist metaphor gathers the various dramatic strands and relates them to the basic theme of social resurrection.

Odets, then, was never primarily a realist. *Awake and Sing!* and his next play, *Paradise Lost,* are essentially allegories of middle-class decay. It was the inability to recognize this fact which was primarily responsible for the critical furor which attended the production of the latter play. The Broadway critics, who had greeted *Awake and Sing!* in uniformly commendatory tones ("a triumph for the Group and . . . Mr. Odets," "Something of an event, not to say a miracle," "a stirring play") now turned their guns upon Odets' new play, most finding it marred by "frowzy characterization, random form and . . . inchoate material."[23] Nor did Odets receive any consolation from the radical press. For the most part, Marxist critics rejected the play on the grounds of unsound social analysis. Stanley Burnshaw, for example, questioned the validity of Odets' portrait of the American middle class. He maintained that the American bourgeoisie "is *not* a homogenous group withering into oblivion. . . . Overwhelming numbers of middle-class people . . . are part and parcel of the advancing social group. . . . Can their life be truthfully conveyed by such symbols as sexual impotence, heart disease . . . barrenness and arson, larcency, racketeering, cuckoldry, feeblemindedness and sex neuroses?"[24]

The Marxist attacks were predicted on a literal interpretation of the dissolution of the Gordon family as a result of economic pressures. Under such an interpretation it is obvious that physical disease cannot fairly be credited to capitalism. But as Clurman, the play's director, noted, neither in direction, acting nor set design was *Paradise Lost* naturalistic: "The 'reading' I have given the script gives the play a definite *line* or what certain reviewers would call a propagandistic slant."²⁵ And, despite the fact that the play displeased the left, the "line" was clearly Marxist: "The middle-class carries out the orders of the ruling class with the illusion of complete freedom."²⁶

At the beginning of Act III of *Paradise Lost*, Clara Gordon relates to her dying son, Julie, the parable of the golden idol:

Well, Moses stayed in the mountain forty days and forty nights. They got frightened at the bottom. . . . What did those fools do? They put all the gold pieces together, all the jewelry, and melted them, and made a baby cow of gold. . . . Moses ran down the hill so fast. . . . He took the cow and broke it into a thousand pieces. Some people agreed, but the ones who didn't? Finished. God blotted them out of the book. Here today, gone tomorrow!²⁷

Paradise Lost is itself Odets' parable of the decadence of contemporary capitalism, and his idolators are as surely condemned as those who worshipped the golden calf. The characters in the play are all condemned—some by disease, some by economics—but they are all presented as denizens of a world made unreal by false hope and futile illusion. The image is starker than that of *Awake and Sing!* because the seeds of redemption, although present in the play, are not allowed to flower. Ralph, Moe, Hennie escape to attempt to create a better world; despite his realization that he must do the same, Leo's final affirmation has come too late. He, too, is condemned. Thus, redemption must come from without, in the creation of a world unmarred by the abortiveness and sickness which dominate the world of *Paradise Lost*.

Such a vision is unquestionably grim, and *Paradise Lost* is a grim play, relieved but briefly by the humor that characterized much of *Awake and Sing!* The several characters, despite particularization, are more overtly allegorical; all represent to a greater or lesser degree the smothering of the individual by capitalist society. For example, Ben, the oldest son of the Gordon family, is, like Biff Loman in *Death of a Salesman*, destroyed by the illusion of facile success and by his inability to accept the fact that this success is not forthcoming. The world, he states, is on his doorstep, but in reality he is condemned. Once a champion runner, the doctor has told him that he can run no more, and this medical verdict symbolizes the general failure which awaits him. Married to a cheating wife, he allows himself to be shot down in a desperate attempt to obtain money by robbery. In his final scene he reveals his will to die: "Are we living? . . . the world is flat, like a table—Columbus was wrong—we're being pushed over the edge" (p. 204).

One by one, Odets pushes his characters over the edge. Sam Katz, Leo's aggressive business partner, hides his impotence behind the mask of avarice; the love affair between Pearl and Felix is doomed by economic realities; even the radical spokesman in the play, Pike, is condemned because, although he is able to diagnose the malady of his civilization, he is unable to provide the necessary remedy. Although articulate in his condemnation of capitalism and war, when he is asked by Leo the most vital of all questions, "What is to be done?" Pike does not draw the revolutionary moral. "I don't know," he answers confusedly, "I mean I don't know." Odets seems to be implying that protest is not sufficient; Pike's accusations lead nowhere, or rather to extinction, to a resting place "at the bottom of the ocean" where "the light is soft, food is free" (p. 192).

The image which pervades *Paradise Lost* is the "sweet smell of decay." The world of the Gordons is a microcosm of the "profound dislocation" of the middle class in capitalist society. Leo Gordon, a man of fundamentally noble instincts, comes finally to recognize that he is the representative of a dying class. Throughout the play he is appalled by the misery which he sees around him and is determined not to build his happiness on the exploitation of others. But his fortune and his family are crushed by personal tragedy and his refusal to recoup the loss of his business by approving an arranged insurance fire. "So in the end," he laments, "nothing is real. Nothing is left but our memory of life" (p. 244). But, despite his condemnation, he is allowed one glimpse of the new future that will replace the false paradise:

No! There is more to life than this! . . . There is a future. Now we know, we dare to understand. . . . I tell you the whole world is for men to possess. Heartbreak and terror are not the heritage of mankind! No fruit tree wears a lock and key. . . . The world is in its morning . . . and *no man fights alone!* [pp. 229-30]

Despite dramaturgic preparation, there can be no denying that this peroration is inconsistent with the basic metaphor of *Paradise Lost*. Perhaps Odets feared that if he did not explicitly state what was generally implied in the play, it might have been open to the criticism of "negativism." And yet, even without the obviousness of Leo's final awareness, it is apparent that the very frustration which dominates the play implies a social protest. As John Gassner has pointed out, "Airing one's discontents is a patent form of rebellion, dramatization of frustration is already a form of acting out, exposing a situation is criticism and often a challenge to action."[28]

The unreality which critics of the play objected to is a reflection of the dream world constructed by the middle class in its futile attempt to escape the economic realities of capitalism. The Marxist metaphor lies at the heart of *Paradise Lost*; it is basic to its very conception. The very title implies that there is a paradise to be regained. The play also represents the end of Odets' period of overt political commitment, the last expression of the bitter years of anonymity which preceded his emergence. Downcast by the bad critical reaction to the play, which long remained his favorite, he wrote a short biographical piece in which he lamented the vagaries of sudden success:

The young writer comes out of obscurity with a play or two. Suppose he won't accept the generous movie offers. Why, that means he's holding out for more. Suppose he accepts—he's an ingrate, rat, renegade. . . .

If he's written two plays about the same kind of people every-one knows that's all he can write about. . . .If the reviewers praise him Tuesday, it's only because they're gentle, quixotic fellows. But watch them tear him apart on Wednesday! . . . The young writer is now ready for a world cruise![29]

And as Clurman pointed out, "for a New York playwright this means almost inevitably Hollywood."[30]

The problem of artistic integrity is necessarily difficult to define; it invariably mires the critic in the quicksands of the intentional fallacy. But biographical concerns are not neces-sarily extrinsic to an evaluation of literature. In the case of Odets, for example, it is crucial to an understanding of much of his later work—in particular *Golden Boy* and *The Big Knife*—to recognize the ambivalent attitudes which he dis-played toward the symbol of American success, Hollywood. Indeed, we are faced here with a not unfamiliar problem: if the roots of an artist lie in the fact of his knowledge of an environment which is economically deprived, how is he to prevent the withering of these roots by the fact of his new-found success? Is the artist, by virtue of his status as celeb-rity, now cut off by this very status from the sources of his previous vitality? These questions have relevance not only to Odets but to many others of his generation. Hollywood's siren song dashed the talents of many young radical writers on the rocks of hack screenwriting.

In the case of Odets, Hollywood meant not only separa-tion from the roots of New York radicalism, but separation as well from his theatre, the Group. Odets' debt to the Group was manifest: it produced all of the plays that he wrote in the thirties. Odets is one of the few playwrights of our time to have a theatre which enabled him to speak in a consistent voice. In the direction of Clurman and the acting talent of the Adlers, Carnovsky, Bromberg, Garfield, Cobb, *et al.*, he was fortunate in having a well-trained ensemble which offered the perfect medium for the expression of his dramatic vision.

Perhaps for several reasons—the failure of *Paradise Lost*, the lure of the fantastic salary ($2,500 a week), the desire to explore that most powerful of mass media—Odets, to the dismay of the Group, went to Hollywood in 1936 to "look around"; as he himself stated to Clurman, he had a need "to sin."[31] Thus began a tortured love affair between Odets and the film capital which lasted until his death there in 1963. Ironically enough, his last work of any significance was his screenplay for the cynical *The Sweet Smell of Success* (1957). Alternately praising and reviling Hollywood, Odets was never able either fully to accept or reject its values. He viewed the cinema alternately as a medium particularly suited to the dramatist because of its directness, fluidity, and universality, and as a medium which, because of its subjugation to commercial exigencies, vitiates and destroys artistic integrity.

On the one hand, Odets offered the justification that Hollywood, by virtue of its fantastic salaries, might serve as the new patron which would free the writer for his more creative work; while, on the other, he continually recognized that isolation from the source of his material was the artist's real danger.[32] Ironically, less than a year before he went to Hollywood for the first time, Odets wrote: "Shortly I'm getting to the coal fields and the textile centers. Let New York see the rest of the country. Hollywood too. Play material enough to keep six dozen writers going. . . ."[33]

Odets' major, and only, dramatic effort for the year 1936 consisted of the film, *The General Died at Dawn;* it was eagerly awaited by radical circles in the hope that the fair-haired boy of leftist drama had succeeded in striking a few blows for the revolutionary cause. Sidney Kaufman reported upon the film's progress in the *New Masses*: "This melodramatic yarn rings like a coin from the nickelodeon mint," he admitted, "but, godalmighty, what a different face it wears."[34] This different face was, for Kaufman, reflected in several speeches of implied social consciousness. An examination of the script, however, reveals them as hardly inflammatory. Judy (played by Madeleine Carroll) has decoyed O'Hara (Gary Cooper) into a train compartment.

Judy: Why do they make these attempts on your life?
O'Hara: Politics. A certain honorable tootsie roll named Yang thinks he has a right to control the lives of tens of thousands of poor Chinese.
Judy: How?
O'Hara: Military dictatorship! Taxes! You put, he takes! You protest, he shoots! A head-breaker, a heart-breaker, a strike-breaker! Altogether a four-star rat![35]

The General Died at Dawn found few champions in either the radical or nonradical camps, and the artist in Odets soon recognized that the media of the film and the stage were not equally hospitable to seriousness, that the powers that controlled the film industry were not interested in fully utilizing the talent in their employ. The stage, and the Group, beckoned, and Odets returned to New York with *Golden Boy*. But while he was anxious to be free of the encumbrances of the film colony, Odets was excited by the possibility of applying film technique and subject matter to the medium of the stage. The cinema was indeed "the authentic folk theatre of America," but producers were not interested in presenting their material significantly; on the contrary, "their chief problem is the one of keeping the level of human experience in their pictures as low as possible." But the film has opened up the possibility of a true portrayal of American life by virtue of the range and color of its subject matter and technique. Inasmuch as Hollywood will not permit the serious use of this authentic material, it remains the task of the playwright to do so within the freer confines of the stage: "It is about time that the talented American playwright began to take the gallery of American types, the assortment of fine vital themes away from the movies."[36]

This is precisely what Odets attempted to achieve in *Golden Boy*. "Where is there a more interesting theme in this country than a little Italian boy who wants to be rich? Provided, of course, you place him in his true social background and . . . present the genuine pain, meaning and dignity of life within your characters." In short, Odets took as his self-appointed task the infusion of a typical Hollywood theme with a sense of reality, "to tell the truth where the film told a lie. . . ."[37] The difficulty with such an approach is that the triteness of the traditional subject matter may negate the seriousness of theme. *Golden Boy* treads the uncertain line between cliché and seriousness. But, on the whole, one must, in the case of this play, acknowledge Odets' success in achieving his avowed purpose. Although the story of Joe Bonaparte's rise and fall is indeed sheer Hollywood—it is the stuff of a hundred fight films—Odets has succeeded in covering the bones of melodrama with sterner stuff. He has done so by reverting to his role of allegorist.

Golden Boy is not primarily concerned with the decay of a class; it is concerned with the decadence of an ideal, success. The very nature of Odets' personal situation in Hollywood offered him his theme; for Joe Bonaparte in gaining the world loses his soul, and he loses it because he relinquishes his artistic integrity for immediate success in the world of the quick buck. It is not my intention to draw any invidious biographical parallels, but it is apparent that Joe's dilemma to a great extent parallels Odets'. The worlds of the prize ring and the motion-picture studios betray uncomfortable similarities. Both exploit talent for specifically commercial ends; both deal in forms of mass entertainment. But in the case of Joe Bonaparte the choice is not ambiguous; the pugilistic talent which he must employ to achieve success is clearly demarcated from his ability to play the violin. The Hollywood screenwriter could bask in the illusion that he was pursuing the dramatic craft.

Whether or not the world of the prize ring is intended to represent the world of Hollywood, it is apparent that the values of both are those which Odets had previously attacked in his early plays. The theme of *Golden Boy* is made meaningful in terms of a specific condemnation of the values of a society in which false values are able to pervert man's better instincts.

Joe Bonaparte's decision to fight, to show the world, is given credence by a society in which "five hundred fiddlers stand on Broadway and 48th Street, on the corner, every day, rain or shine, hot or cold."[38] In such a world the artistic gesture appears futile, and if success must be gained at the expense of art, then art must be sacrificed. But Joe's success, based upon false values, is doomed to prove insubstantial. Slowly he is turned into that which runs against his better nature, a killer; ultimately no longer faced with an alternative, he must fight because that is the only thing he can do. Joe has become a killer in spirit: "When a bullet sings through the air it has no past—only a future—like me! Nobody, nothing stands in my way!" It is not long before he becomes a killer in fact, the fit companion for the homosexual racketeer, Fuseli; in the course of a fight he knocks out his opponent and finds that the blow has killed him. Remorse has come too late; Joe recognizes that in the act of violence he has killed as well the man he might have become. Too late he realizes that it is not the kings and dictators who conquer the world, but "the boy who might have said, 'I have myself; I am what I want to be!'" (p. 315)

Joe's death in an auto crash is not gratuitous; it is the fitting conclusion to a life which he chose to lead according to the laws of the jungle. The final verdict is delivered by Joe's union-organizer brother, Frank: "What waste!" The creative energy which might have produced beautiful music has been destroyed in a false crusade. Joe's killer instinct had been bred in a world in which such talent is highly prized. If Joe was destroyed by his false image of success he was not entirely culpable; this image was created by a society in which man's basest instincts are glorified.

Such are the implications of Odets' parable. It is apparent that beneath the surface melodrama lies the familiar Marxist metaphor, albeit somewhat diluted by personal considerations. Odets' involvement in the problem of success, however, reveals more than merely personal concerns; it reflects his awareness of its mythic role in our society. It is significant that Joe was presented with an alternative. Although he rejected it because of the pressure of false values, the alternative nonetheless exists: to refuse to acquiesce in these values, to build a society in which art has a place. This conclusion is not directly affirmed, but it is strongly implied, particularly in the person of Frank, who serves as a foil to Joe's destructive energy. It is noteworthy that Odets should turn Hollywood subject matter and technique (the short, cinematic scenes, the use of fadeouts) against itself, in order to combat the mythic Hollywood success story (and Hollywood, in retaliation, reversed Odets' logic by putting a "happy ending" upon the screen version of *Golden Boy*). The moral of Odets' allegory might not be overtly revolutionary, but it is nonetheless rooted in severe social criticism.

Odets was not, however, through with Hollywood. Over the course of the next decade he was alternately to make his peace with the film colony and then reject it anew.[39] (A 1944 interview was entitled "Going Their Way Now? Clifford Odets Has Given Up Tilting at the Hollywood Windmill, or So He Says.")[40] In 1948, for example, he returned to Broadway after a seven-year absence, and castigated the movie colony in the harshest terms possible. He deeply resented the accusations of "sell out" which had plagued him ever since he initially left for Hollywood, and offered several explanations for his long defection: he wanted to recoup the "small fortune" he had invested in the Group in its dying years, to forget "the distress of several misplaced personal allegiances"; he was looking for a period of "creative repose: money, rest, and simple clarity."[41] But Hollywood, he averred, offered few consolations beyond the monetary; since his talents were still ignored, he came to detest the lethargy into which he had fallen; he consoled himself with the plays he was going to write, "took my filthy salary every week and rolled an inner eye around an inner landscape." Apparently Odets never quite escaped the sense of guilt born of accepting Hollywood gold, and was performing an act of purgation in returning to the New York theatre, "where personal affiliation with one's writing (the first premise of truth) does not constitute lese majesty."[42]

Odets' specific act of contrition was represented by his play *The Big Knife* (1949), in which he attempted to expose the mendacity of Hollywood and the corrosive effect of its guiding ethic. "The big knife," he stated, "is that force in modern life which is against people and their aspirations, which seeks to cut people off in their best flower,"[43] but, we must ask, in what precisely does this force reside? For the difficulty with the play is that we are never exactly sure what the playwright is railing against. In *Golden Boy*, Odets used some of the conventions of melodrama in order to construct an allegory which depicted the pernicious effect of a destructive ethic; in *The Big Knife* he attempts much the same thing, but fails to demonstrate the play's thesis through dramatic action. Joe Bonaparte is destroyed because society has made him a killer; why does Charlie Castle destroy himself? Hank, the New York writer who symbolizes the man of integrity, presents Charlie's eulogy: "He killed himself . . . because that was the only way he could live." Charlie's suicide was "a final act of faith."[44] Faith, however, in what? Castle's predicament, as revealed in the play, seems magnified beyond all dramatic credibility precisely because it is forcibly wedded to melodramatic circumstance instead of arising inexorably from a genuine moral dilemma. The real issue involved is simple: should the artist, luxuriating in material splendor at the expense of his artistic integrity, chuck it all to return to a meaningful existence? Stated in these terms, the issue seems hardly one to induce suicide. But Odets obviously felt that the problem was not dramatically sufficient, and therefore felt constrained to project this dilemma in terms of a plot which deals with intrigue and suggested murder. The difficulty with this scheme from a dramatic viewpoint is that the real issue—the acceptance or rejection of Hollywood values— is in no way related to the machinery of the plot. If Charlie Castle is blackmailed into signing his contract, what happens to the element of choice which is crucial to the larger, more serious, dramatic issue?

Thus the prevalent tone of *The Big Knife* is hysteria. Odets attacks many evils of the Hollywood scene—the malicious gossip-monger, the amoral aide-de-camp, the hypocritical, vicious producer—but he fails to achieve what he succeeded in accomplishing in *Golden Boy*, to relate these specific evils, and the drama's basic structure, to a guiding metaphor which clarifies the main lines of the intended allegory. The boxing world becomes, in *Golden Boy*, a microcosm of the larger society of which it is a part; Hollywood, in *The Big Knife*, fails not only as a microcosm, but as a realistic portrayal of the film capital. God knows there are sufficient grounds for criticism without implying that producers and agents are would-be murderers.

The crucial fact is that *Golden Boy* presents a social alternative; *The Big Knife* does not. "Does the man in your book get out of here?" cries Charlie to Hank. "Where does he go? What, pray tell, does he do? (*bitterly*) Become a union organizer?" This alternative, objectified in the person of Frank in *Golden Boy*, has become unthinkable (p. 112). Charlie's anguish springs from the recognition that he is a part of the world which he wants to reject. The problem with the play resides in this very ambivalence. Odets—in the character of Castle—alternately villifies and accepts Hollywood captivity. Charlie wants to reject the malicious world of which he is a part, but feels unable to substitute another. Although he recognizes that "everyone needs a cause to touch greatness" (p. 137), he has lost his capacity to believe in causes. He has, as Hank points out, sold out, and is consequently tormented by guilt: "Look at me! Could you ever know that all my life I yearned for a world and people to call out the best in me?" (p. 140). In short, although Odets *has* a theme, he is unwilling to face its direct implications. For the real question, left unanswered in *The Big Knife*, is in what or in whom does the responsibility lie for the destruction of Charlie Castle? In society? In his own weakness? Perhaps Odets was too personally involved in Charlie's dilemma to objectify it truthfully. As Clurman noted, the play "is neither the true story of Odets nor the clear account of a freely conceived Charlie Castle. Its subjectivity is muddled by its pretense of objectivity; its objectivity is compromised by the author's inability to distinguish between his creature and himself."[45]

The importance of Odets' political commitment from a dramatic point of view resided in its affording him an intellectual substructure upon which to construct his several dramas. Since Odets' virtues were never primarily intellectual, his social orientation enabled him to relate his characters and themes to a coherent world-view. Either explicit or implicit in all his dramas of the thirties lies the metaphor born of his Marxist commitment. At first overtly stated, it later becomes the philosophical undercurrent which relates his several portraits of frustration to a gesture of protest. The Marxist eschatology provided the dramatist with a structural referent, for implicit in the dialectical struggle is an essential drama, the vanquishing of the old class by the new. It is this dialectic which informs Odets' Depression dramas; either explicitly in *Waiting for Lefty* or implicitly in *Rocket to the Moon*, they all offer the hope of the future against the frustration of the present. The structural failure of *The Big Knife* lies in Odets' inability, after the loss of political commitment, to substitute a suitable unifying dramatic metaphor. With the absence of the substructure of social protest, the drama flounders in a sea of hysteria. I am not implying the *necessity* of a social metaphor in drama, but merely pointing out the crucial role it played in Odets' career as dramatist. Odets has lost his status as major dramatist because, unlike Tennessee Williams, for example, he failed to suggest in his later dramas that he was presenting us with a vision of reality which transcended his several plays.

The consequences of the loss of metaphor may be observed in a comparison of two domestic dramas written in the thirties and the fifties respectively. *Rocket to the Moon* (1938) is not an overtly political play. In fact, the Marxist critics complained that "Odets has stopped listening to the people he knows so well."[46] It is concerned with the frustrations of a middle-class dentist and his futile love affair with his young secretary. But despite Odets' essentially personal concerns, despite his emphasis upon psychological rather than social factors, there can be no denying that beneath the play resides the basic social metaphor.

The very positing of the metaphor of the rocket to the moon—the illusion of escape—has meaning because it is an illusion, because there is an alternative. Cleo, the young secretary, rejects both Stark and Prince, the denizens of a dying world, to seek fulfillment elsewhere:

Don't you think there's a world of joyful men and women? Must all men live afraid to laugh and sing? Can't we sing at work and love our work? It's getting too late to play at life; I want to *live* it.[47]

Thus *Rocket to the Moon*, despite its psychological emphasis, is still structured by the redemption motif which characterizes Odets' earlier plays. And the redemption resides both in an affirmation and a rejection, since the one predicates the other. The play succeeds, therefore, in relating the confusion and frustration of its major characters to the larger world of which they are a part; Stark, Prince, Belle, and Cleo speak in the authentic voice of the Depression generation, reaching, grasping for a way out. But personal problems are grounded in a larger social context; Ben Stark cannot really love because his bourgeois world is rooted in futility and illusion. Odets draws the social moral—the moral Clurman chose as the "spine" of his production of the play:

Who's got time and place for "love and the grace to use it?" [asks Stark] Is it something apart, love? . . . An entertainment? Christ, no! It's a synthesis of good and bad, economics, work, play, all contacts. . . . Love is no solution of life! . . . The opposite. You have to bring a whole balanced normal life to love if you want it to go! [p. 404]

It is revealing to compare *Rocket to the Moon* with Odets' later domestic drama, *The Country Girl* (1951). Although in the latter play Odets again treats the themes of frustration and redemption, he does so this time within a self-contained personal world removed from social causation. Odets formally acknowledged his restriction of emphasis in an interview in the New York *Times*. In omitting "social significance," he admitted that he may have taken "a step backward" as a playwright. However, by insulating his characters from the raging complexities of the world beyond their own private heartbreak, he believed that he was able to write more proficiently than ever before. He deliberately undertook to limit himself to but one aspect of life, the search for personal values. He acknowledged the self-imposed limitation, but mused, "It may be that limitation is the beginning of wisdom."[48]

The Country Girl is endowed with virtues hitherto unassociated with Odets; it is neat, well-ordered, and theatrically sound—a *pièce bien faite*. "I wanted to take simple elements and make something sharp and theatrical about them. I stated a fact, the story of these two people, rather than speculated about the fact."[49] But in restricting his scope, Odets robbed the play of his salient virtue, the necessary connection between the characters on the stage and the world of which they are a part. Frank Elgin's redemption is portrayed but it is never related to any specific cause. The key questions, left unanswered, are why did he go to pieces and why was he saved? The esthetic difficulties in *The Big Knife* resulted from Odets' inability to realize Charlie Castle's real anguish in effective dramatic terms; the esthetic difficulty with *The Country Girl* is that one is never fully convinced of Elgin's anguish. Since he remains the skeleton of a character rather than its flesh and bones, his redemption by his faithful wife seems, in the context of the play, almost gratuitous. He might well have gone on another bender and failed to achieve his theatrical triumph. At the end of the play Georgie, the country girl of the title, herself admits that "neither of us has really changed," but none the less discerns some "new element of hope," although she is not sure what.[50] Neither are we as audience or reader convinced of this new possibility of hope because we are never presented with any dramatic alternative except that of the conventional backstage drama: will Frank Elgin succeed in making a comeback or not?

Insofar as there is a theme, it involves the fact of human responsibility, the necessity of looking forward not back. Georgie attempts to make Frank look life in the eye, to emerge from behind the myriad of evasions with which he has buttressed his life. But this theme is itself evaded because the roots of Frank's irresponsibility—symbolized in his alcoholism—are never explained. Responsibility implies a correlative: responsibility to what, and evasion of what? Frank's theatrical triumph does not arise out of the fact of his coming to terms with himself; it is merely presented. The last scene of the play might well have demonstrated his inability to cope with the responsibilities of opening on Broadway without marring the essential logic of the play.

In *Rocket to the Moon* the outside world continually intrudes, but in *The Country Girl* the social metaphor has been eschewed, exposing the bare bones of theatrical contrivance. It is as if Odets were saying to Broadway: "You want me to meet you on your terms? Very well, I'll show you that I'm able to do so." But in accepting Broadway's terms—an acceptance rewarded by commercial success— he surrendered the very real virtue which distinguished his earlier work, the adamant refusal to be confined by the structure of the conventional Broadway play, the fervent desire to change the theatre, and ultimately the world outside it.

Odets, in losing his political commitment, enacted the drama of his generation. It is not inappropriate that disenchantment with Marxist principles should have specific esthetic results, for Marxism had indeed attempted to create a specific esthetic. We have observed that although Odets never adhered rigidly to the strict logic of the doctrine of proletarian literature, none the less his Depression dramas are rooted in the *metaphor* of the Marxist dialectic. Thus the theme of redemption or resurrection is wedded to the concept of the necessary vanquishing of the old class by the new. Odets' problem as a dramatist, although never explicitly viewed as such, was to find a substitute metaphor to order the various elements of his artistic experience. Once the Marxist metaphor had lost its validity, once the substructure of the Marxist dialectic no longer sufficed, Odets was deprived of the structural framework upon which he had consciously or unconsciously built.

The consequences of the absence of this framework may be observed in an examination of Odets' last play with the Group, *Night Music* (1940). Although certain persistent Odetsian themes appear in the play, in particular the redemption of the young by the old, they are no longer related to a guiding, thematic concept; instead Odets attempts to substitute an esthetic metaphor, musical structure, for thematic structure, and the resultant play is characterized by a general diffuseness and uncertainty which robs its social implications of any vitality. In attempting to portray contemporary homelessness and uncertainty, Odets committed the esthetic mistake of being himself uncertain and erratic.

Odets possessed an aural rather than a visual imagination; his plays have always been characterized by the specific quality of their dialogue, the authentic sound of colloquial, urban speech. In commenting on New York City, he once noted that "I don't see it visually—though it's beautiful enough—so much as I hear it and feel it."[51] And in the story of Steve Takis' erratic weekend on the town, Odets attempts, in *Night Music*, to record the sounds and music of twentieth-century New York and, by extension, America. But the myriad variations of the play serve to muddy rather than to clarify the theme. Hearing the sound of crickets, Fay, the young heroine, remarks, "Night Music . . . if they can sing, I can sing. . . . We can sing through any night!"[52] This faith in the ability of the human being to transcend his difficulties is, at best, most generally stated. True, the play raises some specific social issues. Steve's predicament, for example, is given an economic base, since his aggression is motivated by the fact of his deprivation. The "big international question" for him is still "when do we eat?" (p. 178). But a sense of man's inability to confront reality and change the world vitiates the social implications of *Night Music*. If there is one essential theme it is that of homelessness, the individual's inability to find someone or something to belong to. Although Steve Takis is indeed a proletarian, despite occasional outbursts of indignation, he displays no real sense of class. He is a boy without credentials, the "All-American bum," striking back at friend and foe alike with a defensive hospitality, which is merely a mask for his sense of homelessness. The theme of *Night Music* is, thus, not the determination of the economically deprived to gain their deserved rights, but rather a despairing acknowledgment of the futility of gestures of protest. Not merely Steve and Fay, but *all* the characters in the play, regardless of class, are characterized by this similar sense of dislocation. Where previously dislocation had served Odets as a class image, it now informs *all* strata of society.

Odets seems to acquiesce in the mood of futility which

pervades the play. His attempt to dispel it, in the person of the Guardian Angel, the detective Rosenberger, is so generalized in its optimism as to be fundamentally unconvincing. For Odets' answer seems to be nothing so much as to affirm a blind faith in man's possibilities. Rosenberger's role in the play serves merely to demonstrate the gratuitousness of his solutions; whenever the young couple finds itself in difficult straits, he appears to set the situation right, and to present them with his optimistic gospel: "Where there is life there is hope, in my humble opinion. Only the living can cry out against life" (p. 168).

It is precisely this sense of false solution—of conquering life by merely living it—which provides the play with the Saroyanesque note that many of the critics noted ("Now that Odets writes like Saroyan," wrote Atkinson, "doomsday is near"). Rosenberger's relationship to Steve is not unlike that of Jacob to Ralph, but whereas the latter's redemption was predicated on the acceptance of a specific road out of the frustrations of the present, Steve's redemption is based upon his acceptance of the vaguest kind of social philosophy: "In the time of your life, live." Although Saroyan's particular talent was able to inform this false optimism with a kind of wistfulness and nostalgia which made it work theatrically, Odets' talent did not lend itself to such manipulation. Ultimately, despite his attempt at wistfulness, his world is a real one, and demands real solutions. *Night Music* is one of those works which catches a specific moment in history; the spirit of the thirties had disappeared, employment was up, and the European war hovered ominously on the horizon. The major social issue was soon to become the simple act of survival. In such a world, in which catastrophe appeared imminent, it is not strange that the playwright should turn to themes of uncertainty, despair, and a desperate optimism. But Odets' dramatic dilemma was to find a means of structuring these various themes. He failed, despite the musical metaphor, because the implications of the various elements in the play continually led him in different directions. Thus the play is alternately wistful, nostalgic, bitter, farcical, optimistic, and despairing. The theme of redemption seems gratuitous because it does not seem warranted; if there is any moral in Steve's redemption, it lies in the cliché, love conquers all. Yet the seriousness of much of the play makes us unwilling to accept the conventional romantic ending. Rosenberger advises Steve to "make a Party-To-Marry-My-Girl." Even as a comic statement, it is significant that Odets' specific political solution to Steve's problems should be marriage.

In *Clash By Night* (1941) the vision of uncertainty and homelessness which found whimsical reflection in *Night Music* had turned stark and grim. The war clouds which had appeared on the horizon in the earlier play now seemed poised to drench the American landscape, and, in fact, less than one month after the play was produced in November, 1941, the Depression era found its violent interment in the cataclysm of world war.

The mood of the play may be gathered from Odets' diary notes pertaining to its genesis:

July 27: The climate of the . . . play will be exactly that of the weather here. Muggy, foreboding, the never bursting open sky Why? I feel it must be that way. It is weather in which anything can happen. All courses of conduct are possible, men and women may suddenly weep, reverse their entire lives under this leaden sky; relaxed amiabilities, hatreds, exquisite tenderness . . . sudden murderous wrath, all may happen. . . . Out of a long chain of seeming dull trivia is born a shattering explosion that is the line of the new play.

.   .   .   .   .   .

August 8: The theme is taking shape in my mind, intensely personal but generally significant feeling behind it. The theme . . . has to do with the need of a new morality, with a return to voluntarily imposed morals, to voluntarily assumed forms in a world . . . where there are no forms but plenty of appetite and irresponsibility.

.　　.　　.　　.　　.　　.

October 21: Part of the theme of this play is about how men irresponsibly wait for the voice and strong arm of Authority to bring them to life. . . . Nothing stands for Authority and we wait for its voice! . . . The children are looking for the father to arrange their lives for them![53]

Clash By Night represents Odets' final testament to the themes which informed his earlier dramas. The vision which had celebrated human possibility has turned sour, and the image of redemption is overshadowed by that of death. Like Odets' early characters, the people whose struggles are recorded in *Clash By Night* are frustrated by circumstance. Mae, like Hennie, is trapped in a loveless marriage; Earl's bluster, like that of Moe and Steve, masks a basic insecurity; the good-hearted Jerry wants nothing so much as to feel that he is needed. The dream of love, the desire to escape a life which is devoid of joy—"a life lived on the installment plan"—these pathetic gropings set the stage for the enactment of the love triangle which constitutes the plot of the play. But whereas Hennie, Moe, and Ralph were able to escape, Jerry, Mae, and Earl are condemned. There is no escape afforded them; Jerry, goaded by the fascistic Kress, is overwhelmed by jealousy and kills Earl rather than lose his wife.

Odets attempts to use the redemption theme by posing, in opposition to the tragedy of his major characters, the healthy relationship of a young couple, Joe and Peggy. Unlike Earl or Jerry, Joe "knows his address," he is not torn away from the roots of life. He states what, we may assume, Odets intended as the moral of the play:

We're all afraid! Earl, Jerry, Mae, millions like them, clinging to a goofy dream—expecting life to be a picnic. Who taught them that? Radio, Songs, the Movies . . . paradise is just around the corner. . . . But . . . we know the facts, the anti-picnic facts. We know that Paradise begins in responsibility. . . . Yes, its a time to learn, a time to begin—its time to love and face the future![54]

We must ask in what manner this theme is realized in *Clash By Night.* Despite this statement, and Mae's final advice to the young couple—"You're young and strong, you got a future" (p. 241)—it is apparent that Odets is merely going through the motions. He had become so acclimated to the structural support of the Marxist-redemption metaphor that he used it in this play as a dramatic device even though it is never validated. The drama of Earl, Jerry, and Mae is in no way logically connected to the drama of Joe and Peggy. Indeed, the latter might well have been eliminated without impairing the play one iota. Nowhere in the play is it implied that the dilemma of the principal characters is motivated by the false ideals which they have learned from society. Nowhere is the corrosive influence of radio, songs, and the movies manifest. Mae, Jerry and Earl are trapped by circumstances, by the inexorable fact that in a love triangle someone's fingers must be burned. Is the desire to escape from the frustration of the present necessarily a false ideal? Nowhere does Odets imply this. The metaphor of social redemption which served as a dramatic aid as long as Odets accepted the implications of Marxism, serves, in the case of *Clash By Night,* to falsify the play; for all elements of the play enforce the conviction that there is no escape. The world is seen, in Arnold's image as "a darkling plain . . . where ignorant armies clash by night." All the characters in the play confirm this pessimistic view, even the untormented Peggy, who states, "It's a nervous world, a shocking world. I don't understand it, I just don't understand it" (pp. 122-23).

The ritual of violence which Odets enacted in *Clash By Night* was soon enacted in the world at large, and the world war which inaugurated the forties fittingly ended both the decade and the Great Depression itself. We have already traced much of Odets' subsequent career. Like many of his generation he was unable to replace the faith which had made him one of the most representative dramatists of the Depression era; and what is more significant for his art, he was unable to find a new dramatic metaphor to replace the one born of his political commitment. The failure of *The Big Knife* brought forth the compromise of *The Country Girl*, in which the rebel in Odets deferred to the Broadway craftsman. And yet his dissatisfaction with the compromise is attested by his last play, *The Flowering Peach* (1954), in which we find the playwright groping towards a new metaphor he never succeeded in finding.

Once again, Odets is concerned with an allegory of redemption; but redemption in this case is not born of a specific act of faith, but rather the attempt to replace the loss of faith. For in *The Flowering Peach* Odets attempts to define the dilemma both of his generation and of his own art. It represents that moment in an artist's career when reassessment seems to be demanded, when the artist must stop and take stock of his personal and esthetic resources. "I'm not a kid anymore," Odet acknowledged to a *Times* interviewer in 1954, "I'm 47. And at this age I began to ask myself, what happened? Do you want to begin all over again? Who are you and where are you?"[55]

The significance of the play lies in the fact that Odets finally attempted to come to terms with the esthetic consequences of the loss of his political commitment. It was an acknowledgment long overdue, for, as we have observed, the attempt to exploit the structural advantages of the Marxist metaphor after rejecting its meaning vitiated Odets' post-Depression plays. The essence of *The Flowering Peach* is the acceptance of the loss of political faith. If there is one key line in the play it is perhaps Rachel's cry to the idealistic

Japheth: "There is idealism now in just survival."[56] Odets affirmed this conviction in the *Times*:

When you start out you have to champion something. Every artist begins as if he were the first one painting, every composer as if there were no Beethoven. But if you still feel that way after ten or fifteen years, you're nuts. . . . I couldn't have written ten *The Flowering Peach* twenty years ago. As you grow older, you mature. The danger is that in broadening, as you mature, you dilute your art. A growing writer always walks that tight rope.[57]

Odets' utilization of the Noah myth is not subject to a one-to-one allegorical interpretation. There can be no doubt, however, that the play represents an intensely personal statement. Odets is basically concerned with man's reaction to cosmic injustice, his attempt to construct a means whereby he can *accept* this injustice. It is this concept of acceptance which dominates *The Flowering Peach*. Despite everything, Noah accepts the will of God, the fact of human destruction. The rebel, Japheth, prefers to remain off the ark rather than accept the divine edict, but Noah knocks him unconscious and carries him aboard; thus man, Odets, implies, must accept the inequities of life; the gesture of protest must not be carried to extremes. And yet the rebellious gesture is not futile. It is Japheth's insistence that the ship have a rudder, his skill in fixing leaks, which saves the ship from foundering. Man must not merely accept, he must act. He cannot assume that God will necessarily prevent catastrophe; he must have faith in himself, for he can never be sure what God wants. Noah, however, *does* know what God wants. He wants to prevent the extinction of life, to provide the basis for the construction of a new world. The necessity of this preservation—and the acceptance of the capriciousness of divine law—transcends the meaning of Japheth's gesture of protest. Ultimately, he too must accept the way of the world. The rebel may attempt to guide his destiny, but

he cannot change it. Significantly, the world which is renewed at the end of the play, it is implied, will not be very
different from the world which was destroyed. Shem, who
symbolizes man's acquisitive nature, has not been changed
by the catastrophe. At the beginning of the play he was
loath to accept Noah's demand to aid in the construction of
the Ark because it meant the sacrifice of his worldly pos-
sessions; during the voyage he had planned for the future
by saving the manure of the animals in anticipation of the
time when fuel would be needed and he could sell dried
manure briquettes. But Noah, who had previously berated
Shem's avariciousness, finally, and significantly, comes to
live with it. Previously Noah had attacked Shem's desire to
live again by the principle of exploitation, but after his initial anger at his son's attempt to "begin a new world . . .
with manure," at the risk of endangering the safety of the
ark, Noah finally comes to accept his wife's logic: "Shem
made a useful thing from nothing. . . . Why kill the man with
brains? No, make him use it for the *family!*" (p. 197). Ultimately it is *not* the rebel, Japheth, that Noah goes to live
with in the new world; it is Shem. "Why? It's more comfortable" (p. 203).

Thus, the rebel in Odets came to accept the futility of
the radical gesture; there is sufficient idealism in the fact of
survival. "You say to the eagle, fly!" cries Noah to God at the
moment of his designation, "Even to a little bitty of an eagle
like me, fly, fly, higher and higher! You have shrinked away
his wings and he couldn't do it! Why did You pick me?" (p.
184). But every man is chosen, and every man must face the
contradiction between his aspirations and his achievements.
The fire of youth is gone, the desire to change the world is
gone; but the world endures. And what has Noah learned
from his journey through catastrophe? "To walk in humility,
I learned. And listen, even to *myself* . . . and to speak softly,
with the voices of consolation" (p. 204).

Thus redemption is ultimately born of acceptance, not protest; Agate Keller had cried in *Waiting For Lefty* that "when we die they'll know what we did to make a new world! Christ, cut us up to little pieces . . . put fruit trees where our ashes are!" But Noah accepts a small branch of the flowering peach as a "precious gift . . . from the new earth." Regeneration indeed, but this time without the ashes of man's effort.

8

S. N. BEHRMAN: NO TIME FOR COMEDY?

It is relieving, if not morally profitable, for an American writer to contemplate people who can recreate the semblance of gaiety in the face of lamentably inappropriate circumstances.

ROBERT SHERWOOD, Preface to *Reunion in Vienna*

Manner—divorced from justice—the Hell with that!

S. N. BEHRMAN, *No Time for Comedy*

CHAPTER EIGHT

THE AMERICAN temperament has never been particularly hospitable to high comedy; our wit has always remained too equalitarian to accommodate the epigrams and mots of a leisure class. It is not surprising, then, that S. N. Behrman in his attempt to produce an American comedy of manners should look to British examples, nor that the comic world which he in fact created should be peopled perennially with the flower of the Anglo-American theatrical aristocracy: the Lunts, Jane Cowl, Ina Claire, etc. Nor should we burden ourselves with a too-intense search for the sounds and smells of a specific locale. Behrman's world, whether it be London, or New York, or Mexico, or Maine, is always the same; the drawing room is always elaborately furnished and the grand piano offers perpetual solace for world-weariness. Against the backdrop of this fashionable world the perennial intrigues of sophisticated comedy are enacted. Love is always the prime mover, but it is never ventured into precipitately, for this would impede the flow of wit released by the continual discussion of its complications. In the world of high comedy articulateness is all.

I do not wish to denigrate the genre, but merely, in affirming several of its salient features, to indicate the paradox in which S. N. Behrman was necessarily involved. For it is extremely important in the world of sophisticated comedy that situations appear more portentous than they in fact are. High comedy thrives on trivia; dependent upon a core of dramatic conventionality which serves as the framework upon which the playwright embroiders verbal witticisms, it is concerned less with the demonstration of human folly and absurdity than with the witty comment upon them. Comedy of manners is, therefore, dependent upon a very specific set of social values. The laughter which it provokes has its roots in Bergsonian superiority. Gaucherie, maladroitness, pretension—these are the salient vices of its world; cleverness, articulateness, *savoir faire*—these are the prescribed virtues. Above all, the wit must preserve a degree of detachment from the follies which he witnesses and assails verbally. Involvement would be fatal; it might, after all, demonstrate the ridiculousness of his own position.

For these several reasons one would not expect the genre to flourish in a period of intense social dislocation. In a world of crises, in which old values are crumbling and new ones asserted, it would seem that its very foundations would be undermined. In a world which demands action, the necessarily static and detached form of high comedy might well seem anachronistic. For witty laughter is apt to seem most trivial in a world of insecurity, and the surface mannerisms of social life may appear supremely unimportant in the context of social conflict.

And yet S. N. Behrman's major comedies of manners were written during one of the most convulsive periods of recent history. If there was ever a time unpropitious for high comedy, it would appear to be the thirties. The world was deadly serious; it was, as Behrman himself observed, "no time for comedy." Drama was illumined by the flame of social protest, not by the fire of wit. And yet, as Behrman has consistently affirmed, it is precisely in such a period that laughter is most needed; for when man loses his ability to laugh at himself, he has most surely surrendered to his more ignoble instincts.

This then was Behrman's esthetic dilemma: his forte was undeniably sophisticated comedy, and yet the world seemed to strike at the very roots of the genre by destroying the possibility of detachment. How was the serious comic dramatist to retain the genre and still express a necessary concern with the vital issues of the age? Note the qualifying adjective "serious"; had Behrman been merely a hack there would indeed have been no problem. His task would quite simply have been to turn out quite pleasant trifles within the dictates of an established formula. But Behrman, despite the closeness with which he toed the Broadway line, was much more than a hack in the thirties. Clurman has written wistfully of "the poet buried in him that he himself hardly knows,"[1] and this "poet" emerged time and again to challenge the Broadway craftsman. Despite his dedication to well-made comedies, Behrman's major plays have demonstrated a consistent involvement with serious themes.

It is not our purpose to pursue the reason why Behrman continued to utilize the conventions of high comedy to express his very serious opinions upon the social upheavals of his age. Surely, these concerns with fascism, communism, and liberalism strain the genre at times almost to the breaking point. Perhaps he felt that laughter must be provoked at all costs in a humorless world; or perhaps he recognized, quite realistically, that his particular talent was best expressed through the forms of high comedy. What concerns us is that Behrman was determined to retain the genre, and yet deal seriously with serious problems. What emerges dramatically is, therefore, a unique hybrid. The form is still that of high comedy, since most of the traditional conventions are retained. Lovers are still wonderfully articulate, and mots are casually exchanged. But although the world delineated is still that of the leisure class, it is a world besieged. Social philosophy as well as amorous intrigue affords food for table talk. Young radicals appear—sometimes in the form of the young scions of the upper class itself—to drag most disquieting subjects into the drawing room. But although ideas abound, Behrman never attempts to create a Shavian comedy of ideas. In Shaw ideas themselves determine the form of drama. Comedic devices are utilized insofar as they facilitate and embody the clash of various intellectual or social positions. Shaw runs the comic gamut from high comedy to burlesque, continually adapting forms to his specific intellectual and dramatic needs.

Behrman, on the other hand, although he is involved with ideas, continually attempts to make them conform to the dictates of a specific genre. He is never the *farceur*; in his plays situations themselves are rarely comic; they are in fact most serious, for were they otherwise the world of wit might abdicate before the world of low comedy. Behrman is determined to *use* ideas as he uses dramatic situations, as the means for the exploitation of wit. He attempts to make ideas and social conflict conform to high comedic demands by never forgoing the essential qualities of the form. Thus the very seriousness of the ideas involved continually threatens to destroy the trivial base upon which his wit is perched. One is asked to accept the triviality of his characters as well as the seriousness of the problems in which they are involved.

In Behrman's pre-Depression plays this problem does not present many difficulties. In *The Second Man* (1927), for example, we are not compelled to accept anything extrinsic to the demands of high comedy. We are fully aware that Storey's problem—whether to marry his wealthy mistress or a young ingénue—is the stuff of comedy. We are not asked, nor do we aspire, to accept Storey's dilemma as very portentous. We acquiesce in its triviality because we accept the rules of the game. "In the end everything is reduced to cliché."[2] This is Clark Storey's credo, and it is the credo of *The Second Man*. But, as we have indicated, plot cliché is essential to the unbridling of wit, and in the character of Storey, Behrman has created a perfect comic mouthpiece: "Real emotions and real feelings are destructive. I've learned to do without them. That's civilization" (p. 70).

But the exploitation of verbalisms and the familiar amatory intrigues are not the only stuff of *The Second Man*. There *is* a theme, and it is expressed in the very title of the play. Storey reveals to Monica that cynicism is contrary to his better nature: "There's someone else inside me—a second man—a cynical, odious person, who keeps watching me, who keeps listening to what I say, grinning and sophisticated, horrid. . . . He never lets me be—this other man . . ." (p. 48). But we cannot accept Storey's protestation very seriously; it is apparent that this theme is itself a device. Storey is never humanized, nor should he be, for were his dilemma a real one the play would assume a decidedly uncomic tone. Thus from the very outset although Behrman demonstrated his ability to exploit elements of seriousness, these elements are, in *The Second Man*, confined within the limits of the genre. Storey's attack of integrity is, in the context of the play, about as important as Monica's spurious pregnancy. Both move the machinery of plot and allow the wit room to maneuver.

One element which characterizes this and Behrman's subsequent plays, and which demonstrates his tendency to exploit dramatic conventions for the purposes of wit, is the puritanism which lies behind the facade of his characters' sophistication. Time and again, Behrman's major characters are faced with either marriage or abandonment. Rarely does the possibility of a casual affair seem to be entertained. Storey, for example, despite his man-of-the-world stance, states, "If I were a cad I should have an affair with Monica. But regrettably I am a Puritan. Can't help it. It's in my blood" (p. 63). Lael, the heroine of *Rain from Heaven*, similarly says, "though I'm intellectually sympathetic to any indulgence, emotionally I'm fastidious and even puritanic."[3] And Paula to her boy friend, Will, in *End of Summer*: "What a Puritan you are!"[4] Even Gaylord in *No Time for*

Comedy: "Damn it, Linda—I've got to marry Mandy or somebody because its the only way I can be unfaithful to you!"[5]

One might well question the accuracy with which Behrman delineates the mores of the upper classes, and inquire why this continual assertion of the puritanic nature of most of his major characters? Perhaps the playwright recognized that without their puritanic morality his characters would be totally inert. Were they casual in their love-making, Behrman would be deprived of his perennial plot device, the momentousness of amatory choice. In Behrman's plays the machinery of plot is perpetually wedded to sentimental premises. As in much of popular art, the glamour of illicitness is exploited within the strict confines of public morality.

We are not overtly troubled by these premises in the context of *The Second Man* or *Serena Blandish* (1929) or *Brief Moment* (1931); they are essentially trifles. It is in the context of Behrman's later plays that his devices become bothersome, for Behrman seems dramatically unwilling to forego the formula with which he had achieved success in *The Second Man*. The Behrmanian formula might be stated as follows: take a man or woman of the world (elegantly played either by Alfred Lunt or Ina Claire), make him or her the object of the attention of several worthy suitors of the opposite sex; add the fillip of indecision (the various suitors present different virtues) and sprinkle generously with the spice of witty self-analysis. Needless to say, this formula is hardly original with Behrman. What Behrman attempts is to retain his successful commercial formula and yet use it as a means whereby he can take a serious look at the issues of his time. The technique suffices as long as he can retain the detached position of the wit; one can comment even upon a changing world. The difficulty arises when Behrman himself becomes involved, when the pressure of events—in particular the rise of fascism and the persecution of the Jews—dislodges him from the position of un-involvement. It is then that the foundations of sophisticated comedy begin to crumble and the machinery of device to appear insubstantial.

The intrusion of social concerns into the world of high comedy may be first seen in *Biography* (1932), in which Behrman introduces for the first time a characteristic figure of the decade, the radical. In Richard Kurt, Behrman draws the portrait of a type he comes to dislike thoroughly. It is not the radical's viewpoint on social issues which disturbs Behrman, since he is, in fact, in substantial agreement on many particulars. The quality possessed by Kurt in *Biography*—and later Chris in *Wine of Choice*—which Behrman disavows is an inhumanity born of dogmatism. The radical, Behrman continually affirms, is "really at home only in protest."[6] He will not allow his better instincts to break through the facade of his toughness, for this would threaten the simplicity of his world. Kurt's fanaticism leads to the rejection of his basic goodness, and Marion, his lover, recoils before this rejection. "Studying you," she tells him, "I can see why so many movements against injustice become such absolute tyrannies" (p. 173).

In *Biography* Behrman initiates his attempt to write a form of comedy which takes cognizance of contemporary social issues, but which does not depart from the necessary detachment of wit. Although he retains the form of *The Second Man*, he attempts to infuse it with the life blood of social comment. Above all, in the face of an intolerant world he tries to raise the banner of sanity, to demonstrate that wit is still possible—in fact, necessary. If one villain emerges from the corpus of his work, it is the authoritarian fanatic—either communist or fascist—who, like Kurt, denies the humanity of both himself and others.

Yet Kurt is not totally unsympathetic; on the contrary, within the context of the plot he is, indeed, the hero.

Behrman rejects his means, not his ends. In *Wine of Choice* (1938), however, the radical prototype is thoroughly excoriated. For Chris, the proletarian novelist, has drowned almost all his humanity in class hate. Wilda, the young ingénue who falls in love with him, notes that Chris does not judge those outside his class as human beings: "You wrote about us exactly as if we were all wild animals or foreigners. . . . As though, for you, we were in a different category altogether—a non-human category." And Chris answers, "Perhaps for me you are."[7] Kurt, at least, was not completely humorless. His aim in publishing Marion's biography was "to laugh the powers that be out of existence in a great winnowing gale of laughter" (p. 150). Bitter laughter indeed, but at least laughter. Chris, however, has no respect for any humor, ameliorative or otherwise. "Humor is a vice," he asserts, "it cushions suffering" (p. 86).

Having rejected the capitalist world, Chris is ready to write its denizens off completely. They are members of a dying class and will hardly be missed. He rejects in toto all the values which seem to him an irrelevance, and which to Behrman represent qualities the world can scarcely do without: charm, grace, tolerance. But the world which Chris wishes to destroy is obviously not without its virtues; although the aristocracy is indeed an anachronism in an age of social change—"on the one hand inhibited by a code, on the other emasculated by charm" (p. 166)—as represented by the charming but ineffectual Laddy, for example, it is not vicious. Ryder, the play's *raisonneur*, points out that if he must fight in order to defend the worthwhile values of the old order against Chris he will do so: "You make me feel suddenly that there is something marvelously worth preserving in Laddy. Against you and your kind I would preserve not his indolence but his chivalry—not his indifference but his generosity—" (p. 134).

Yet Ryder recognizes that the old order, with all its many

virtues, can no longer avoid the facts of social change; he affirms that charm is no longer enough, that the time has come to make a new start. He attacks Laddy for enduring a friend's parasitism:

You support him in his miserable . . . self-indulgence to divert you from the horrors on the surface of which you live. The spirit of man causes him to brave fires and snows for the divine impulse to truth that burns in him, . . . but to Binkie [the friend] . . . this is an eccentricity! To him and to the society which he represents this immolation is an eccentricity, a lapse in style. [p. 50]

Obviously style in itself no longer suffices. If the virtues of the world of grace and charm are to be retained, they must be grounded in the new virtue of social justice.

Thus *Wine of Choice* represents Behrman's most overt espousal of what he terms "the skepticism of Democracy." Although Ryder recognizes that change is necessary, he cannot accept Chris's revolutionary alternative. Therein lie the pitfalls of fanaticism and greater evils than the ills of the old order. For in the name of the ideals of justice the dogmatist is willing—almost obliged—to commit the gravest acts of injustice. Ryder tells Chris:

You are locked deep in the cold fastnesses of theory—on that surface nothing can take hold . . . neither love nor friendship nor affection. I see now how people like you can condemn to death their best friends—because equally well you can condemn yourselves to lovelessness, to abnegation, to death. [p. 205]

To Chris's assertion that Ryder's liberalism is sentimental, the latter replies that it is he himself who is sentimental. "Your sentimentality is the most perverted of all because it ignores the most powerful impulse in people—to be free—to choose . . ." (p. 207). True, mankind can be convinced of the stupidest of follies; it can behave cruelly, absurdly, viciously, but the answer does not reside in acting inhu-

manely ourselves. There is always an alternative: "We suffer and succumb to our suffering. We are capricious, we are
adolescent and fallible. But we emerge from our weakness
and retain our dream" (p. 208).

At the other end of the political spectrum from communism lay, for Behrman, an even more vicious threat to man's
humanity, fascism. As the war clouds loomed ever nearer,
Behrman became increasingly concerned with the nature of
the authoritarian personality until, in the plays written during the war years, it became his major dramatic concern.
Behrman demonstrated an early interest in the power-rid-
den fanatic; in his early play, *Meteor* (1929), he explored
the personality of a man who rises inexorably and ruthlessly
to the top of the financial heap in boom-age America.
Raphael Lord, guided by a conviction of infallibility, justi-
fies economic ruthlessness on the grounds of necessity:
"There's a lot to be said for blood and iron. If Russian Communism is a success, it'll be because the leaders are first-
rate executioners—the first Utopians who knew how to
handle machine guns."[8] But Lord is not a radical; he has, in
fact, but one obsession, the possession and enjoyment of
power. It is this obsession which distinguishes Behrman's
protofascist from his radical characters. The latter possess
specific ideals which in themselves are not reprehensible.
In fact, several of his radical characters are treated quite
sympathetically; for example, Will in *End of Summer* and
Avis in *The Talley Method*. Behrman does not reject the
radical's humanitarian ideals, but fearing that the use of
inhumane means may well pervert these ends, he proposes
instead the liberal's gradual route to social reform.
Behrman's protofascist figures, on the other hand, are intoxi-
cated with the possession of power for its own sake. They
are rarely presented, as are the communists, as ideologists.
When they are—such as Hobart in *Rain from Heaven*—the
portrait is apt to be drawn in the simple outlines of carica-

ture. Behrman is less concerned with the specifics of fascist doctrine than with the psychology of fascist mentality, with the anatomy of the will to manipulate, to possess, and to destroy. Lord, drawn before the advent of Naziism, is the prototype of this figure, which reappears in Behrman's later plays as Dr. Rice in *End of Summer*, Clay Rainier in *Dunnigan's Daughter*, and, in less extreme form, Axton Talley in *The Talley Method.*

Behrman's most successful portrayal of the fascist mentality is Kenneth Rice, the charlatan psychiatrist in *End of Summer* (1936). Rice uses the jargon of psychoanalysis and his own not inconsiderable charm to present a facade of calm detachment, behind which lies a core of ruthless opportunism. He cynically woos Leonie in order to obtain her fortune, the money necessary to realize his dream of power. Rice has no use for liberal or radical ideals; he is firm in his conviction that in a predatory world, only the fittest survive:

When I hear the chatter of your friends, it makes me sick. While they and their kind prate of cooperative commonwealths, the strong man takes power, and rides over their backs—which is all their backs are fit for. Never has the opportunity for the individual career been so exalted, so infinite in its scope, so horizontal. House painters and minor journalists become dictators of great nations. Imagine what a really clever man could do! See what he has done! [p. 358]

As Behrman states in a stage direction, "This man is the enemy" (p. 359). Paula, Leonie's daughter, to whom Rice makes this self-revelation, comes to a similar recognition and is determined to stop him from marrying her mother. To achieve this Paula traps Rice, who has confessed a passion for her, into revealing this passion to Leonie. The revelation dooms his scheme, and Rice exits fuming. Thus we may observe how Behrman utilizes the stock devices of high comedy (in this case, the unmasking of the philanderer) in order to comment seriously upon a social phenomenon. The dramatic difficulty, however, lies in the fact that the conventional machinery does not seem to sustain the weight of Behrman's purpose. The rejection scene, in the context of the seriousness which preceded it, smacks of artifice, and we cannot fully assent to the summary disposal of the hitherto all-powerful psychiatrist.

Yet whether completely successful or not, we cannot deny the seriousness which lies at the heart of *End of Summer*. Behrman attempts to anatomize the fascist danger. In an age of unrest, the ruthless cynic may offer the illusion of security; but these panaceas can only be achieved at the expense of human freedom. Will, the young radical in love with Paula, in attacking Rice, points the moral:

Some men are born ahead of their time, some behind, but you are made pat for the instant. Now is the time for you—when people are unemployed and distrust their own capacities—when people suffer and may be tempted—when integrity yields to despair—now is the moment for you! [p. 348]

Curiously, in the light of the portrait of Chris in *Wine of Choice*, if there is an antidote to Rice's cynicism it lies in the fervor of the young radical, Will. In fact, the money which was initially to finance Rice's sanatorium eventually goes to subsidize a radical paper which Will and a friend are contemplating. But then, Will is not presented as a doctrinaire communist; in fact his position is not far removed from Ryder's liberalism. It is the dogmatism into which radicalism often degenerates which Behrman rejects, not the radical premises themselves.

The relationship between Will and Paula is another in the series of romantic misalliances which characterize Behrman's work. Again, as in the case of Marion and Kurt in *Biography*, we are presented with a relationship between an upper-class woman and a man of lower social position. But whereas Marion and Kurt were of conflicting temperaments, Paula shares Will's social faith. "Don't you realize," she tells him, "that since I've acquired your point of view about things, my life has had an excitement and a sense of reality it's never had before" (p. 286). The difficulty between them (and again we must ask if this difficulty is not deliberately intensified in order to satisfy the exigencies of plot) lies in Will's refusal to accept her money, and the dependence which he feels such an acceptance would entail.

Supposing you weren't rich? Is it a world in which, but for this, I'd have to sink? If it is, I'm going to damn well do what I can to change it. I don't have to scramble for the inheritance of dead men. . . . I don't want this damn fortune to give me an unfair advantage over people as good as I am who haven't got it. [p. 363]

It is apparent that Behrman presents Will's fervor as the foil to Rice's cynicism. The world which Leonie represents is dying; she herself, in her acceptance of Rice, demonstrates her desperate need to find meaning in her life. Above all, she wishes "I could dedicate myself to something—something outside myself" (p. 369). In the end money is more of a curse than a solace; it "gives the illusion of escape —but always you have to come back to yourself" (p. 364). In contrast to Behrman's other female characters—who usually embody his most cherished virtues—Leonie is the victim. Behrman seems to be sounding the death knell of the class she represents, and speculating as to whether Rice or Will reflects the image of the future. Although he fervently prefers the triumph of the latter, Behrman fears that we are living in the Age of the Charlatan. The gratuitous defeat of Rice almost seems to represent an act of deliberate exorcism.

Behrman drew his last portrait of the fascist mentality in *Dunnigan's Daughter* (1945). In the person of Clay

Rainier, the playwright finally succeeded in exorcising the figure. Rainier, like Lord and Rice, worships power for its own sake, and has, as the others, again abdicated his humanity. Again he sees himself above the common herd; if human beings, inevitably weak and fallible, were not led by the strong man, the result would be anarchy. "The mass is an animal that can be led in only two ways—a feed bag in front, a stick from behind. Power can't be distributed."[9] And the enjoyment of power is the "most continuously satisfying" emotion (p. 131). In short, Rainier operates on the theory of human maliciousness. The reforming instinct is doomed to failure because man is innately evil. But Clay's impulse to possess human beings and objects is not merely socially destructive; it is personally destructive as well. In the end, he is deserted one by one by the individuals whom, in his perverse way, he loves: Enid, his fiancée, and Zelda, his daughter. The last view we have is of a deserted, broken man. But the principle which Clay embodies is perpetually dangerous, even if temporarily thwarted. Although fascism may be defeated, Behrman implies, mankind must be ever vigilant against its recurrence, for "we live in a time when one warped individual with a grievance, provided he has the knowledge and provided he has the power, can destroy the world" (p. 123). To counteract this danger it is necessary to affirm the liberal, humanitarian dream, for knowledge without responsibility will again "blow the roof off the world" (p. 183). The difficulty lies in the recognition that while "evil is mobilized, goodness is not." Goodness is confused, irresolute, and forever susceptible to defeat by fanatic evil. Man must, then, recognize his fallibility—"the serpent in the garden of Eden"—and build upon the foundation of this recognition. But in this very recognition there is, as Miguel asserts, a form of grandeur. Clay maintains—as do the frustrate who inspire evil to feed their own inadequacies—that without power man is nothing. Miguel counters with the following affirmation of faith in man:

Look at this poor creature—man. He knows he is insignificant, yet can conceive to be noble. He knows that he is mortal, yet can dream into the infinite. He knows that he is evil, yet can hope to be good. He is loveless and alone—yet feels the need of love and the need of his kind. Is this what it is to be nobody? [p. 179]

Behrman's detestation of fascism arises time and again to destroy the pose of his detachment. He is quite capable of retaining this pose in his consideration of the radical temperament; he sympathizes with the radical gesture but offers the corrective of wit against its dogmatic excesses. But against the threat of fascism he is unable to remain uncommitted; he feels compelled not merely to anatomize the fascist mentality but to take sides actively against it. In *Rain from Heaven* (1934), for example, he was aroused by an incident in the persecution of the Jews to write a play which might depict the human consequences of this persecution. The incident in question concerned a meeting between the Jewish critic, Alfred Kerr, and the celebrated German playwright, Gerhardt Hauptmann. Kerr had been partially responsible for Hauptmann's early reputation, and in time of danger went to his old friend for help and advice. The Grand Old Man, however, had accepted Naziism and turned his back on his former friend, as he did on all his previous associates who did not measure up to the new standards. Behrman saw in this confrontation the essential horror of fascist perversion, and, in his own words, was "condemned to write" *Rain from Heaven.* For there in Hauptmann's study lay the betrayal of nobility.

In the great man's quiet study, one might hope for the emergence of a spirit and an understanding transcending the clamors and ferocities of the marching, lustful mobs. Here . . . might

arise an emanation so distilled and powerful that miraculously
it might delethalize those other and headier exhalations from
. . . the heated breaths of the demagogues. Because if not from
this room, from where else? That it did not come—this for me—
was the essential tragedy.[10]

Note the word "tragedy." The comic spirit, if not the comic
machinery, is overwhelmed in *Rain from Heaven* by the intensity of Behrman's involvement with the tragedy of surrender to fascist brutality. And yet the form of the play remains that of sophisticated comedy. The plot again centers
upon amatory intrigue: Phoebe, who is married to Hobart,
is in love with Hugo, who is in love with Lael, who is, in
turn, loved by Rand, etc. The crucial incident of the rejection of the Jew, represented in the play by Hugo, is never
presented on stage; it is narrated in passing. Again Behrman, at home only in the leisured world of high comedy,
seems unwilling to essay new dramatic forms. Thus *Rain
from Heaven* alternates between scenes of conventional
sophistication and scenes of serious import. The very seriousness of the latter causes the former to lose much of
their comic effectiveness.

Behrman affirms that commitment cannot be avoided.
Hauptmann, for him, symbolizes those who in the guise of
practicality make their peace with evil by attempting to
ignore it. Hugo Willens, in the play, had gotten himself
into difficulties by consciously attacking the Nazis' anti-
Semitic policy in a pamphlet entitled "The Last Jew," in
which he related a parable of the extermination of the Jews
(in 1934 direfully prophetic). When all the Jews but one
are killed, the fascists realize that this survivor is the most
valuable man in the country, since the government's entire
policy is based upon the use of the Jew as a scapegoat. "Let
this man die and their policy is bankrupt. They are left
naked, without an issue, without a programme. . . . The Jews
gone and still no millennium" (pp. 204-5). Hugo himself

is not Jewish, although he acknowledges a Jewish great-grandmother, but the Nazi "chromosome hunt" and his pamphlet had forced him into the world of the exiled.

But Hugo does not acquiesce in this exile. At the end of the play he decides to return to Germany to fight the evil on its own home ground. Lael tries to persuade him to remain: "You're an artist, Hugo. What have you to do with feuds and hatreds and rebellions? Can't you try to see it as I see it? . . . I believe in muddling through. I believe . . . that in the main people are reasonable and corrigible and sweet . . ." (pp. 271-72). But Hugo will not accept Lael's gradualism; the artist cannot exempt himself from man's suffering and inhumanity. He must face the cruel facts, and act:

No, I'm determined at last to view the world—including myself —completely without illusion. It's a matter of life and death. I see now that goodness is not enough, that liberalism is not enough. I'm sick of evasions. They've done us in. . . . [p. 272]

Behrman's pose of detachment is shattered, and *Rain from Heaven* represents his most intense anti-fascist statement. It is not sufficient to recognize the evil of fascism; it must be actively combatted. For Behrman—as for others, Jew and non-Jew alike—the madness of racism presaged the wholesale destruction of humanity, the Jew being merely the first victim. Unless racism was opposed wherever it appeared, the fascist danger would necessarily increase. In the name of economic order Hobart champions a native fascist movement. Therein lies the real danger: that we ignore the enemy within. "You think its because you killed Christ that we fear and hate you," Hobart tells Hugo. "No! It's because you gave birth to Lenin!" Thus the fascist justified anti-Semitism on the grounds of anticommunism.

By the time that Behrman wrote *The Talley Method* in 1941 it indeed appeared that man's darkest apprehensions were being fulfilled. With the outbreak of the European war the Age of Terror had most certainly arrived, and *The Talley Method*—although it too goes through the motions of sophisticated comedy—is too bitter, too involved with the spectacle of human destruction to be legitimately termed comedy at all. "These days, I'm afraid, charm isn't enough," says one of the characters (p. 53), and it is apparent that Behrman's comic vision has turned most grim. The veneer of flippancy has all but disappeared: "We live in a time when the truest voices are struck dumb by the loudest" (p. 43). If there is one persistent note struck in the play it is the insensitivity of humanity to man's suffering.

In *Rain from Heaven* Hugo returned to Germany to fight, but such a gesture is no longer possible. Manfred, the refugee writer in *The Talley Method,* finds himself rejected by all sides and takes the one road left to him, suicide. He is the victim of a world dominated by cruelty. "Why is there so little kindness?" Philip, the younger generation, asks Enid, the older. She answers, "Perhaps because cruelty is at the heart of things. . . ."[11] But man cannot accept the immutability of cruelty. He must continually strive to transcend it. "I know there are no facile consolations," Enid tells Talley, "but it is true, I think, that often the victims survive their murderers. I must cling to that belief—or I'll sink" (p. 167). Talley, humane only in his professional capacity as physician, represents the individual who has immunized himself to human suffering. That is, in fact, the Talley method: detachment from anything not specifically germane to one's personally limited goals. Talley can feel no sympathy for Manfred's plight. "If those people couldn't control a system they despise, they must take the consequences. . . . As they took no interest until it was too late about . . . who should govern them and how—why should we now pull their chestnuts out of the fire for them?" (pp. 150-51).

In the end, of course, the Talley method is ineffective; it cuts Talley off not only from humanity in general but from those he loves as well, Enid and his children. But while Talley's situation seems to parallel Clay Rainier's exactly, it is apparent that there is a vital difference. Talley is not, like Rice or Rainier, obsessed with power; he is not motivated by the desire to manipulate. His sin is indifference, the refusal to involve himself with the problems of human beings other than in a professional capacity. In the end, however, indifference as well as opportunism achieve the same result. In a world of global conflict no man is an island; evasion is no longer possible. Manfred surrenders, but Enid affirms, "We will not! We . . . are still free" (pp. 166-67).

Thus Behrman's esthetic dilemma is again asserted: although, on one hand, he desires to retain the form and detachment of high comedy, on the other, he feels compelled to deal with serious themes. It takes all his dramatic skill to permit him to walk the tightrope between these conflicting aims. That he himself was aware of his dilemma is apparent from his play *No Time for Comedy* (1939), in which he attempts, not uncharacteristically, to exploit it for comic purposes. He is successful in that the play is consistent; the serious core does not, as in *Rain from Heaven*, run away with the play. In forcing his very real dilemma to serve the purposes of sophisticated comedy (in much the same manner that the issue of integrity is exploited in *The Second Man*), Behrman answers Gaylord Esterbrook's dilemma (Is there indeed time for comedy in a humorless world?) with a resounding "yes." But, significantly, he does not do so within the context of the play. Gaylord's decision to continue to write comedy does not result from any intellectual realization; it seems based upon his romantic preference for Linda rather than Mandy. The perennial triangle is the dramatic core of the play. Behrman's answer lies, cleverly, not in any overt demonstration of the need for comedy, but rather in the fact of the comedy itself.

But, as we have seen, Behrman does not persevere in this detachment. If in *No Time for Comedy* he is able to exploit

Gaylord's dilemma for the purposes of comedy, at other times he seems to acquiesce in his self-deprecation:

While I'm imagining these charming variations . . . people are dying—the innocents are being slaughtered. . . . No . . . I *must* get something *clear* and *outside* myself to be enlisted for. I'm sick of the triviality, sick of ringing changes on what I've already written, sick of the futility theme. . . . [p. 105]

The problem of detachment from or involvement in the social and political issues of one's time—in short, the problem of political commitment—thus plays a crucial role in the drama of S. N. Behrman. From one point of view this involvement adulterated the form of Behrman's art; sophisticated comedy could not completely withstand the seriousness of the issues involved. Yet from another point of view Behrman's concern with the social issues of his age raised his drama beyond the level of triviality and made him, in fact, a more serious dramatist than he perhaps intended to be. Surely Behrman's subsequent dramatic record does not confirm the assertion that social considerations vitiated his art. Since the war Behrman has been almost exclusively concerned with adaptations: *The Pirate* (1942), based upon Ludwig Fulda's *Die Seeräuber; Jacobowsky and the Colonel* (1944), a collaboration with Franz Werfel; *I Know My Love* (1949), a vehicle for the Lunts based upon Marcel Archard's *Auprès de ma blonde; Jane* (1952), based upon a story by Maugham; *Fanny* (1955), based upon the plays of Marcel Pagnol; *The Cold Wind and the Warm* (1959), a nostalgic reminiscence of his boyhood based upon his own *The Worcester Account;* and *Lord Pengo* (1962), a free adaptation drawn from Behrman's biography of the art dealer, Lord Duveen. In all of these the Broadway craftsman is dominant; the frequent choice of other people's material suggests that Behrman has abdicated from serious playwriting. Some men are born serious and others achieve seriousness; perhaps Behrman had seriousness thrust upon him.

9

ELMER RICE AND THE SERIOUS-NESS OF DRAMA

The pressure of commercial theatre may become a tyranny. In that event the artist can know but one relationship to it: the relationship of antagonism. In such an era the playwright is either a rebel and an artist or a yes man and a hack.

ERIC BENTLEY, *The Playwright As Thinker*

CHAPTER NINE

IF S. N. BEHRMAN questioned the appropriateness of comedy in an age of crisis, Elmer Rice questioned the very credentials of drama itself. Unlike Behrman, Rice was not committed to a specific dramatic genre; he was not faced with the problem of accommodating harsh social realities within the context of a frivolous form. On the contrary, he had demonstrated his ability to utilize such divergent forms as expressionism, naturalism, melodrama, and farce. The dilemma which confronted Rice in the mid-thirties was more fundamental: could American drama, as represented on Broadway, rightfully claim the virtue of seriousness, or did formal and economic exigencies render it, in fact, subliterary? The issue is not without contemporary significance; our most influential literary critics, by virtue of their total unconcern with American drama, have affirmed the latter half of the question; and even our more astute dramatic critics, such as Eric Bentley and Francis Fergusson, have concentrated their interest upon European drama. It is not our purpose to pursue this debate, but it is surely significant that American dramatists themselves have time and again raised the issue of the seriousness of the genre in which they are engaged. (One recent playwright to do so has been William Gibson, who, in *The Seesaw Log*, ironically relates the compromises necessary to achieve Broadway production.)

That Elmer Rice should, in the thirties, raise his voice in protest against the conditions that Broadway imposed upon the dramatist is particularly revealing; for Rice, throughout both his previous and subsequent theatrical career, presents us with a body of work which is perhaps unique in American drama in its inconsistency, its alternation of seriousness and conventionality. On one hand, we have such serious plays as *The Adding Machine, The Subway, Street Scene, We the People,* and *Not for Children*; on the other, such conventional Broadway products as *On Trial, Cock Robin, Wake Up Jonathan,* and *The Grand Tour*. That Rice himself was never quite sure of his role is revealed by his different public statements. In 1934 he wrote, "I was disenchanted with the commercial theatre long before I was ever in it. . . . I have always been, and still am, interested in the drama as an art form, a social force and a medium for the expression of ideas."[1] However, in 1938 we find this statement: "Fortunately for myself, I have never had a very high opinion of myself as a dramatist, nor have I ever thought of myself . . . as a candidate for the suffrage of posterity. . . . This youthful recognition of my own limitations . . . made it possible for me to devote myself to the utilization of what . . . is a pretty definite talent for constructing plays."[2]

Significantly—and not surprisingly—Rice's period of most intense concern with the problem of the seriousness of drama coincides with the early thirties when the Depression was at its worst and social solutions seemed imperative. Rice, like many liberals, allied himself with the radicals as a gesture of protest against the social chaos which prevailed, and his condemnation of Broadway—melodramatically proclaimed in the New York *Times* under the heading "Elmer Rice Says Farewell to Broadway"—was quoted favorably by Joshua Kunitz in the *New Masses*. For Rice, the drama could not treat life seriously because the powers that control the theatre would not allow it to do so:

The theatre is in the hands of business men, of real estate operators and entrepreneurs, whose chief interest is to capitalize the creative talents of the authors and actors and turn them into dollars and cents. . . . And so the drama, once the high priestess of religion, becomes the bond maiden of commerce. Between the creative artist and his potential auditors stands the sordid and ugly barrier of the commercial theatre. Here, as everywhere in our civilization, the profit system stifles the creative impulse and dams the free flow of human vitality.[3]

But Rice never completely assented to Marxian analysis. His "Farewell to Broadway," despite its Marxist tinge, never uses the familiar communist vocabulary; the words "bourgeois," "proletariat," "masses" are conspicuous by their absence. In fact, Rice's analysis of the deficiencies of the dramatic genre—as revealed in the introduction to and the play *Not for Children*—considers economic pressure as but one of the factors which prevent the drama from fulfilling its serious potential. Indeed, although Rice condemns both the "idle and frivolous amusement seekers" and "the artist who . . . panders to the tastes of the ruling class," he does not offer the familiar revolutionary corrective. The lot of the dramatist is not necessarily happier in those countries where the philosophy of individualism is not in favor and where the machinery of the theatre is under governmental control or regulation. "Here, commercial enterprise gives way to political expediency. The theatre becomes an arm of the state and we find that the criterion is no longer box-office value but political orthodoxy."[4]

The difficulties which assail the serious dramatist are not merely economic, but inherent in the dramatic form itself. The dramatist cannot present his vision of reality directly to the audience, as can the painter or writer; he must work through the cooperative efforts of a series of transmitting artists: the actor, the director, the scenic designer. The physical limitations of his playhouse impose specific restrictions on the scope of his imagination. He is bound by temporality, by the necessity of creating a theatrical illusion instantaneously; he is never permitted to ignore the collective psychology of his audience, and, as Rice points out, "the collective behavior of a crowd varies greatly from the customary private behavior of the individuals who compose it." Thus the playwright is denied the artistic prerogative of expressing himself seriously upon political, racial, economic, religious, or sexual problems, for "doubts and heresies which are freely held and expressed by hundreds of thousands of individuals are greeted by an audience with the frightened hostility of a panic-stricken herd."[5]

These several factors, which combine to rob the drama of its requisite creative freedom, present the playwright with his "real dilemma": "Like every other artist, he is interested in projecting reality as he sees it. But he finds himself dependent upon an interpretative medium which is essentially artificial, conservative and conventional."[6]

Rice attempted to give this dilemma dramatic form in *Not for Children* (1934), the very title of which revealed his conviction that most American drama was infantile. The play attempts to combine Shavian intellectual comedy and Pirandellian illusionism, unfortunately not very successfully; for in using the device of having two characters both comment upon and participate in the stage action, Rice has not succeeded in balancing these dual functions; the commentary, rather than the participation, becomes the play's *raison d'être,* and one emerges with the feeling that perhaps Rice might have dispensed with the "play proper" entirely. Unfortunately Rice does not demonstrate either Shaw's ability to make ideas work theatrically, or Pirandello's skill in balancing illusion and reality. What concerns us, however, is not so much the esthetic success of *Not for Children* as its assertion of Rice's belligerently antitheatrical attitude. It may be noted that even at the moment of his most intense disillusionment with drama,

Rice feels compelled to express this disillusionment dramatically.

In *Not for Children* Rice personifies his esthetic dilemma in the personages of Ambrose and Theodora, who function as a dual chorus in commenting upon the play proper, which is a Behrmanesque comedy of manners. Theodora presents the protheatre point of view, while Ambrose upholds the negative. In answer to Ambrose's contention that the theatre can no longer be taken seriously, she rejoins:

You complain that the theater is unrelated to reality. It is precisely that which gives the playhouse its charm. Reality is harsh, forbidding, painful, confused. But in the theatre all is neat, orderly, pre-arranged and . . . readily apprehended by a bright child of eleven. How delightful that is. . . . How restful, how satisfying, how reassuring. [p. 9]

But it is soon apparent, from the sheer weight of dialogue if nothing else, that Rice is in sympathy with Ambrose's point of view. It was not a time for delight, rest, or reassurance. The theatre stands condemned, in Ambrose's words, "because it is so essentially false. Because it is so unrelated to reality. Because its emotions are so hollow, its characters so two-dimensional, its speech so hackneyed, its intellectual pretensions so ludicrous, its puppets so mechanical, its philosophy so trite" (p. 9). Or as Rice himself stated in his "farewell": "The theatre game as it is played on Broadway is so pitiably adolescent. . . . It is a trivial pastime, devised by 'grown-up children' for the delectation of the mentally and emotionally immature."[7] Thus Rice's moral is unequivocally stated in a play specifically aimed "not for children": "The more nearly a play is good theatre, the less likely is it to be a reflection of reality. In short, the theatre and life are antithetical" (p. 124).

Obviously Rice, in this last statement at least, surrendered to overstatement born of his reaction against the triviality of the commercial theatre. As a firm admirer of Shaw, Ibsen, Hauptmann, he could scarcely uphold the proposition that the theatre and life are necessarily antithetical. The significance of the polemic from our point of view lies in Rice's vehement assertion of the serious playwright's dilemma: if he wishes to comment seriously upon the world of which he is a part—and for Rice, as others in the thirties, this inevitably implied social comment—can he do so in the context of a frivolous theatre? Lawson threw his energies into criticism and political work; Behrman effected a tenuous balance between frivolity and seriousness. Rice was too much a man of the theatre to forsake it, and he, too, effected his theatrical compromise.

But theatrical compromise was nothing new to Elmer Rice. His work, as we have indicated previously, is supremely inconsistent. It is curious that his fervent condemnation of the commercial theatre should come from one whose talent has always been best expressed within its confines. It is at the *craft* of the theatre that Rice has always excelled; although he has been equally at home in many dramatic forms, this formal experimentation seems less the result of a desire to expand the bounds of conventional drama (as in the work of O'Neill) than the delight of the craftsman in demonstrating his technical facility.

Rice's eclecticism may be observed in his use of expressionism (*The Adding Machine, The Subway*), naturalism (*Street Scene*), sophisticated comedy (*The Left Bank*), psychological drama (*Cue for Passion*), allegorical fantasy (*American Landscape*), and the list may be extended. Perhaps the most persistent (and the most commercially successful) of Rice's forms has been the courtroom melodrama; he has continually exploited his legal background for theatrical purposes. *On Trial, It is the Law, For the De-*

fense, Judgment Day, all derive their form from the court-room trial; and *Counsellor-At-Law* owes much of its success to its behind-the-scenes revelation of the life of a big-time lawyer. Except for the courtroom melodrama, Rice has scarcely employed the same dramatic form twice. Such versatility is not only admirable; it is almost unique. Most dramatists have been content to develop facility in but a few forms, usually moving logically from one to another. Ibsen, Strindberg, and O'Neill pass from realism to symbolism when they have, from their point of view, exhausted the possibilities of the former. But Rice fails to afford the dramatic critic any such orderly development. It is difficult to find in the sum total of his work the consistent dramatic vision which informs the work of the major dramatists. As with many other minor writers, his significance appears to be seismographic; *The Adding Machine, We the People, Flight to the West,* and *Cue for Passion,* seem less the work of a consistent artistic personality than the faithful reflection of the intellectual climate of the twenties, the thirties, the forties, and the fifties.

But it is not merely the change of viewpoint which makes a critical evaluation of Rice's work difficult. The very issue which he raises in the thirties concerning the seriousness of drama must be considered in our critical judgment, for Rice himself has continually vacillated between seriousness and conventionality, many of his plays springing, in his own words, from "no nobler impulse than a realistic desire to make a comfortable living."[8] Although this mundane consideration need not, of course, invalidate a work of art, an examination of the bulk of Rice's work soon reveals that much of it is unworthy of serious consideration. Yet the serious core remains as a worthy contribution to American drama. Indeed, in *The Adding Machine* Rice succeeded not only in absorbing the form of expressionism, but in creating a character, Mr. Zero, who came to epitomize the contemporary antihero. And in *Street Scene* he drew a slice of New York life with such fidelity and compassion that it is still convincing.

If Rice's salient virtue is indeed seismographic, there can be no denying that his serious plays of the twenties reflect the contemporary concern with the dehumanization of man by society. In *The Adding Machine* (1923), *The Subway* (1929), and *Street Scene* (1929), we find variations upon that not uncommon theme of the age, reflected elsewhere in such plays as Lawson's *Roger Bloomer*, Sophie Treadwell's *Machinale*, Kaiser's *From Morn to Midnight*, and Toller's *Masse-Mensch*. In each of the plays man is crushed not so much by an oppressive social system as by the sheer weight of modern industrial civilization. From a social point of view, it is significant that Rice poses no political alternatives. We do not find the sense of class division which informs the early work of John Howard Lawson. Zero, Sophie, Mrs. Maurrant are destroyed by a dehumanized society. Zero is dwarfed by the gigantic adding machine he finally is condemned to operate; Sophie by the mechanical monster which hurls itself through manmade subterranean caverns; Mrs. Maurrant by the huge tenement which denies her the elemental freedom of privacy.

In *The Adding Machine* Zero is condemned not merely in life, but in death as well. He can never be free because he is a product and, consequently, has meaning only insofar as he is useful. Nurtured on hatred of "dagoes, catholics, sheenies and niggers," brutalized by the mechanical function he must perform, tortured by inaccessible dreams of sex, he represents man as victim. He cannot accept the possibility of freedom offered in the Elysian fields; he is troubled by the very air of serenity which prevails, and nature appears beautiful only in relation to the standards of a mechanized world. "Look at the flowers!" shouts Daisy,

Zero's potential paramour. "Ain't they just perfect? Why you'd think they was artificial, wouldn't you?"[9] Brutalized in life, Zero remains in death prey to the perverse puritanism represented by Shrdlu, who cannot understand why the Elysian fields are peopled, not by the defenders of religious morality, but rather by men who "spend all their time . . . telling stories and laughing and singing and drinking and dancing . . ." (p. 101).

Zero cannot accept life's joys because he has never experienced them; he remains a perpetual suppliant to the God of the Machine, eager to serve again by operating with the big toe of his right foot a lever which will set in motion the "superb, super-hyper-adding machine" which represents the nightmare of the technological future. It is only when faced with the truth about himself that Zero rebels. Although he wants only to serve, he is told that even in this service he is a failure:

You're a . . . waste product. A slave to a contraption of steel and iron. The animal's instincts, but not his strength and skill. The animal's appetites, but not his unashamed indulgence of them, . . . the raw material of slums and wars—the ready prey of the first jingo or demagogue or political adventurer who takes the trouble to play upon your ignorance and credulity and provincialism. [p. 107]

Zero, when faced with the bitter truth, begs to remain in the world of the dead, but is persuaded to return to the endless cycle of futility by the illusion of Hope in the form of sex. Thus man palliates his servitude and remains the eternal victim.

Similarly, in *The Subway*, Rice uses a modified form of expressionism to present another victim of modern mechanization. Sophie Smith, like Mr. Zero, also responds to the forces which are crushing her with an act of violence. But it is an act performed upon herself; she offers herself as a sacrifice to the God of the Machine by throwing herself in the path of a subway train. What better symbol of the animistic power of the machine? "A monster of steel with flaming eyes and gaping jaws, . . . the beast of the New Apocalypse. . . ."[10] The image which dominates the play is that of "all mankind joining the mad mechanistic dance . . . bondsmen to the monsters they have created . . . slaves to steel and concrete" (pp. 94-95).

Rice's vision, like that of the New Playwrights, is apocalyptic. In *The Adding Machine* Charles ironically relates the tortured history of evolution which for millions of years labored through plants, reptiles, amphibians, and mammals to achieve that paragon of animals, Mr. Zero. In *The Subway* the artist relates a parable of destruction in which scientists of a future age uncover the relics of our present civilization:

They dig down to the subway . . . down to the bones of these civilized millions. . . . Nothing but bones and a glass eye and some false teeth and a handful of blackened coins and a steel key that unlocked a steel box in a steel vault . . . and a pair of jade earrings from the five-and-ten cent store, . . . all that remains of Western Civilization. . . . [p. 97]

The subway, far beneath the surface, reflects man's remoteness from nature. Significantly it is not nature itself that is cruel; Zero denies the Elysian fields, and Sophie yearns for a house in the country "with flowers . . . violets and roses and daisies . . ." (p. 51). The horror of modern life resides precisely in its denial of the forces of nature, of love and beauty, of sunlight and fresh air and room to breathe and the ability to live one's own life. In *Street Scene*, a play in the quite different form of naturalism, Rice emphasizes, though not so overtly, the same theme. Sammy, despairing of his life in the New York slums, cries to Rose, "Everywhere you look, oppression and cruelty! It doesn't come from nature, it comes from humanity—humanity trampling on itself and tearing at its own throat."[11]

The forces which built the adding machine and the subway also built the slums, in which life is similarly dehumanized. Although Mrs. Maurrant's appeal for simple human understanding is denied, Rose and Sammy represent those who will not be content to become victims. They will rise above the sordidness which surrounds them. Rose, unlike Sophie Smith, leaves the slum in an attempt to find "a chance to breathe and spread out a little" (p. 187), and *Street Scene* does not end on the note of hopelessness which characterizes Rice's expressionistic plays.

Rice's serious plays of the twenties, then, accurately reflect the prevailing fear that machine civilization was succeeding in dehumanizing mankind. It is not surprising that most who presented this indictment should, with the onset of the Depression, turn towards political radicalism, for their initial attack was essentially a gesture of protest. The villain became not the machine, but the owner of the machine, and mankind's victimization was seen, not as an immutable fact of the law of social evolution, but rather as the deliberate act of an exploiting class.

Although Rice never fully accepted Marxist theory, his need for social protest caused him to affiliate with many left-wing causes.[12] But throughout his fellow traveling Rice always retained his liberal attitude. His public stands have invariably concerned the issue of censorship. From 1930 until the present day he has continually spoken out when forces of repression seem to threaten the civil liberties of the theatre or society. In 1931 he denounced J. S. Sumner, Cardinal Hayes, and Dr. Manning for their views on stage decency; in 1936 he resigned as regional director of the Federal Theatre because of the government censorship of the Living Newspaper production of *Ethiopia*; in 1945 he resigned as director of the New York City Center because of the banning of *Trio*; in 1953 he protested the ban on *The Moon is Blue*; in 1955 he urged amnesty for sixteen communists imprisoned under the Smith Act; in 1956 he attacked the "subtle censorship" by pressure groups which represented, in his view, a serious menace to "complete freedom of expression."[13]

In short, from the thirties onwards, Rice has been *un homme engagé*; he has been perennially involved with social and theatrical questions, and has consistently registered his protest against encroachments upon civil liberties. He has, moreover, been involved in various attempts to provide an alternative to Broadway. In 1933 he proposed the establishment of a People's Art Theatre which would "attempt not only to set the leaven of art at work in the masses but to drag the artist into the forum, face to face with his times." Rice's proposed theatre would have a social base; every play to be presented would be judged not only according to its dramatic and literary merits but also according to its social value. "No play would be presented which, in a general sense, does not possess social significance." But Rice was quick to indicate that he was not proposing a doctrinaire theatre:

The People's Art Theatre would not be committed to any specific policy or economic program, nor would it be animated by any doctrinaire philosophy. It would be an organ of propaganda only insofar as its general policy would favor the establishment of a new social order in which existing economic and social injustice is eliminated.[14]

It is not surprising, then, that with the formation of the Federal Theatre Project in 1935 Elmer Rice should have been selected as regional director for the New York area. In reporting upon the project, Rice optimistically predicted the demise of the commercial theatre: "The rugged individualism so beloved by Mr. Hoover is now a museum piece. It is no longer a part of the social scene. The old system in the theatre is finished."[15]

In what manner were these social concerns reflected in

Rice's dramas of the thirties? His concern with the seriousness of drama is consistent with the articulate protest born
of his renewed social conscience. But Rice could not fully
ally himself with the revolutionary theatrical movement;
he could not, for example, turn toward the composition of
proletarian plays. Although infused with social indignation,
he could not acquiesce in the communist solution. He has
continually voiced his suspicions of the adverse effects of
doctrine upon art. And yet he is compelled to involve himself with social issues. Each of his plays of the thirties (except *Not for Children* which, as we have seen, is concerned
with the fundamental problem of the legitimacy of the
dramatic form) has at its core a social problem. *We the
People* is Rice's most slashing attack upon the social chaos
bred by the Depression; *Judgment Day* condemns the
Reichstag fire trial and Nazi injustice; *Between Two
Worlds* presents the conflict of the old social order and the
new; and *American Landscape* affirms American liberalism's answer to fascism and social injustice.

"You couldn't live in the Depression and fail to be
touched by it,"[16] Rice told an interviewer in 1958, and
surely *We the People* (1933) represents an almost documentary attempt to portray the image of America during
the early thirties. But Rice is not content to record; he must
protest, and *We the People* is his most overtly didactic
drama.

We the People was not written for Broadway [he wrote defiantly in the *Times*]. . . . It was written for the people who believe that the theatre can be something besides a place of entertainment and forgetfulness, that art can serve a useful social
function, that the stage is a legitimate forum for the discussion in
emotional and dramatic terms of problems that affect the lives
and happiness of millions. . . .[17]

Rice's method of attack is panoramic. During the course
of twenty scenes, he attempts to demonstrate how every

area of American life has been affected by the Depression. Not restricting himself to class, he penetrates into the inner sanctums of big business and big education, as well as into the factory, the school, the farm. He attacks, from a basically Marxist point of view, every social abuse that he can discover: the plight of the worker dispossessed by unemployment; the tenuous economic position of the white collar worker; the impoverishment of the farmer; the use of the Jew, Negro, and foreigner as economic scapegoats; the inability of young people to live a normal life because of lack of money; the relationship between war and economics; the failure of organized religion to provide adequate social answers; the impact of the failure of the banks; the denial of academic freedom to dissenters; the connivance between the police and the ruling classes; the shooting down of demonstrating workers; the conspicious consumption of the rich while the poor starve. If his fervor is vitiated it is because of the furious indiscriminateness of his attack, for no sooner does he raise one social issue than he must counterpose another. Consequently, from a dramatic point of view, he presents rather than demonstrates his indictment.

There can be no denying, however, the implication of his attack. *We the People*—two years before *Waiting for Lefty*—is almost an agit-prop; but it differs from the communist agit-prop in that its call to action, despite the catalogue of social evils which the play reveals, is not revolutionary. The play represents, rather, the aroused liberal's cry of protest against social injustice, against the misery of the poor. The final words of the play are spoken by Carter Sloane, scion of an old American family, who has sided with the oppressed and resigned his university job in protest against the suppression of academic freedom. He speaks at a public meeting, which, in the agit-prop tradition, allows the dramatist to address the audience directly.

His appeal is not a call to revolutionary action, but rather to a return to the original principles of American liberty and justice:

I find it necessary to take this platform, in order that I may raise my voice against acts that are committed in contravention of those ideals and those rights. . . . The right to live . . . that is all any [man] asks. And no social system that denies him that right has a claim to a continuance of its existence. . . . We are the people, ladies and gentlemen, we—you and I and every one of us. It is our house: this America. Let us cleanse it and put it in order and make it a decent place for decent people to live in![18]

We have observed that the two social conditions in the thirties which forced many individuals to commit themselves politically were the Depression and the rise of fascism. It is appropriate, therefore, that Rice should follow his militant call for social justice in *We the People* with a bitter attack upon Naziism in *Judgment Day* (1934). Protest did not force, however, formal consistency upon the playwright; the form of *Judgment Day* in no way resembles that of *We the People*. In fact, Rice uses the familiar form of the courtroom melodrama in order to present his indictment. In the machinations surrounding the burning of the German Reichstag in February, 1933, Rice had, in real life, a plot replete with melodramatic intrigue and chicanery. He even had a ready-made hero, Georgi Dimitroff, the Bulgarian communist whose defiance of the mock-trial electrified the world. And he also had a happy ending, because the Nazis, still insecure in their political position in 1933, were not able to ignore either the facts of the case or the pressure of world public opinion, and so freed the defendants. In fact, the difficulty with the play is that Rice's re-creation (he set the play in an undesignated Balkan country and changed various details of the actual case) pales in comparison with the documentary facts.

At the end of *Judgment Day* Judge Slatarski, one of the few presiding judges who will not bow to totalitarian pressure, shoots Vesnic, the thinly-veiled version of Adolf Hitler, and cries, "Down with tyranny! Long live the people!" This act, coupled with the surprise appearance of a character presumed dead, unfortunately melodramatizes a situation which, in reality, was already replete with sensation. The act of wish-fulfillment in destroying the Hitler figure serves to remove the entire play from the realm of actuality. Rice thus damages his indictment by making the very real facts of the case appear equally incredible. A perusal of contemporary accounts reveals no need to heighten reality to achieve dramatic effect, as the following excerpt from an eyewitness report by Eva Lips indicates:

> . . . a workman . . . told of a Party meeting in Freienwalde. . . . They had intended to form units to attack the counter-revolution if it should march upon Berlin.
> "The counter-revolution," pipes Bünger. "What was that?"
> "The Nazis," whispers Dimitroff to the microphone.
> "I forbid you to use that word," roars Werner.
> "Beg pardon!" says Dimitroff politely, "The National Socialists . . ."
> "Hold your snout!" from the Judges table.
> Dimitroff's hand moves in a gesture of pained resignation.
> "Proceed witness! . . . Take your eyes from Dimitroff!"
> "Excuse me, I can't go on," groans workman Felix. He is led off clinging to his two guards.[19]

Yet even if the actual facts of the case were more dramatic than Rice's presentation, *Judgment Day* was an effective weapon against Naziism. Scheduled productions in France and Holland were cancelled at the insistence of the Hitler government, and in Norway performances were prevented by rioting by the Norwegian Nazis. Rice's indictment was obviously strong enough to arouse fascist ire. In the character of George Khitov, the Dimitroff figure in the play, Rice had a ready-made *raisonneur*; for Dimitroff himself had used the trial as a public forum in which to condemn fascism openly. He knew the eyes of the world were upon Leipzig, and he spoke to influence world opinion beyond the confines of the courtroom. Thus Rice uses Dimitroff-Khitov as the mouthpiece for his fervent indictment of fascism:

I stand here [states Khitov in his final defense] . . . to charge Gregor Vesnic . . . with tyranny, cruelty, ruthlessness, and whole-sale slaughter. . . . I charge him with destroying the precious heritage of our science and our art and with sending into exile the flower of our intellectual life. I charge him with sowing the seeds of terror and hatred. I charge him with racial and religious fanaticism, with deliberately endangering the peace of the world. I charge him with the murder of the thousands of innocent men and women who have perished on the scaffold, in the torture chamber and in the concentration camps.[20]

Rice, like many liberals of the time, respected the communists for their anti-fascist fervor and made common cause with them on many issues. But he, like Behrman, distrusted their dogmatic intensity. Again like Behrman, he was attracted to Marxist ideals, but repulsed by Marxist methods. Rice, as *We the People* indicates, strongly felt the need for a new social order to replace capitalism, but he was unwilling to throw out the baby with the bath. As a convinced libertarian, he could not deny basic freedoms even to those he detested. Thus in *Between Two Worlds* (1934) he presents the clash of representatives of the old world and the new, and suggests the need for a rapprochement which would combine the social fervor of Marxism and the individual liberties of capitalist democracy.

Again Rice portrays a cross-section of humanity, but this time within the confines of an ocean liner bound for Europe. It is apparent from the outset that the playwright has little sympathy for most of the first-class passengers whose activities he chronicles. They are a frivolous, useless group, with little wit or charm to redeem their vulgarity. Rice centers his attention upon a few of the passengers who represent various contemporary types: Elena, the Czarist exile, who clings to the illusion of a dead world; Lloyd, the young esthete, who yearns for a world of gentility and charm; Edward, the liberal advertising man, who hates himself for accepting the debased values of a business culture; and, finally, the two protagonists, Margaret, who like Lawson's gentlewoman and Behrman's Leonie, represents a leisure class that recognizes its futility, and Kovolev, the communist film director, the blunt, unsentimental harbinger of a new order.

Although the relationship between Margaret and Kovolev is the key plot element in the play, Rice is concerned with more than the conventional shipboard romance. Margaret comes to recognize that there is a great deal of truth in Kovolev's indictment of the values of her class. Part of Kovolev's fascination for her lies in his possession of what she lacks, a strong sense of social purpose, a cause in which to believe. But although the alternative which Kovolev represents has many virtues, Margaret realizes that in the very intensity of its attack upon the values of the old order it has sacrificed the essential human trait of tolerance. The following exchange points up the dangers of the radical's dogmatic faith:

Margaret: What's your idea? . . . To level everybody down, until we're nothing but a lot of machines?

Kovolev: To level, but not down. To use machines to liberate the oppressed classes and to build a classless society.

Margaret: Yes, and I suppose it doesn't matter how many people you torture and kill while you're doing it.

Kovolev: It is all a question of which people you kill.

Margaret: There's no justification for cruelty and cold-blooded murder.

Kovolev: You call it murder—we call it class-justice. It depends upon whether you are killing or being killed.[21]

But the brief romance between the Russian director and the American girl does have a positive result. She emerges with a renewed sense of social purpose, and a clearer picture of the wrongs which she has previously ignored. He recognizes that in one's desire to alleviate social evil one cannot completely neglect the virtues of tolerance and pity. Social fervor without regard for the value of the individual can itself degenerate into oppression. Rice affirms the liberal position: he wants a new world, but not one built upon the ashes of the old.

Rice returned from his self-imposed theatrical exile in 1938 with *American Landscape*, a play which he characterized as "a plea for tolerance, for freedom of the mind and spirit, . . . an affirmation of the American tradition of liberty and of the American way of life."[22] The form which Rice now assays is that of allegorical fantasy—a half realistic, half fantastic parable of the return of the ghosts of the American past to defend the traditions which they died for. Again Rice the polemicist knows no half-way measures; in *We the People* he attempted to encompass all contemporary social evil, and in *American Landscape* he allegorizes simultaneously the plight of the American home, farm, and factory. If the structure of the play seems cut to measure, perhaps it is again the fault of Rice's overzealousness; but, from a historical point of view, it once more indicates Rice's sensitivity to the intellectual climate of his time. The wave of protest which in the early thirties had thrown many liberals into the radical camp had waned. The vogue of "Americanism" had begun; the liberal had become somewhat disenchanted with communist intransigence (although the real disenchantment was still to come with the

Nazi-Soviet pact), and affirmed a native liberalism born of America's tradition of freedom. Looking to the American past, the new liberal patriotism—reflected in such plays as *Abe Lincoln in Illinois* and *Prologue to Glory*—found in our tradition much that was worth defending: our revolutionary origin, our heterogeneous population, our Bill of Rights, our tradition of dissent.

American Landscape uses as its symbol of America the estate of the Dales, a New England family rich in tradition. The present scion of the Dale clan, Captain Frank Dale, is determined to sell the family factory rather than submit to unionization, a social innovation he finds repugnant to his paternalistic concept of employer-employee relations. He also intends to dispose of the family farm, for it, too, is not making money in an economically precarious age; and finally, he is contemplating an offer by a native Nazi group to purchase the old homestead for use as a youth camp for the training of young fascist adherents. To prevent this dissolution of family property and tradition the ghosts of the illustrious Dale past return to attempt to dissuade Captain Frank. The property must not be abandoned; its precious heritage must not be betrayed. Rice affirms in a time of crisis that America's tradition of freedom must be retained. Changes are indeed needed; old concepts of rugged individualism, as represented by Frank's point of view, must be replaced by new social theories; thus Connie, the youngest member of the family, falls in love with Joe, a proletarian who is involved in the fight for unionization. Captain Frank —and America—must recognize the facts of economic change, and build upon them. But if the factory, and the welfare of its workers, is threatened by economic conditions and Frank's refusal to accept new economic solutions, the threat to the homestead is far greater. For Stillgebauer, the Nazi, is determined when in control of the Dale house to remodel it drastically to remove its inconveniences: "Our modern German-Americans prefer that everything should be more up to date and comfortable" (p. 81). The fascist threat, from within and from without, can conquer if America betrays its fundamental principles. Obviously, the Dale property cannot be sold; the American cannot abrogate his heritage. Captain Frank dies before he can make his decision, the property passing on to the younger generation, the old order replaced by the new. And the new generation is strengthened in its determination to put the factory and the farm back on a paying basis by instituting long-needed social reforms. The Dale heritage reaffirmed, the play concludes with the ghosts of the past warning the present that if it wishes to assure the continuity of the ideals it cherishes it must be ever vigilant:

Beware of those who seek to enslave you and to force you and your children into uniform, whether of the body or of the mind. You have sharp brains and strong hands. Use them to create, to build, to make things grow—not to slaughter and destroy. . . . I leave you a tradition that is rich and deep and alive: a tradition of freedom and of the common rights of humanity. It's a priceless heritage. Cherish it! . . . And be prepared to defend it. . . . [141-42]

That the principles of freedom would, indeed, very soon have to be defended by force is an unfortunate fact of recent history. As war erupted in Europe and the Nazis engulfed one free nation after another, the defense of America seemed even more imperative. In *Flight to the West* (1941) Rice chronicles the end of an era. Again he presents a cross section of contemporary types within a confined locale; but unlike *Between Two Worlds* this time the journey takes place on an airplane bound from Europe to the United States. In the earlier play the two worlds presented were a malfunctioning capitalism and a resurgent communism; in *Flight to the West* the two worlds are simply the world of slavery and the world of freedom.

Rice articulates the liberal's dilemma in the face of incipient world conflict. Although he had been nurtured on the concept that war was essentially an imperialistic device for the obtaining of new markets,[23] now there seemed no alternative to the fascist threat. A young liberal seeks counsel from an elder spokesman of the generation of the thirties:

You taught us how some old men in Washington shut us out of the League—and then what happened afterwards. And it made us resolve that no old men were ever going to lead us down the path of war. So we joined up with something called the youth movement. We had the red tag pinned on us, though most of us weren't reds at all, but just young people who wanted the right to lead lives in which war had no part.[24]

The rapes of Finland and Norway and France have changed all that. Since the young liberal, Charles, has seen the horror of aggressive war at first hand, pacifism no longer seems tenable. But if the young man is confused by the change in his views demanded by the world situation, the old liberal, Ingraham, finds it necessary to revise the intellectual convictions of twenty years:

A man doesn't readily throw overboard the convictions of a lifetime. For twenty years, I've devoted myself to decrying war and the war makers, agitating for disarmament, for a world commonwealth. But more and more, I began discovering to my horror that my facts and my arguments were being used in ways that I never intended, by the rabid isolationists, by the critics of democracy, even by the Nazi propagandists. And . . . it's knocked the props from under me. [pp. 22-23]

Ultimately, however, in the course of the plane journey, in which the Nazi consul, Walther, reveals clearly the imminent danger of the fascist threat, both Charles and Ingraham have their confusion dispelled. There can be no compromise with evil; one cannot do business with Hitler as the businessman, Gage, suggests. The only answer is to combat him in the name of liberty. Symbolically, Charles, who is Jewish, throws himself impulsively in the path of a bullet intended for Walther, thus affirming the free man's defense of the individual, however much he may be detested personally. Ingraham's final advice to Charles and his pregnant wife is that they should not fear to bring a child into a world torn by strife. In fact it is upon their children that the future of mankind depends: "Bring your child into the world with . . . a faith in the future and in the eventual triumph of sanity and decency. Because your faith and your courage will help make it come true"(p. 151).

The thirties had demanded seriousness, and Elmer Rice, acutely attuned to the intellectual vibrations of his age, had responded. Yet his dramas of the decade survive less as works of art than as social documents; he was never quite able to forge a form which could dramatize rather than present his social convictions. Did the deficiency lie in the fact of his commitment or in the simple lack of art? Surely one cannot escape the feeling that ideas lie on top of his work, that they are never fully imbedded in the fabric of the play. Only in *The Adding Machine* has he been successful in fully integrating form and idea; and in that case he had before him sturdy European forbears. But Rice demands respect for the fervor with which he involved himself in the conflicts of his age. One senses that at heart he recognizes his esthetic limitations, but continually yearns to transcend them. A talented craftsman, he has continued to demand that American drama rise above facile craftsmanship. A paradox: but we are richer for its being posed.

10

THE POLITICAL PARADOX OF
MAXWELL ANDERSON

I have to believe
there's something in the world that isn't evil
I have to believe there's something in the world
that would rather die than accept injustice—
something positive for good—that can't be killed—
or I'll die inside.

Key Largo

. . . This thing that men call justice,
this blind snake that strikes men down in the dark,
mindless with fury, keep your hand back from it,
pass by in silence—let it be forgotten, forgotten!

Winterset

CHAPTER TEN

WHATEVER ONE'S final verdict as to Maxwell Anderson's dramatic contribution, there can be no denying the integrity with which he practised his art. With the sole exception of O'Neill, no American playwright so consistently affirmed a personal dramatic vision within the confines of the commercial theatre, nor as steadfastly refused to compromise his dramatic faith. For him the drama was nothing if not serious:

> Unless you and your play have a dream—or a conviction—and unless you can defend that conviction against death and hell and the wiles of experienced tricksters, your play isn't worth producing.
>
> Unless you are willing to make nearly every possible business and artistic concession to the play-producing set-up, you will probably never get your play on at all.
>
> But if you let these concessions touch and injure the dream (or conviction) that animates your play (and those you deal with will try their damnedest to get at it) it isn't worth putting on your play at all.[1]

But respect for a writer's integrity does not, unfortunately, necessarily predicate respect for his work. The sad fact is that much of Anderson's work now seems less experimental than derivative, and while one must credit his attempt to revitalize verse drama, one cannot help wishing that his not inconsiderable literary talents might have included a poetic ear. However, it is not our purpose to analyze Anderson's poetic deficiencies; we are concerned, after all, with the playwright's involvement in his art with the social and political issues of his age.

At first glance, Anderson might seem a particularly uncommitted playwright. Most of his plays, after all, are historical, not contemporary; his very attempt to reinstate verse drama represented a reaction against the "journalistic social comment"[2] which, in his view, dominated American drama in the thirties. Moreover, Anderson was always a confirmed rugged individualist; he never felt comfortable within the confines of a specific political ideology. He distrusted and inveighed against all political organizations, whether Communist, Fascist, Democratic, or Republican. The political man, his plays and essays have proclaimed, is invariably a scoundrel and opportunist. And yet, despite his suspicion of political action, it is significant that Anderson never avoided political issues; on the contrary, man, as he emerges from Anderson's work, is essentially a social, not a psychological animal. Most of Anderson's plays, particularly those written in the thirties, are involved with the problem of man in conflict with social and political forces. The persistent dichotomy which rings throughout them is a political one: the lust for power in conflict with the desire for freedom; the rebel-reformer—Essex, Rudolf, McLean, Macready, Gregor, Mio—is one of his perennial protagonists.

Anderson's work, despite his formal attempt to write historical verse tragedy, is inextricably bound with the social forces of his age. "A playwright," he has declared, "is driven more directly than any other writer or artist to make up his mind about his world or be silent until he can make up his mind."[3] And Anderson has never been silent; indeed he has been amazingly prolific. The testament of his work has been a ceaseless attempt to define the boundary between man's acknowledgment of the immutability of social evil and his faith in the ability to change or transcend it. This is the paradox that must be faced: man sees evil born of man himself, and despite his desire to eradicate it, is forced to recognize the futility of the effort. And yet without the attempt man has abdicated his humanity. "The concepts of truth and justice are variables approaching an imaginary limit which we shall never see; nevertheless, those who have lost their belief in truth and justice and no longer try for them are traitors to the race, traitors to themselves, advocates of the dust."[4] Thus Anderson recognizes the necessity of the gesture of protest while simultaneously proclaiming it invalid.

And yet the gesture must be made; despite his pessimism, Anderson never *accepts* social injustice. The difficulty arises in attempting to determine how much social evil resides in transformable institutions and how much in the black heart of man. It is the continual shifting from one emphasis to another which obscures Anderson's dramatic vision. There can be no denying that despite his abhorrence of political dogma, Anderson does affirm a political position. Time and again he asserts the destructive influence of all organized government, the inevitable tyranny of authority, and the necessary resistance to all organized authority in defense of personal freedom. In short, Anderson's position is anarchistic, a compound of ideas derived from Rousseau (a benevolent primitivism and a sporadic faith in the goodness of man), Proudhon (property is theft), Thoreau (civil disobedience as the corollary of freedom), and Jefferson (that government is best which governs least). But Anderson is never, in the tradition of Kropotkin or Bakunin, a revolutionary anarchist; one of his perennial themes is the futility of revolutionary action.

Thus we have stated Anderson's essential paradox: he was continually engaged in the struggle against social injustice (as revealed personally in his defense of Sacco and Vanzetti, his loss of academic position because of pacifist opinions, and his vocal opposition to Hitler and Franco). Since he invariably attributes this evil to the coercive and brutalizing effect of organized authority, the logical result of this position is political action against encroachments upon man's individual freedom. And yet, behind the necessity of this action lies the recognition that all action is essentially futile. Behind the anarchist resides the fatalist: "The writer of tragedy knows that there is no immediate way out. He knows that the burning questions of reform are all old, that men have sought the answers since the morning of history, and that the answers will not be found in his time, that nothing final will come of anything he does or says."[5]

The paradox may be observed in Anderson's two plays based upon the Sacco-Vanzetti case. In *Gods of the Lightning* (1928) written shortly after the execution of the two anarchists, the prevalent tone is that of protest. As in Rice's *Judgment Day*, the playwright takes considerable liberties with the facts of history. Although Vanzetti is more or less accurately delineated in the person of Capraro, Anderson chooses for his fellow victim, not another foreign-born anarchist, but rather an American Wobbly, Macready. Mac is, in fact, unlike either Sacco or Vanzetti, a militant radical portrayed as actively engaged in an attempt to bring off a strike. But Mac's radicalism is a far cry from the Marxist variety, and while in many ways he presages the defiant hero of proletarian drama, he is not imbued with class consciousness, for he continually attacks not only organized government and religion, but the cowardice of the working class. The character of Macready enables Anderson to articulate a militant anarchism not reflected in the public utterances of either Sacco or Vanzetti. And Anderson uses Capraro, his Vanzetti figure, as the spokesman for a pacifism born of the conviction that belligerent patriotism is the camouflage for economic exploitation: "When we are young boys we look on the flag and believe it is the flag of liberty and happy people—and now I know it is a flag to carry when the old men kill the young for billions."[6] Thus Anderson's use of both Macready and Capraro as more articulate foes of social evil than either Sacco or Vanzetti reveals a desire to reinforce the social lesson which he drew from the celebrated case: the men were condemned, not because their opinions were nonconformist, but because organized society could not tolerate threats to its oppressive authority. Yet, while Anderson takes liberties with the characters of his protagonists to reinforce his social analysis of their martyrdom, his version of the actual mechanics of the trial sticks closer to the record. But again Anderson underscores the conspiratorial aspect. The district attorney, Salter, and Judge Vail (Anderson's re-creation of Katzmann and Thayer) are portrayed as willfully distorting the processes of justice in order to assure condemnation of the radical defendants.

To affirm further the fact of frame-up Anderson introduces another character, who has no counterpart in the actual case. Suvorin is indeed a strange figure; Dostoyefskian in his mixture of prophetic fervor and criminality, he serves as the counterbalance to Macready's militancy. Mac operates on the theory that society is evil and that it must be changed; Suvorin operates on the theory that society is evil and it can't be changed. Equally anarchistic, Suvorin reveals the core of fatalism at the heart of Anderson's radicalism:

The world is old, and it is owned by men who are hard. Do you think you can win against them by a strike? Bah! They own this government, they will buy any government you have. I tell you there is no government—there are only brigands in power who fight for more power! It has always been so. It will always be so. [p. 34]

It is, in fact, Suvorin who was involved in the murder of the paymaster for which Macready and Capraro are on trial. And at a crucial moment he confesses his deed. Yet even in the face of that confession, the state cannot allow its victims to escape. It merely implicates all three in the murder, affirming Capraro's conviction that "there is no answer to the anarchist who says the power of the State is power for corruption" (p. 92).

Thus the paradox of Anderson's dilemma is asserted. In the face of evil man must protest; he is impelled to social action. But behind the protest lies Suvorin's mocking recognition that all human action is condemned to failure. Protest, if you will, but realize that you cannot succeed in changing the way of the world. The last lines of *Gods of the Lightning*, spoken by Rosalie after the news of the execution, sum up the paradox: "Shout it! Shout it! Cry out! Run and cry! . . . Only—it won't do any good—now" (p. 106).

In *Winterset* (1935) the core of protest remains, but it now serves as a symbol upon which Anderson attempts to construct his first contemporary verse drama. The heat of the moment has dissipated, and Anderson is less involved with the social implications of the Sacco-Vanzetti case than with the eternal problems of justice, redemption, and faith. But the issues raised by *Gods of the Lightning* have not disappeared. In the opposition of Mio's fervent desire for justice and Esdras' talmudic fatalism we find reenacted the essential conflict of Macready and Suvorin. Mio's life is dedicated to the vindication of his father. It is the faith by which he lives.

> Will you tell me how a man's
> to live, and face his life, if he can't believe
> that truth's like a fire,
> and will burn through and be seen
> though it takes all the years there are?
> While I stand up and have breath in my lungs
> I shall be one flame of that fire;
> its all the life I have.[7]

But Esdras' answer, not unlike Suvorin's, is that life is based upon the fact of injustice: "There's not one title to land or life, / even your own, but was built on rape and murder. . . . / it would take a fire indeed / to burn out all this error" (pp. 70-71).

The conflict is thus defined; but the difficulty with *Winterset* is that Anderson does not follow the logic of this conflict. In the end it is Esdras' fatalistic vision which prevails, and which Mio accepts: "We live our days / in a storm of lies that drifts the truth too deep / for path or shovel . . ." (p. 121). But by what path did Mio arrive at this conviction? He had come determined to vindicate his father, to prove conclusively his innocence, and he had, in fact, received the information that he desired. For a time Judge Gaunt almost makes him doubt his cause, but the intervention of Trock and the reappearance of Shadow leave no doubt about the actual perpetrators of the crime for which Romagna, the Vanzetti figure, died. Thus the fact of injustice is proven, and Mio's resolution to vindicate his father should, if anything, be strengthened. The fact that he is thwarted by evil—represented by Trock and his hoodlums —might well symbolize Anderson's view of the impotence of individual protest; but, considering the logic of the play, why is the gesture of protest itself denied? Mio, instead of being confirmed in the righteousness of his cause by the fact of his father's innocence, has "lost . . . my taste for revenge." His love for Esdras' daughter, Miriamne, has replaced his desire for vindication, and his death—in the light of his rejection of the meaningfulness of his cause— smacks almost of gratuitousness.

Perhaps Anderson tried too consciously to follow a formula of what he conceived the ideal tragedy to be. In the preface to *Winterset* he writes: "A play should lead up to and away from a central crisis, and this crisis should consist in a discovery by the leading character which has an in-

delible effect on his thought and emotion and completely
alters his course of action."[8] But the problem in *Winterset*
lies in the fact that the central crisis presented—the recognition scene in which the truth about the Romagna case is
revealed—leads logically not to an alteration of Mio's passionate resolve but rather to its affirmation. Had it been discovered that Romagna had indeed been guilty, Mio's pessimism would have made more dramatic sense. Thus Anderson asserts a fatalistic position without demonstrating it.

Unlike the protagonists of classical tragedy, Mio is destroyed less by his inner contradictions than by external
realities. One of the basic themes in *Winterset* is the op-
pressiveness of authority. Mio's friend, Carr, states that the
State is always right because it can't afford to admit it is
wrong, that all justice is corrupt. And Judge Gaunt stands as
the symbol of guilt born of an oppressive legality. The forces
which afflict man are more often without than within, and
Anderson's tragedies—despite their attempt to follow clas-
sic patterns—are more of his age than he might have
acknowledged.

The playwright's involvement in the social and political
issues of his day may be explicitly observed in two nonverse
dramas written in the thirties. In *Both Your Houses* (1933)
and *Knickerbocker Holiday* (1938) Anderson is at his most
polemical. The target in both instances is again organized
government. In the first play, as the title indicates, Anderson surveys the political situation and finds in both parties
nothing but graft and corruption. In the second he takes for
his specific target the paternalistic philosophy represented
by the New Deal, and makes a fervent appeal against the
tendency towards increased governmental control. In the
preface to *Knickerbocker Holiday*, he leaves no doubt as to
his anarchistic position, a position which he consistently
reaffirmed.

... a civilization is a balance of selfish interests, and a government is necessary as an arbiter among these interests, but the
government must never be trusted, must be constantly watched,
and must be drastically limited in its scope, because it, too, is a
selfish interest and will automatically become a monopoly in
crime and devour the civilization over which it presides unless
there are definite and positive checks on its activities.[9]

In *Both Your Houses,* produced two days after Roosevelt's initial inauguration, Anderson has as yet no specific
political target. He rakes all politicians unmercifully in an
attempt to demonstrate that all government has its roots in
corruption. Each member of the House Committee on Appropriations is engaged in an attempt to saddle a forthcoming appropriations bill with his own pet scheme, and
while the Congressmen attempt to legitimize their personal projects on the basis of national need, Anderson leaves
no doubt that their motives are hardly grounded in altruism.
That government is best which governs, and taxes, least is
Anderson's perennial refrain, and to illustrate his thesis he
sends his own Mr. Smith to Washington, in the person of
Alan McLean, to take on the nest of nepotistic vipers. Mc-
Lean, an intellectual idealist, had been appointed to the
committee on the assumption that he would support the
appropriations bill, but the members had not counted upon
the young man's intransigent honesty. Plagued with inner
doubts, McLean had investigated his own election and had
come up with disquieting facts not only about his own supporters but about those of the other members of the committee as well. He comes to the conclusion that the appropriations bill will benefit no one but the congressmen and
their supporters, and consequently is determined to defeat
it. Anderson's political solution for the ills of the Depression
is strictly one of laissez faire; Alan asserts that he was
elected to decrease, not to increase, public expenditure. But

Alan's political efforts to defeat the bill by overloading it with useless expenditures fail; and, unlike Mr. Deeds and Mr. Smith (Frank Capra's cinematic representatives of the average man against organized society), he comes to realize the impotence of individual idealism. He has learned the bitter lesson that self-interest will always be placed above the nation's welfare. Beyond the fact of economy Anderson offers no specific political remedy to this unfortunate situation. "Who knows what's the best kind of government?" asks the disillusioned Alan, "maybe they all get rotten after a while and have to be replaced."[10] Anderson's political platform seems to consist of one strongly-held plank, turn the rascals out—all of them: "There are a hundred million people who are . . . disgusted enough to turn from you to something else. Anything else but this" (p. 179).

But the American people had turned to something else, the New Deal; and as the decade wore on Anderson found this alternative even more repugnant than the last. At least corruption, because of the clash of selfish interests, was inefficient. Government may have been robbery, but it was not despotism. "Whatever the motives behind a government-dominated economy," writes Anderson in the preface to *Knickerbocker Holiday*, "it can have but one result, a loss of individual liberty in thought, speech and action" (p. vi). And in the play itself he attempts to demonstrate through the usually frivolous medium of the musical comedy the dangers inherent in the New Deal.

Knickerbocker Holiday represents Anderson's attempt to write an American *Threepenny Opera*, and his musical collaborator was in fact Kurt Weill. Many of the ballads, following the Brechtian tradition, are political, but whereas Brecht's principal target was the social inequality bred by an oppressive economic system, Anderson's target is the philosophy of benevolent despotism:

No man shall want for food,
Nor ditto any wife;
All hail the bright, the good,
The regimented life! [p. 43]

In the character of Pieter Stuyvesant, the benevolent despot who comes to usher in "the age of strength through joy," Anderson draws a figure for whom it was not difficult to find a contemporary parallel. "My dear fellows," counsels Stuyvesant in Anderson's parody of the Roosevelt manner, "under my system there is no such thing as ruin, and no such thing as bankruptcy; there is only a slight financial sophistication supported by unlimited government credit" (p. 85). And Anderson leaves no doubt that such a doctrine can only lead to dictatorship. Stuyvesant states that the government, in extending credit, will naturally become a partner in any business which it guaranteees, and as a result taxes will have to be rather high to support it. A man objects, "But maybe ve couldn't pay dem high taxes and high vages, so nobody vorks, so nobody buys anything, so nobody makes any profit, so it stops going!" (p. 86). In that case, Stuyvesant maintains the government would naturally have to take over. As Anderson explicitly states in his preface: "Social Security is a step toward the abrogation of the individual into that robot which he has invented to serve him —the paternal state" (p. vi).

In opposition to the benevolent despotism represented by Stuyvesant, Anderson juxtaposes the rugged individualism of Brom Broeck, who embodies the Andersonian political virtues, "A person with a really fantastic and inexcusable aversion to taking orders, coupled with a complete abhorrence of governmental corruption" (p. 30). Brom, a born rebel, recognizes the fact that "all governments are crooked, vicious and corrupt," but at least a democracy "has the immense advantage of being incompetent in villainy and clumsy in corruption" (p. 100). Anderson's defense of democracy is based upon the theory of the lesser evil. Since by his definition all government is evil, the less government the better. Tyranny may substitute the illusion of order but only at the expense of man's most cherished liberties. In actuality, the "order" of totalitarianism is only superficial; it is merely "efficiently vicious and efficiently corrupt." Thus Anderson's political answer is to "throw out the professional and go back to the rotation of amateurs! Let's keep the government small and funny, and maybe it'll give us less discipline and more entertainment!" (p. 101).

But despite the fervor of his political beliefs, Anderson was never primarily an anarchistic muckraker; on the contrary he consistently denigrated the theatre of social protest. His effort to reinvigorate poetic drama may be observed as a direct reaction to the challenge of the prosaic leftist theatre. It is, I suspect, no accident that Anderson's career as verse dramatist should *exactly coincide* with the decade of the thirties. His first major poetic play is *Elizabeth the Queen* in 1930; his last, *Journey to Jerusalem* in 1940. None of Anderson's pre- or post-thirties plays are written in verse, not even those on historical subjects (such as *Anne of the Thousand Days, Joan of Lorraine,* or *Barefoot in Athens*). Anderson's effort, then, represents a conscious attempt to re-emphasize the role of individual heroics in a world—and in a theatre—in which the individual seemed to exist only as a representative of larger social forces. In the world of Anderson's dramatic imagination, the protagonist is invariably a man or woman of high station fighting a losing battle against hostile—usually evil—social forces.

Even in Anderson's early poetic dramas—particularly in the Tudor plays, *Elizabeth the Queen* (1930) and *Mary of Scotland* (1933)—the playwright is continually concerned with the problem of power. In both plays the machinations of statecraft prevent the protagonists from following the free dictates of their passion. The love affair between Elizabeth and Essex is thwarted by the intrigues of Cecil and Raleigh as surely as the love affair between Mary and Bothwell is thwarted by Elizabeth herself. Both plays are commentaries on expediency and political survival. Elizabeth survives, according to Anderson, because she is willing to sacrifice her love to the dictates of power; Mary is defeated precisely because her tolerant personality is unable to credit the clever machinations of her enemies. In *Elizabeth the Queen* it is apparent that Elizabeth loves Essex, but she also recognizes that he is a born rebel, a man who can never be content with but a portion of power, and that his martial temper would not only embroil England in useless wars which would be a drain upon national resources, but that Essex's lust for power would ultimately cause her own deposition. This she cannot endure, and sacrifices her passion for political survival. The objection might be raised that Anderson, in opposition to the data of history, has magnified the role of passion in political conflict. Surely both Tudor plays are unabashedly romantic—a romanticism which rings hollow against the backdrop of Websterian intrigue which informs the general world of these plays. The criticism is not without validity, and it is significant that in several of his later verse dramas Anderson de-emphasizes, though never completely eschews, the power-passion dichotomy, and shifts his dramatic emphasis to the conflict between power and liberty.

Even in romantic terms Anderson is involved with the contradiction between freedom and authority. The Elizabeth that emerges in *Mary of Scotland* has completely committed herself to the laws of expediency. It is as if Anderson were describing (in opposition to chronology) the hard, passionless woman that the Queen had become because of the disillusionment of her affair with Essex. Remorseless, adaptable, ("Aye, times have changed, / And we change along with them"), she skillfully baits the trap into which the unwary Stuart is led. Mary Stuart is destroyed because she lacks Elizabeth's political resiliency. Her credo—"to rule gently is to rule wisely"—cannot survive in a world of vipers. Her tragedy lies in her distaste of power and her hatred of intolerance. She refuses to placate the fanatic Knox, and instead chides him for his messianic fervor. A lover of beauty, a hater of violence, she affirms her faith in the triumph of good, a faith which unfortunately is not justified: "This is my faith . . . that all men / Love better good than evil, cling rather to truth / Than falseness, answer fair dealing with fair return. . . ."[11] But at the murder of her favorite, Rizzio, Mary comes to the fatal realization that goodness is not enough, that the fact of evil is an inescapable element in the universe:

> Now I see it. Before I reign here clearly
> There will be many men lie so for me
> Slain in needless quarrel. Slain, and each one
> With blood to spill but once, like his. And yet
> One steps on into it—steps from life to life
> Till the heart faints and sickens, and still goes on
> And must go on. [p. 93]

In Anderson's early historical verse dramas—in the Tudor plays and *Night Over Taos* (1932)—he attempted to utilize history as myth: that is, the materials of history served as the framework upon which he attempted to construct traditional tragedies according to Aristotelian dictates. The result is inevitably *pastiche*, and is saved from inconsequence by Anderson's romantic theatricality (which undoubtedly explains much of his considerable commercial success) and, what is more significant, by his own bleak vision of the paradox of power. But as the decade wore on and the threat of totalitarianism seemed to Anderson more manifest in both domestic and foreign affairs, he became less concerned with history as myth and more concerned with history as prophecy. The facts of history no longer served as the backdrop upon which classical tragedies were to be reconstructed; they now seemed to point a direful lesson, and the playwright was determined to reveal the moral. Consequently, many of Anderson's later historical dramas assume the double vantage point of past and present. His protagonists—often famous historical figures—invariably display prophetic vision; and inasmuch as the subject matter of Anderson's dramas more often than not deals with rebellion, the prophetic vision which the plays reveal is inevitably the same, the revolution betrayed.

Not only has Anderson continually exploited the theme of rebellion in his historical tragedies (indeed the only historical play written in the thirties which does not touch the theme is *Wingless Victory*, which deals with the problem of racial intolerance), but he has written dramas which explicitly treat of the most momentous revolutions of the modern era: the French, American, and Russian revolutions. In the first and last instances, Anderson's theme is the betrayal of revolutionary idealism, and even in *Valley Forge*, his drama of the American Revolution, the forces of betrayal, as we shall shortly see, almost succeed.

In *The Feast of Ortolans* (1937), a group of French intellectuals and liberal aristocrats gather on the eve of the French Revolution to celebrate the annual ceremony of the Pompignan family. True children of the Enlightenment, they look forward to the realization of man's illimitable potentialities as prophecied by the *philosophes*. "The new era . . . of freedom and reason" is about to begin, man will be freed of institutional evil. Philippe of Orleans envisages a government which will reform social injustice and hearken to all legitimate grievance; Lafayette affirms a Rousseauistic faith in a brave, new world based upon social justice. But it is soon apparent that this optimistic faith is to be denied.

Resorting to his role as prophet, Anderson uses the character of La Harpe to intimate the disaster that is to befall all present. Lafayette had dreamed the anarchist's dream of a world in which there will be "no kings, / No capitalists, no nobles, and no armies,"[12] but this dream, La Harpe prophesies, will not come to pass: ". . . the revolution will devour its children, / And those who fostered it" (p. 20). Condorcet, Bailly, Desmoulins, Chénier, Lafayette will all be either executed or driven into exile. In the name of the ideals just enunciated the greatest barbarities will be committed. It will be a crime to have been or to have spoken with an aristocrat; it will be a crime to oppose the government in any way, or to speak one's mind. In the name of tolerance, intolerance will reign supreme.

> Those who rule
> Will be philosophers, and will repeat
> All you have said about the bright new world
> In which men are free; in that world's name
> You and your children will be put to death,
> Till the executioners are wearied out
> With chopping . . . [p. 21]

And the final result will be a greater tyranny than that overthrown. On the tide of violence and chaos, a new leader will ride in who "will set himself to master all the world / By preaching our own doctrines . . . till he makes himself / An emperor, and all his brothers kings" (p. 24). Thus the revolutionary dream ends in Napoleonic tyranny; and, to confirm La Harpe's dire prophesy, the woodcutters presage the bloodshed that is to come by murdering the host and ending for all time the feast of the Ortolans.

Similarly in *Second Overture* (1938) Anderson describes the betrayal of the ideals of the Russian Revolution. Gregor, who had participated in the abortive revolution of 1905, counsels a group of Russian aristocrats, with whom he has been accidentally imprisoned, that they need not fear for their lives because the triumph of the Bolsheviks will ensure "free speech, civil rights . . . and the abolition of arbitrary and tyrannical power, such as was exercised by the Czar. . . ."[13] But Charash, once Gregor's fellow revolutionist and now the officer in command, explains that although the aristocrats have technically committed no crime, they are still guilty by virtue of their class and must be executed. He defends the necessary bloodshed on the grounds of expediency. In order to fulfill the revolutionary dream all vestiges of the old order must be expunged; in the name of the final ideal, the most reprehensible means are regrettably justified. "The task now," the communist asserts, "is a cleansing of the empire of the filth of a thousand years" (p. 17). Gregor, however, cannot accept Charash's logic. He observes that evil means cannot produce virtuous ends, that in the name of the highest ideals of justice, Charash is contributing towards a tyranny greater than the Czar's.

> You strangle with your own hands
> All hope for the revolution. . . . Justice—
> To attain justice you revoke all justice—
> To attain mercy you repudiate
> The principle of mercy—blood will breed murder,
> Murder breed blood—the evil means we use
> For a good end, will bring down only more evil
> And curses at the end. [pp. 16-17]

At the end of the play Gregor helps the aristocrats to escape, although he himself remains behind. He is willing to die because in the betrayal of the revolutionary ideals he has lost his reason for existing. The revolution is dead and he is content to die with it.

Anderson further treats of the theme of revolutionary failure in his reworking of the Rudolf-Vetsera affair in *Masque of Kings* (1937). But the ill-fated romance of the

lovers of Mayerling is not the major subject of the play.
The dramatic conflict is not, as in *Elizabeth the Queen*, between power and passion, though at times it might seem so.
The essential conflict of the play rests in the contrast between the wily, politic monarch Franz Joseph and the
idealistic young rebel, Rudolf. The romantic elements, as
in much of Anderson's work, tend to obscure rather than
clarify his main theme, which is again the failure of the revolutionary dream.

Rudolf, like the French *philosophes*, dreams of a society
in which man is naturally free. He acquiesces in revolutionary intrigue against his father in the hope of enacting
necessary social reforms: the granting of autonomy to the
Hungarian provinces, the opening of the franchise to all
men of voting age, the elimination of restrictions on free
speech and press, the release of political prisoners, the abrogation of arbitrary parliamentary power, and, finally, the
relegation of monarchy to an exclusively advisory capacity.
Like most of Anderson's rebel-heroes he has a passionate
dislike for authority, an inner yearning to be his own man
in a world removed from the vicious intrigues of the powerful. But the Emperor is the champion of *real-politik*; he is
not a vicious man, but he recognizes the logic of authority.
In the play's most crucial scene, after Rudolph's successful
seizure of power, Franz Joseph logically demonstrates to
his son that the consequences of power cannot be avoided,
that his revolutionary ideals are doomed to failure if he is,
in fact, determined to rule. He explains to Rudolf that if he
would be king thousands of men in both Hungary and
Austria must be killed, including the king himself. Very
well, Rudolf acquiesces, let them die. But the Emperor
points out that Rudolf is too idealistic to kill indiscrimin-
ately; he will let some live who will then plot with renewed
vigor to overthrow his regime. Rudolf insists that he will be
thorough. Franz Joseph's logic cannot be denied, and al-

ready the ideals of freedom begin to crumble. The Emperor does not relinquish his advantage. What will Rudolf do with the property of the men he will be forced to execute? Again Rudolf swallows the bait: it will be distributed among supporters of the rebellion.

Thus the Emperor progressively forces Rudolf to recognize the logic of power. One cannot rule innocently. As Rudolf agrees to one suppression after another, Franz Joseph ironically observes that Rudolf is sanctioning repressions that will give the present regime, in retrospect, "the air / of a golden age. . . ."[14] At last Rudolf recognizes the corner into which he has been inexorably driven. An honest man, he sees he has been led to Franz Joseph's conclusion that "all reforms are counters in the game / of government . . ." (p. 110).

> I see in one blinding light
> that he who thinks of justice cannot reach
> or hold power over men, that he who thinks
> of power, must whip his justice and his mercy
> close to heel. . . .
>   I have been taken upon a crest of time
> and shown the kingdoms of the world, those past,
> those present, those to come, and one and all,
> ruled in whatever fashion, king or franchise,
> dictatorship or bureaucrats, they're run
> by an inner ring, for profit. Its bleak doctrine . . .
> but its savagely true. [pp. 111-12]

Like Gregor, Rudolf cannot surmount the dashing of his ideals, and he willingly surrenders his power back to his father. Thus revolutionary idealism is forever compromised by the logic of power, and the anarchist's dream of a Rousseauistic millennium is shattered by the Hobbsian conviction that the evil in man will triumph over the good.

In only one revolutionary situation is this social pessimism denied, the American Revolution. But it is significant that

Anderson's dramatic recreation in *Valley Forge* diverges from his other parables of revolutionary failure only in the vital fact of outcome. Again the anarchistic dream is almost thwarted by the intrigues of politics; again the representatives of government, both British and American, are depicted in terms of the greatest contempt; again the idealist's vision is countered by the facts of commercial aggrandizement. In fact, from all points of view the dramatic logic of *Valley Forge* leads toward the inevitable defeat of Washington and the dream he represents. Anderson saves the revolution—after all, a historical necessity—not by the logic of character and situation, but, rather, by the cheap, theatrical trick of thrusting Mary Phillips gratuitously into the barren camp at Valley Forge. Not merely does she intrude an incongruously romantic note, but her final revelation to Washington that the French have decided to enter the war (the *crucial* dramatic fact: for Washington is about to acquiesce to Howe's terms) is not even dramatically justified (Howe had made a conscious effort to keep the news from her). Thus the dénouement of *Valley Forge* is totally spurious as Anderson indulges in the most flagrant forms of sentimentality and flag-waving.

The play collapses because Anderson cannot accept the logic of the situation he has presented; he is obviously tied to the facts of history. Surely the subject matter of the American revolution might well serve as the symbol of a necessary fight for libertarian ideals, and Anderson affirms that this is his aim. But the situation which he presents works towards a quite contrary conclusion. Congress is described, and depicted, as a group of selfish merchants concerned only with economic advantage, and the American Revolution is viewed essentially as a trade war, not a libertarian uprising. Harvie, the Congressman, bluntly tells Washington that since the continuation of hostilities could only have the most disastrous commercial results, it would be better to reach a settlement with the English. Howe concurs; he has no stomach for violence and is willing to compromise. Indeed, he is depicted as a true child of the Enlightenment.

> What beasts we've been,
> We English-speaking brothers, to gash and stab
> and drill each other's brains out all these years
> over one kind of government or another
> when they're all the same! I'm a liberal myself,
> want to see men free. . . . but good Lord,
> when has a king balked freedom, when has the lack
> of a king guaranteed it?[15]

Is this statement inconsistent with the philosophy of government which Anderson has continually asserted? Tench, one of Washington's most militant subordinates, reiterates almost the same view:

> They're all alike, and have one business, governments,
> and its to plunder. This new one we've set up
> seems to be less efficient than the old style
> in its methods of plundering folk, but give them time;
> they'll learn to sink their teeth in what you've got
> and take it from you. [p. 63]

Since both sides are in fundamental agreement as to the aims and practices of government, what reason is there for the war to continue? Anderson asserts the idealist's dream that men "shall walk upright, masterless, doff a hat to none, / and choose their gods!" (p. 164). But beyond the postulation of this ideal—an ideal which in his work has continually been thwarted by the very forces he presents in *Valley Forge*—he demonstrates no dramatic reason why it should triumph. Washington shares all the traits of Anderson's other rebel-idealists—the dream, the distaste for authority, the basic anarchism; but unlike Rudolf or Gregor he triumphs almost by the sheer effort of will (and theatri-

cal contrivance). Although he continually disclaims des-
potic ambition, Washington, as Anderson presents him,
emerges as a "man on horseback," the symbol of popular
antigovernmental discontent—the kind of man who, by
virtue of his personal magnetism and distrust of legally constituted authority (after all, Washington *refuses* to accept
orders from his legal superiors) might well fall into the very
dictatorial pattern that Anderson abhors. Thus the anarchist
dream, by its denial of governmental alternatives, may
facilitate the very tyranny it detests. The mere assertion of
democratic faith does not suffice when the premises of democracy are themselves undermined.

As Anderson progressively delineates the features of the
world about him, either directly or through the device of
historic parable, he likes what he sees less and less. On all
sides he finds individual liberty in danger; man's most
cherished libertarian ideals crumble in the face of authoritarian betrayal. As the decade of the thirties advances,
Anderson recognizes that he must face the problem of how
to cope with the social evil he sees accumulating. What is
man to do in a world in which his individual freedom is
being increasingly restricted? In *High Tor* (1937) and *Key
Largo* (1939) he presents different answers to the question.
In the first instance the playwright proposes escape; in the
second, commitment.

Van Van Horn represents the last defender of the faith
of rugged individualism; he embodies the traditional Andersonian virtues. The mountain, High Tor, his refuge from
encroaching materialism and authority, is being threatened
by speculators who want to cut it up "like a pie" for commercial purposes. At the outset Van steadfastly defends his
right to live as he pleases and turns down all offers for the
rights to his mountain. He despises industrialism and the
regimentation it inevitably creates. The vision which Van
(and Anderson) champions belongs to the past, to an agrar-

ian society of small, autonomous communities in which man has maximum individual freedom. But while Van is unable to retrieve the past, however much he might desire to do so, Anderson, by virtue of his creative prerogative, can do so imaginatively; the ghosts who inhabit High Tor are the playwright's symbolic testament to the superiority of the past to the present. Mankind has become a race of "quick, fierce wizard men / . . . [who] come to drive / machines through the white rock's heart."[16] But the ghosts are of the past and, consequently, do not have to accept this brave, new world; as Lise, Van's phantom love, points out to him "this is your age, your dawn, your life to live" (p. 109). Van himself realizes that perhaps his entire way of life is as anachronistic as that of the ghosts or of the ancient Indian who is waiting to die.

> Maybe I'm a ghost myself
> trying to hold an age back with my hands;
> maybe we're all the same, these ghosts of Dutchmen
> and one poor superannuated Indian
> and one last hunter, clinging to his land
> because he's always had it. [p. 113]

Van wishes to have High Tor back the way it was before the speculators and the gangsters and the authorities came, but he realizes that he is condemned to his age. So, in the end, he capitulates; High Tor is not worth a fight. He accepts the Indian's counsel:

> let them have the little hill, and find your peace
> beyond, for there's no hill worth a man's peace
> while he may live and find it. [p. 128]

Anderson's fatalistic vision prevails: in the final analysis the creations of man are as illusory as the ghost of High Tor. The Indian again points the moral: "Nothing is made by man / but makes, in the end, good ruins." And Van, having relinquished his mountain, finds comfort in this thought: "Well, that's something. . . . I can hardly wait" (p. 142).

But the basic dramatic situation in *Key Largo* arises from the guilt that obsesses King McCloud because he relinquished *his* mountain. In the Prologue to the play, it is related how McCloud refused to fight with his men on a hill during the Spanish Civil War. The Loyalist cause has been lost, and King suggests that there is nothing to do but pull out before the Rebels attack and destroy them. But the men refuse to leave even though they realize that a stand will result in their deaths. Monte maintains that although it wasn't their fight, they had, by volunteering, made it their fight. Although the men have few illusions about the Loyalists, they have committed themselves to the battle and they will remain. King tries to convince them that such a stand is foolhardy. "Was there ever a crusade without an ignominious end?" he asks. Asserting Anderson's familiar thesis of the betrayal of all revolutionary ideals, King can see no logic in dying for a lost cause.

> . . . all the formulas are false—
> and known to be false—democracy, communism
> socialism, naziism—dead religions
> nobody believes in. . . .
> Why should we die here for a dead cause, for a symbol,
> on these empty ramparts, where there's nothing to win,
> even if you should win it?

But Victor points out that without some faith, even if at bottom it is illusory, man cannot live: "I have to believe there's something in the world / that would rather die than accept injustice . . . or I'll die inside."[17] He is willing to die to prove that man will continue to struggle against evil. His faith is not only in himself and in what men are, but in what they may become.

King McCloud leaves the men to their martyrs' deaths,

and the main body of *Key Largo* becomes a drama of his expiation and redemption. The play, in fact, denies the thesis of *High Tor*: that no hill is worth a man's peace. King comes to realize that one must take one's stand against evil, despite the knowledge that evil will never be entirely vanquished. McCloud is tortured by guilt because "there never came a time / when I could say to myself, make a stand here" (p. 63). Ultimately he is presented with a second chance. The gangster, Murillo, personifies the evils of totalitarianism. But at their initial confrontation, King again cannot act; he is still tormented by the fatalistic vision that all ideals are equally invalid, and all action equally futile. D'Alcala, however, echoes the faith of his dead son, Victor, that man must accept the challenge of existence: "To take this dust / and water and range of appetites / and build them towards some vision of a god / of beauty and unselfishness and truth . . ." (p. 112). And King finally comes to recognize that Victor and d'Alcala were right, that without this faith man is nothing; that to live without combatting evil is to acquiesce in all evil.

> . . . In the last analysis one dies
> because its part of the bargain he takes on
> when he agrees to live. A man must die
> for what he believes—if he's unfortunate
> enough to have to face it in his time—
> and if he won't then he'll end up believing
> in nothing at all—and that's death, too. [pp. 117-18]

King sacrifices himself in order to destroy Murillo, and in this act achieves his redemption. Thus Anderson, faced with the monstrous evil of fascism, affirmed that man must act after all. Even if he recognizes the basic futility of all action, in order to survive as a human being he must affirm the possibility of what mankind can become. By this very affirmation Anderson denies his social fatalism, and again we observe the basic paradox of his philosophy. On one hand, Rousseauistic man dreams of a world in which institutional evil is eradicated, in which the coercion of authority is not permitted to thwart man's essential goodness; on the other, Machiavellian man creates ever more complex instruments for self-aggrandizement and oppression. In fighting political evil, man must face the contradiction of becoming that which he detests. And yet he must fight; for to avoid the battle means the abrogation of humanity. It is no accident that this paradox should be most manifest in Anderson's dramas of the thirties. Not only the social dramatists faced the crucial social issues of their time: "It's all of us / in this age of dying fires."[18]

THE PROBLEM TODAY

If prosperity really does come back, life is going to be an awful bore for us revolutionists.

LASHIN and HASTINGS, *Class of '29*

EPILOGUE: ELEVEN

GRANVILLE HICKS, a survivor of the political vicissitudes of the thirties, titled the retrospective memoir of his intellectual development *Where We Came Out,* and it is appropriate that we should attempt, at the conclusion of our investigation, to make a similar discovery. Although the intensity of political debate has diminished, the issues raised by the dramatists of the thirties have by no means vanished. Indeed, as we indicated in the Prologue, the problem of political commitment represents a revival in contemporary terms of the primary esthetic debate of that troubled decade. That the debate is not completely academic in our time may be observed by several of the major tendencies in contemporary theatre and dramatic criticism. Sartre and Camus in France, Osborne, Wesker, Littlewood, and Richardson in England have attempted to respond to the political imperatives of their age by creating a theatre (and cinema) of political commitment. The impetus has been particularly strong in Great Britain, where, since Osborne's breakthrough in *Look Back in Anger,* the younger generation finds itself increasingly dissatisfied with the inequities of a class-conscious society. It is no coincidence that finds most of the younger British playwrights and directors fervently enlisted in the cause of nuclear disarmament. The plays of Osborne and Wesker leave no doubt as to their socialist sympathies, although both playwrights reject the simplistic Marxism of the thirties. Indeed, Arnold Wesker's commitment has resulted in his recent attempt to create a genuine workers' theatre in cooperation with the trade-union movement. Similarly, recent significant British films (e.g., *Saturday Night and Sunday Morning, The Loneliness of the Long-Distance Runner*) have almost exclusively dealt with the more tawdry aspects of provincial working class life—and with the explicit or implicit thesis of social reform.

The wave of political commitment reflected in the work of the angry young English playwrights, directors, and actors finds itself in opposition to another significant tendency in the contemporary theatre. The emergence of the work of Beckett, Ionesco, and Genet in the fifties has created the vogue of what has been termed "the theatre of the absurd," the focus of which is upon man's anguish, fantasies, and alienation. In a world of dust-bins, brothels, and theatrical no-man's lands political gestures are at best irrelevant; man's victimization is the product of the human condition rather than social injustice. The influence of these playwrights of the absurd has not been limited to the fringe of the *avant-garde*. For the first time since the vogue of expressionism in the twenties, conventional theatre audiences have accepted a large-scale assault on the premises of realism. The influence has been particularly strong upon contemporary American drama. Suffering from a much more intense case of radical disenchantment than the English, young American playwrights have remained relatively unconcerned with the theatre of commitment. Such dramatists as Edward Albee, Arthur Kopit, and Jack Gelber have looked to Beckett, Ionesco, and Genet for theatrical inspiration, although it is significant to note that Albee, for one, has revealed a streak of social involvement in such plays as *The Death of Bessie Smith* and *The American Dream*. By and large, however, American radicalism has not recovered sufficiently from its disillusionment to support a social theatre comparable to that flourishing in Great Britain.

That the essentially contradictory social premises of the theatres of commitment and the absurd should produce esthetic debate is inevitable, and it is no surprise that the issue of political commitment in drama should consistently be revived in our time, particularly in England. One of the most interesting forms of this debate occurred in the pages of the London *Observer* in 1958. It began when Kenneth Tynan, reviewing a production of two short Ionesco plays, dismissed them with the claim that they had no relevance to the important issues of society. "M. Ionesco's theatre is pungent and exciting," he admitted, but, because of its remoteness from social realities, "it remains a diversion."[1] The following week Ionesco replied that it was not the business of the playwright to deliver messages to the world. A work of art, he claimed, "has nothing to do with doctrine." He particularly rejected the assertion that his plays were escapes from reality:

The true society, the authentic human community, is extrasocial —a wider, deeper society, that which is revealed by our common anxieties, our desires, our secret nostalgia. . . . No society has been able to abolish human sadness, no political system can deliver us from the pain of living, from our fear of death, our thirst for the absolute; it is the human condition that dictates the social condition, not vice versa.[2]

The debate enlivened the *Observer's* correspondence column for the next few weeks, with many prominent theatre artists entering one side or the other of the controversy. The basic problem, all acknowledged, was specifically that of political commitment. George Devine, who had produced the plays of both Osborne and Ionesco, opted for the latter's dramatic philosophy: "An alive theatre should lead us to know more about ourselves and other people and to question every kind of 'ism' that crops up. Being committed to being committed is a dog chasing its own tail."[3] But Orson Welles and Lindsay Anderson reaf-

firmed Tynan's defense of the necessity of political commitment. Anderson wrote: "Commitment . . . is not a formulated dogma, but a principle of belief and action. It ex-
presses a resolution to relate the arts to contemporary life—
moral, spiritual, social, and political. . . . It does not demand
that the writer should devote himself to propagating a party
line. On the contrary—it demands that he work with his
own awareness of, his own responsibility towards, the revolutionary period through which we are living."[4]

The problem continues to be debated; it does not represent a remote episode in the history of literary esthetics.
Has our investigation clarified this continuing controversy?
Not completely, of course. Since literary history unfortunately lacks the precision of natural science, its findings
cannot always serve the function of prophecy; they are at
best tenuous analogues, rather than blueprints, to the future. I think, however, that the evidence of our investigation of American drama of the 1930's does warrant at least
one conclusion: that political commitment *in itself* is an inadequate test of esthetic effectiveness. The Marxist condemnation of art which is not a weapon is obviously absurd;
yet so too is the contrary assertion that all art which demands political action has abrogated its function. The
crucial fact is *how* the writer utilizes his commitment:
whether, as in the case of Lawson, it is an obvious excres-
cence which has little relation to the artist's experience, or
whether, as in the case of Odets (and we might add Brecht,
Silone, and Malraux), the organic structure of his work is
dependent upon and rises from the artist's political convictions. The act of political obligation has apparently been
disastrous for many artists; it has imposed upon their work
considerations alien to their authentic talents. But in other
cases political commitments have served to order the
artist's anarchic tendencies, to offer a structural framework
upon which to build. Martin Esslin writes of Brecht: "The

act of *engagement* . . . can therefore be seen as having been of considerable importance in the mechanism of his creative process. It gave him the reason, the justification, and the incentive to work."[5]

Perhaps we might clarify the problem by considering for a moment the analogous problem of religious commitment. Surely one need not take new vows in order to appreciate a work by an artist of a religious persuasion different from one's own. Even the most zealous religionist would hardly maintain that only Catholics can enjoy Claudel, Protestants Milton, and Jews Shalom Aleichem. When we read a successful literary work, one in which the artist's commitment is intrinsic to his experience, we briefly become his fellow communicants. If the artist's vision of life is genuine, if it is authentically his own, we are obligated to accept it on his terms. If we do not do so, if we demand that art conform to our particular beliefs and prejudices, then we find ourselves in the predicament common to those who endeavor assiduously, and absurdly, to prove that Shakespeare was either a secret Catholic or a pre-Marxist social rebel. Gerard Manley Hopkins was a good poet; Joyce Kilmer was not; although both were good Catholics, the success of their poetry bears no direct relation to the degree of their personal piety. Both Lawson and Brecht were avowed Marxists, but the latter's literary stature has steadily increased, while the former's has steadily declined. Thus, let us not ask to what the artist is committed, but rather how he is committed. Although neither sound ideology nor sound theology can fill the void of esthetic deficiency, let us not commit the contrary heresy of damning those works whose commitments we reject.

A SELECTED BIBLIOGRAPHY

EDITIONS OF PLAYS [*]

Anderson, Maxwell. *Both Your Houses*. New York, 1933.
———. *Eleven Verse Plays, 1929–1939*. New York, 1940.
———. *Knickerbocker Holiday*. Washington, 1938.
———, and Hickerson, Harold. *Gods of the Lightning*. New York, 1928.
Ardrey, Robert. *Thunder Rock*. New York, 1941.

Behrman, S. N. *Dunnigan's Daughter*. New York, 1945.
———. *Four Plays*. New York, 1955.
———. *Meteor*. New York, 1934.
———. *No Time for Comedy*. New York, 1939.
———. *Rain from Heaven*. New York, 1934.
———. *The Talley Method*. New York, 1941.
———. *Wine of Choice*. New York, 1938.
Brecht, Bertolt. *Mother*.[*] 1935.

Clarke, Harold, and Nurnberg, Maxwell. *Chalk Dust*. New York, 1936.

De Rohan, Pierre (ed.). *Federal Theatre Plays*. 2 vols. New York, 1938.

Fulton, A. R. (ed.). *Drama and Theatre: Seven Modern Plays*. New York, 1946.

Gassner, John (ed.). *Twenty Best Plays of the Modern American Theatre, 1929–1941*. New York, 1941.
Gold, Michael, and Blankfort, Michael. *Battle Hymn*. New York, 1936.
Green, Paul. *The House of Connelly; and Other Plays*. New York, 1931.

Lashing, Orrie, and Hastings, Milo. *Class of '29*. New York, 1936.
Lawson, John Howard. *The Internationale*. New York, 1928.
———. *Loud Speaker*. New York, 1927.

[*] Asterisks designate MSS located in the Theatre Collection of the New York Public Library.

————. *Marching Song.* New York, 1937.

————. *Processional.* New York, 1925.

————. *Processional,*° rev. ver. 1937.

————. *Success Story.* New York, 1932.

————. *With a Reckless Preface.* New York, 1934.

Levy, Melvin. *Gold Eagle Guy.* New York, 1934.

Lewis, Sinclair, and Moffit, John. *It Can't Happen Here,*° 1936.

Maltz, Albert. *Black Pit.* New York, 1935.

————, and Sklar, George. *Peace on Earth.* New York, 1933.

Odets, Clifford. *The Big Knife.* New York, 1949.

————. *Clash By Night.* New York, 1941.

————. *The Country Girl.* New York, 1951.

————. Selections from *The Flowering Peach,* in *Best Plays of 1954–55,* ed. Louis Kronenberger. New York, 1955.

————. "I Can't Sleep," *New Theatre,* III (July 1936), 8–9.

————. *Night Music.* New York, 1940.

————. *Six Plays.* New York, 1939.

————. *Three Plays.* New York, 1935.

Peters, Paul, and Sklar, George. *Parade.*° 1935.

————. *Stevedore.* New York, 1934.

Piscator, Erwin, and Goldschmidt, Lena. *The Case of Clyde Griffiths,*° trans. Louise Campbell. 1936.

Rice, Elmer. *American Landscape.* New York, 1939.

————. *Flight to the West.* New York, 1941.

————. *Seven Plays.* New York, 1950.

————. *The Subway.* New York, 1929.

————. *Two Plays.* New York, 1935.

————. *We the People.* New York, 1933.

Saul, Oscar, and Lantz, Louis. *The Revolt of the Beavers.*° 1936.

Shaw, Irwin. *The Gentle People.* New York, 1939.

Sifton, Paul, and Sifton, Claire. *1931–.* New York, 1931.

Stavis, Barrie, and Stavis, Leona. *The Sun and I.*° 1937.

Wolf, Friedrich. *The Sailors of Cattaro.* New York, 1935.

PERIODICALS AND NEWSPAPERS

Anvil (New York), *Drama Magazine* (Chicago), *Federal Theatre Magazine* (Washington), *Fight* (New York), *Fortune* (New York), *Harper's* (New York), *Liberty* (New York), *London Magazine*

(London), *Manchester Guardian Weekly* (Manchester, England), *Modern Quarterly* (Baltimore), *Nation* (New York), *New Leader* (New York), *New Masses* (New York), *New Republic* (New York), *New Theatre* (New York), *New Yorker* (New York), *One-Act Play Magazine* (New York), *Partisan Review* (New York), *The Periodical* (London), *Saturday Evening Post* (Philadelphia), *Theatre Arts Monthly* (New York), *Les Temps modernes* (Paris), *Times Literary Supplement* (London), *Workers' Theatre* (New York), *Zeitschrift für Anglistik und Amerikanistik* (East Berlin); the following New York newspapers: Brooklyn *Eagle, Daily Mirror, Daily News, Daily Worker, Evening Journal, Herald Tribune, Post, Sun, Times, World Telegram.*

MAJOR SECONDARY SOURCES

Aaron Daniel. *Writers on the Left.* New York, 1961.
Allsop, Kenneth. *The Angry Decade.* New York, 1958.
Anderson, Maxwell. *Off Broadway.* New York, 1947.
Auden, W. H. *Collected Poetry.* New York, 1945.

Beals, Carleton, and Odets, Clifford. *Rifle Rule in Cuba.* New York, 1935.
Blake, Ben. *The Awakening of the American Theatre.* New York, 1935.
Block, Anita. *The Changing World in Plays and Theatre.* New York, 1939.

Clurman, Harold. *The Fervent Years,* rev. ed. New York, 1957.
———. *Lies Like Truth.* New York, 1958.
Cogley, John. *Report on Blacklisting.* 2 vols. New York, 1956.
Cowley, Malcolm. *Exile's Return.* New York, 1951.

Esslin, Martin. *Brecht: the Man and His Work.* New York, 1959.

Fergusson, Francis. *The Human Image in Dramatic Literature.* Garden City, New York, 1957.
Flanagan, Hallie. *Arena.* New York, 1940.
Flexner, Eleanor. *American Playwrights: 1918–1938.* New York, 1938.

Gagey, Edmond M. *Revolution in American Drama.* New York, 1947.

Hart, Henry (ed.). *American Writers' Congress.* New York, 1935.
———. *The Writer in a Changing World.* New York, 1937.
Hicks, Granville. *Where We Came Out.* New York, 1954.

Himelstein, Morgan Y. *Drama Was A Weapon: The Left-wing Theatre in New York, 1929-1941*. New Brunswick, N.J., 1963.
Hoffman, Frederick. *The Twenties*. New York, 1955.
Howe, Irving. *Politics and the Novel*. New York, 1957.
————, and Coser, Lewis. *The American Communist Party*. Boston, 1957.

Kempton, Murray. *A Part of Our Time*. New York, 1955.
Kozlenko, William (ed.). *The One-Act Play Today*. New York, 1938.
Krutch, Joseph Wood. *The American Drama Since 1918*. New York, 1957.

Lawson, John Howard. *Film in the Battle of Ideas*. New York, 1953.
————. *The Hidden Heritage*. New York, 1950.
————. *A Southern Welcome*. New York, 1934.
————. *Theory and Technique of Playwriting*. New York, 1936.
League of Professional Groups for Foster and Ford. *Culture and the Crisis: An Open Letter to the Intellectuals of America*. New York, 1932.
Lumley, Frederick. *Trends in Twentieth Century Drama*. London, 1956.

Mander, John. *The Writer and Commitment*. London, 1961.
Marx, Karl. *Selected Works*. 2 vols. Moscow, 1955.
Maschler, Tom (ed.). *Declaration*. London, 1957.

Rideout, Walter. *The Radical Novel in the United States*. Cambridge, Mass., 1956.

Sartre, Jean-Paul. *Being and Nothingness*, trans. Hazel E. Barnes. New York, 1956.
————. *What Is Literature?*, trans. Bernard Frechtman. New York, 1949.
Schlesinger, Arthur, Jr. *The Crisis of the Old Order, 1919–1933*. Boston, 1957.
————. *The Coming of the New Deal*. Boston, 1959.

Twelve Southerners. *I'll Take My Stand*. New York, 1930.

Wecter, Dixon. *The Age of the Great Depression*. New York, 1948.
Whitman, Willson. *Bread and Circuses*. New York, 1937.
Wilson, Edmund. *The American Jitters*. New York, 1932.
————. *The Shores of Light*. New York, 1952.

NOTES

ONE: PROLOGUE

1. *Manchester Guardian*, Feb. 18, 1960, p. 11.
2. (New York, 1956), p. 107.
3. "After Commitment," p. 693.
4. Quoted in Kenneth Allsop, *The Angry Decade* (New York, 1958), p. 135.
5. "Theatre and Living," *Declaration*, ed. Tom Maschler (London, 1957), p. 94.
6. Ibid., p. 95.
7. "The Small, Personal Voice," *Declaration*, p. 195.
8. Ibid., p. 190.
9. "Till Rome Burns," *International Literary Annual*, No. 1, ed. John Wain (London, 1958), p. 28.
10. (London, 1961), p. 211.
11. Ibid., pp. 15, 107, 108.
12. Ibid., pp. 12–13.
13. The interest has continued into the 1960's. At the 1963 International Drama Conference at Edinburgh, one of the six daily sessions was entirely devoted to the problem of commitment in relation to the dramatist.
14. "Symposium on the State of American Writing," Aug. 1948, p. 860.
15. Ibid., p. 886.
16. Ibid., p. 879.
17. Ibid., p. 886.
18. "Art and Commitment," Winter 1960, p. 5.
19. Ibid.
20. Ibid., p. 6.
21. Supplement to *The Periodical*, Autumn 1959, p. 1.
22. R. P. Blackmur wrote: "We do not know to what it is we are committed" (p. 865).
23. (New York, 1956), p. 631.
24. See, for example, Erich Kahler, *The Tower and the Abyss* (New York, 1957), p. 238.

25. *Existentialism and the Modern Predicament* (London, 1953), p. 130.

26. "Art and Commitment," p. 6.

27. "Réponse à Albert Camus," *Les Temps modernes*, Aug. 1952, p. 345.

28. *Sartre* (New Haven, 1953), p. 112.

29. "The Pound Case," *Partisan Review*, May 1949, p. 518.

30. Ibid., p. 515.

31. Ibid., p. 517.

32. "The Writer in his Age," *The London Magazine*, May 1957, p. 44.

33. Ibid.

34. *The Human Image in Dramatic Literature* (Garden City, N.Y., 1957), pp. 20–21.

35. *Politics and the Novel* (New York, 1957), p. 16.

CHAPTER TWO

1. (New York, 1951), p. 307.

2. Ibid., p. 308.

3. "New Year's Letter," *Collected Poetry* (New York, 1945), p. 274.

4. "Spain 1937," ibid., pp. 182, 184.

5. Josephine Herbst, quoted in introduction to *American Writers' Congress*, ed. Henry Hart (New York, 1935), p. 15.

6. *The Shores of Light* (New York, 1952), p. 498.

7. (New York, 1932), p. 3.

8. Quoted in Frederick Hoffman, *The Twenties* (New York, 1955), p. 308.

9. Quoted in Arthur Schlesinger, Jr., *The Crisis of the Old Order, 1919–1933* (Boston, 1957), p. 145.

10. Quoted in Granville Hicks, "Communism and the American Intellectuals," *Whose Revolution?* (New York, 1941), p. 90.

11. Walter Rideout, *The Radical Novel in the United States,* (Cambridge, 1956), p. 256.

12. *American Writers' Congress*, p. 11.

13. *The Writer in a Changing World*, ed. Henry Hart (New York, 1937), p. 32.

14. N.Y. *Daily Worker*, June 29, 1936, p. 1. Henceforth abbreviated *DW*.

15. A perusal of the volumes of Burns Mantle's annual record of American drama reveals that of some 1,500 presentations offered by independent managers on Broadway from 1929 through 1941, only about 100 treated themes of social, political, or economic significance; but this figure excludes all of the significant theatrical organizations—the Group Theatre, the Theatre Guild, Theatre Union, the Mercury, the Federal Theatre Project, the Playwrights' Company—from which nearly all significant drama of the period arose.

16. Quoted in Morgan Y. Himelstein, *Drama Was A Weapon: The Left-wing Theatre in New York, 1929-1941* (New Brunswick, N.J., 1963), p. 78.

17. Quoted in "American Writers Look Left," *New Masses*, June 30, 1936, p. 25. Henceforth abbreviated *NM*.

18. *The Radical Novel*, p. 171.

19. Waldo Frank, "Values of the Revolutionary Writer," *American Writers' Congress*, p. 76.

20. "In Defense of a Term," *NM* Literary Section, July 12, 1938, p. 146.

21. "Advertisement for Debate," *NM*, July 1930, p. 3.

22. Paul Peters, George Sklar, *et al.*, "Parade" (New York Public Library, Theatre Collection, typewritten, 1935), n.p. Henceforth abbreviated Thea. Coll.

CHAPTER THREE

1. Quoted in Anita Block, *The Changing World in Plays and Theatre* (New York, 1939), p. 275.

2. "Collective Drama at the Civic Repertory Theatre," Brooklyn *Eagle*, Mar. 29, 1936, p. 17.

3. George Sklar and Albert Maltz, "The Need for a Workers' Theatre," *DW*, Dec. 16, 1933, p. 7.

4. Block, p. 274.

5. The New Playwrights, founded in February, 1927 by John Howard Lawson, Mike Gold, John Dos Passos, Francis Faragoh, and Emjo Basshe, declared that their theatre should be "a clearing house for ideas and a focus for social protest" (Lawson, "The Crisis in the Theatre," *NM*, Dec. 15, 1936, p. 35). Their plays, invariably experimental in form and undogmatically radical in theme, included Emjo Basshe's *Earth* (1927), a play about the conflict between superstition and Christianity in a Negro community; Paul and Claire Sifton's *The Belt*, a drama about a revolt against a Henry Ford-type assembly

line; Upton Sinclair's *Singing Jailbirds* (1928), about an IWW organizer railroaded to prison; and Lawson's *The Internationale* (1938). See Chap. V on Lawson's contribution to the theatre.

6. Quoted in Ben Blake, *The Awakening of the American Theatre* (New York, 1935), p. 23.

7. John Gassner, "The One-Act Play in the Revolutionary Theatre," *The One-Act Play Today*, ed. William Kozlenko (New York, 1938), p. 256.

8. Ibid.

9. "Theatre Union Replies," *New Theatre*, Nov. 1934, p. 12. Henceforth abbreviated *NT*.

10. Ibid.

11. *DW*, Dec. 30, 1933, p. 3.

12. N.Y. *Herald Tribune*, Dec. 24, 1933, p. 45.

13. Margaret Larkin, N.Y. *Herald Tribune*, Oct. 28, 1934, p. 37.

14. "Theatre Union's Project," N.Y. *Times*, Feb. 7, 1937, sect. X, p. 2.

15. Emery Northup, "Meet the Theatre Union," *NT*, Feb. 1934, p. 9.

16. Ibid.

17. Larkin, "On Becoming Acclimated to Broadway," *DW*, Nov. 24, 1936, p. 7.

18. Larkin, "Social Play Gets an Audience," N.Y. *Herald Tribune*, Oct. 28, 1934, p. 36.

19. Ben Compton, "Facts and the Left Theatre," *DW*, Jan. 3, 1937, p. 13.

20. "Collective Drama," loc cit.

21. John Anderson, article, N.Y. *Evening Journal*, Apr. 18, 1934, p. 16.

22. "Collective Drama," loc. cit.

23. *DW*, Mar. 19, 1935, p. 5.

24. Ibid., Jan. 16, 1934, p. 28.

25. "Straight from the Shoulder," *NT*, Nov. 1934, p. 11.

26. Review of *Stevedore*, *NM*, May 1, 1934, p. 28.

27. Apr. 28, 1934, p. 58.

28. Apr. 2, 1935, p. 42.

29. Albert Maltz, *Black Pit* (New York, 1935), p. 105.

30. Quoted in Frederick Wolf, *The Sailors of Cattaro* (New York, 1935), p. iii.

31. "The Most Important Play in New York," Dec. 25, 1934, pp. 28–29.

32. "The Work of Frederick Wolf," *NM*, June 11, 1935, p. 23.

33. *Brecht: the Man and his Work* (New York, 1959), p. 129.

34. Ibid., p. 130.

35. "Principles of Educational Theatre," *NM*, Dec. 31, 1935, p. 27.

36. Esslin, pp. 73-74. Also see Stanley Burnshaw, "Theatre Union Produces *Mother*," *NM*, Dec. 3, 1935, p. 27.

37. N.Y. *Times*, Jan. 26, 1936, sect. IX, p. 3.

38. "Facts and the Left Theatre," loc. cit.

39. Robert Forsythe, "Wanted: A Theatre," *NM*, Oct. 18, 1938, p. 15.

40. "Change the World," *DW*, Oct. 9, 1937, p. 7.

CHAPTER FOUR

1. *The Fervent Years*, rev. ed. (New York, 1957), p. 38.

2. Program to *1931–* (Group Theatre Scrapbook, Thea. Coll.), p. 1.

3. *Fervent Years*, p. 30.

4. "The Group Theatre Campaigns," *Theatre Arts Monthly*, May 1932, p. 347.

5. *Fervent Years*, p. 222.

6. Ibid., p. 46.

7. Ibid., p. 61.

8. Robert Forsythe, "Wanted: A Theatre," *NM*, Oct. 18, 1938, p. 15.

9. Hearings, House Committee on Un-American Activities, May 19–20, 1952 (Washington, 1952), p. 3455.

10. Hearings, Apr. 10, 1952 (Washington, 1952), p. 2407.

11. *Fervent Years*, p. 124.

12. Ibid., p. 127.

13. Ibid., p. 222.

14. "The Case of the Group Theatre," July 1936, p. 5.

15. N.Y. *World Telegram*, Apr. 17, 1936, p. 28.

16. *Fervent Years*, p. 218.

17. For a detailed examination of the plays of Odets see Chapter VI.

18. Erwin Piscator and Lena Goldschmidt, "The Case of Clyde Griffiths," trans. Louise Campbell (Thea. Coll., 1936, typewritten), p. 83.

19. Paul and Claire Sifton, *1931–* (New York, 1931), p. 45.

20. Ibid., p. xiii.

21. Leon Alexander, "The World of Theatre," *DW*, Dec. 4, 1934, p. 7.

22. Stanley Burnshaw, "Theatre," *NM*, Dec. 11, 1934, p. 29.

23. Paul Green, *The House of Connelly; and Other Plays* (New York, 1931), p. 23.

24. Clurman, "The Group Halts," N.Y. *Times*, Jan. 17, 1936, p. 51.

25. Paul Green, *Johnny Johnson*, in *Twenty Best Plays of the Modern American Theatre, 1929-1941,* ed. John Gassner (New York, 1941), p. 142.

26. *Fervent Years*, p. 224.

27. Irwin Shaw, *The Gentle People* (New York, 1939), pp. 40-41.

28. Robert Ardrey, *Thunder Rock* (New York, 1941), p. 21.

29. *Fervent Years*, p. 263.

30. Ibid., p. 265.

CHAPTER FIVE

1. "Entertaining Flood Sufferers," *Federal Theatre Magazine,* II, No. 4 (1937), p. 13.

2. Hallie Flanagan, *Arena* (New York, 1940), pp. 380–430.

3. Elmer Rice, "The Federal Theatre," N.Y. *Times*, Jan. 5, 1936, sect. IX, pp. 1, 3.

4. See *Arena*, pp. 377–436, for complete production record.

5. Ibid., p. 268.

6. Willson Whitman, *Bread and Circuses* (New York, 1937), p. 68.

7. Dixon Wecter, *The Age of the Great Depression* (New York, 1948), p. 71.

8. *Arena*, p. 16.

9. Ibid., p. 19.

10. Ibid., p. 46.

11. Quoted in Whitman, pp. 100–101.

12. *Arena*, p. 256.

13. See, e.g., "Unemployed Arts," *Fortune*, May 1937, pp. 108–17.

14. *Arena*, p. 121.

15. "Unemployed Arts," p. 168.

16. *Arena*, p. 205.

17. See Walter Pell, "Which Way the Federal Theatre?," *NT*, Apr. 1937, p. 7.

18. *Arena*, p. 361.

19. Ibid., pp. 432–33.

20. One additional limitation: we are restricted by necessity to a consideration of those plays which survive either in published versions or in typescript. The following analysis of officially-criticized WPA drama is, therefore, if selective, not arbitrarily so.

21. "The State," *DW*, Jan. 31, 1938, p. 9.

22. John Cambridge, "Toller's Play," *DW*, Jan. 31, 1938, p. 9.

23. Charles Dexter, *DW*, Oct. 29, 1936, p. 7.

24. Barrie and Leona Stavis, "The Sun and I" (Thea. Coll., typewritten, 1937), Act II, Scene iii, p. 11. Paginated by acts and scenes.

25. Harold Clarke and Maxwell Nurnberg, *Chalk Dust* (New York, 1936), pp. 2–3.

26. Ibid., p. 97.

27. Orrie Lashing and Milo Hastings, *Class of '29* (New York, 1936), p. 31.

28. Quoted in introduction to *Abe Lincoln in Illinois*, in *Modern American Dramas*, ed. Harlan Hatcher (New York, 1941), p. 268.

29. E. P. Conkle, *Prologue to Glory*, in *Federal Theatre Plays*, II, ed. Pierre de Rohan (New York, 1938), p. 60.

30. John Cambridge, "Lincoln's Youth and Love," *DW*, Mar. 21, 1938, p. 7.

31. Quoted in *Arena*, p. 173.

32. N.Y. *Times*, Dec. 10, 1949, p. 1.

33. Oscar Saul and Louis Lantz, "The Revolt of the Beavers" (Thea. Coll., typewritten, 1936), Act I, Scene i, p. 2. Paginated by acts and scenes.

34. *DW*, June 29, 1936, p. 1.

35. Michael Gold and Michael Blankfort, *Battle Hymn* (New York, 1936), p. 12.

36. Morris Watson, "The Living Newspaper," *NT*, June 1936, p. 7.

37. Arthur Arent, "Technique of the Living Newspaper," *Theatre Arts Monthly*, Nov. 1938, p. 820.

38. Ibid., p. 821.

39. Ibid., p. 822.

40. "Revolt of the Sharecroppers," *DW*, Jan. 21, 1937, p. 5.

41. Staff of the Living Newspaper, *One Third of a Nation*, in *Federal Theatre Plays*, II, 105.

42. "Not in Despair," *Federal Theatre Magazine*, II, No. 4, 5.
43. Quoted in *Arena*, p. 188.
44. Ibid., p. 334.
45. Ibid., p. 354.
46. Ibid., p. 346.
47. Hearings, House Committee on Un-American Activities, IV (Washington, 1939), 2857–58.
48. Ibid., p. 2873.
49. Quoted in *Arena*, p. 337.
50. Ibid., p. 326.

CHAPTER SIX

1. (New York, 1955), p. 210.
2. *The Fervent Years*, p. 87.
3. Introduction to *Loud Speaker* (New York, 1927), p. ix.
4. "Biographical Notes," *Zeitschrift für Anglistik und Amerikanistik*, IV, No. 1 (1946), 233.
5. Lawson, *Roger Bloomer*, in *Drama and Theatre: Seven Modern Plays*, ed. A. R. Fulton (New York, 1946), p. 233.
6. Lawson, *Processional* (New York, 1925), p. v.
7. *A Part of Our Time*, p. 185.
8. Donald Nash, review, Oct. 26, 1937, p. 28.
9. Gilbert Gabriel, review, N.Y. *Sun*, Mar. 4, 1926, p. 24.
10. Lawson, *The Internationale* (New York, 1928), p. 235.
11. Rideout, *The Radical Novel*, p. 132.
12. "Biographical Notes," p. 75.
13. *Fervent Years*, p. 18.
14. "Biographical Notes," p. 75.
15. *Fervent Years*, p. 87.
16. Lawson, *Success Story* (New York, 1932), p. 207.
17. "A Bourgeois Hamlet of Our Time," *NM*, Apr. 10, 1934, p. 29.
18. Margaret W. Mather, review of *With a Reckless Preface*, *NM*, July 17, 1934, p. 28.
19. Lawson, *The Pure in Heart*, in *With a Reckless Preface* (New York, 1934), p. 63.
20. Lawson, *Gentlewoman*, in *With a Reckless Preface*, p. 213.
21. *With a Reckless Preface*, p. ix.
22. Ibid., p. xvii.
23. "A Bourgeois Hamlet," p. 28.
24. Ibid.

25. "Inner Conflict and Proletarian Art," Apr. 17, 1934, p. 30.

26. Ibid.

27. *Fervent Years*, p. 125.

28. "Biographical Notes," p. 76.

29. Kempton, *Part of Our Time* (New York, 1955) p. 185.

30. Lawson, *A Southern Welcome* (New York, 1934), p. 14.

31. Lawson was among the leadership in the League of American Writers and was active in their congresses and conferences; he was associate editor of the *New Masses* and later *Mainstream* and *Masses and Mainstream*; he was vice-president of the National Council of the Arts, Sciences and Professions; he was involved in the organization of the Screen Writers' Guild and served as its first president; he was one of the organizers of the Conference against Thought-Control, and participated in the Cultural and Scientific Conference for World Peace in New York in 1949 ("Biographical Notes," p. 75).

32. June 1, 1934, p. 6.

33. "The Theatre Guild Plays," *NM*, Jan. 5, 1937, p. 23.

34. "Play on Dimitroff," *DW*, July 23, 1934, p. 5.

35. "Straight from the Shoulder," *NT*, Nov. 1934, pp. 11–12.

36. "Crisis in the Theatre," *NM*, Dec. 15, 1936, p. 35.

37. *Fervent Years*, p. 148.

38. "Lawson's Technique and Re-evaluation of the Drama," *NM*, Apr. 28, 1936, p. 25.

39. *American Writers' Congress*, pp. 123–24.

40. Lawson, *Theory and Technique of Playwriting* (New York, 1936), p. x.

41. Lawson, *Marching Song* (New York, 1937), p. 84.

42. Mar. 2, 1937, p. 7.

43. *Fervent Years*, p. 175.

44. "A Dramatist's Tribute to Helpful Hollywood," uncited clipping, dated 1932 (Group Theatre Scrapbook, Thea. Coll.).

45. See Dorothy B. Jones, "Communism and the Movies: A Study of Film Content," reprinted in John Cogley, *Report on Blacklisting*, I (New York, 1956), 196–233.

46. Kempton, pp. 195–96.

47. "A Bourgeois Hamlet," p. 29.

48. *Where We Came Out* (New York, 1954), p. 57.

49. Joseph Dugan, "Movies," June 28, 1938, p. 27.

50. Jones, op. cit., p. 208.

51. Lawson, selections from the script of *Blockade, One-Act Play Magazine*, Oct. 1938, p. 406.

52. *Fervent Years*, p. 228.

53. See Lawson, "Art Is a Weapon," *NM*, Mar. 19, 1946, pp. 18–20.

54. "Biographical Notes," p. 75.

55. Lawson, *The Hidden Heritage* (New York, 1950), p. vii.

56. Lawson, *Film in the Battle of Ideas* (New York, 1953), p. 21.

57. (New York, 1960), p. xxxii.

58. *Fervent Years*, p. 228.

CHAPTER SEVEN

1. Apr. 6, 1935, p. 18.

2. Mar. 31, 1935, p. 25.

3. *Fervent Years*, pp. 138–39.

4. Gregory Novikov, "Newsboy" (Thea. Coll., 1933, typewritten), p. 5.

5. Art Smith and Elia Kazan, "Dimitroff," *NT*, July-Aug. 1934, p. 20.

6. Review, *NM*, July 2, 1935, p. 39.

7. Clifford Odets, *Waiting for Lefty*, in *Six Plays* (New York, 1939), p. 7.

8. Odets, *Waiting for Lefty*, in *Three Plays* (New York, 1935), p. 42. The stenographer-actor sequence, present in both the original production and the first published version of the play, was omitted from the version included in the 1939 edition of Odets' *Six Plays*. Obviously by 1939 Odets had retreated somewhat from his doctrinaire militancy of the mid-decade.

9. Hearings, House Committee on Un-American Activities, May 19, 1952 (Washington, 1952), pp. 3484–85.

10. N.Y. *World Telegram*, Apr. 10, 1935, p. 28.

11. Review, *NM*, July 2, 1935, p. 40.

12. Odets, *Till the Day I Die*, in *Six Plays*, p. 138.

13. N.Y. *World Telegram*, Mar. 19, 1935, p. 16.

14. Hearings, op. cit., p. 3456.

15. Ibid.

16. Ibid., p. 3462.

17. Preface, p. ix.

18. Odets, "I Can't Sleep," *NT*, July, 1936, p. 9.

19. Carleton Beals and Clifford Odets, *Rifle Rule in Cuba* (New York, 1935), p. 11.

20. N. Y. *Times*, July 7, 1935, sect. II, p. 2.

21. John McCarten, "Revolution's Number One Boy," *New Yorker*, Jan. 22, 1938, p. 25.

22. Odets, *Awake and Sing*, in *Six Plays*, p. 37.

23. Brooks Atkinson, review, N.Y. *Times*, Dec. 29, 1935, sect. IX, p. 1.

24. "*Paradise Lost*: An Obituary," *NM*, Feb. 11, 1936, p. 28. See also Jay Gerlando, "Odets and the Middle Class," *DW*, Feb. 7, 1936, p. 7.

25. "Interpretation and Characterization," *NT*, Jan. 1936, p. 21.

26. Ibid.

27. Odets, *Paradise Lost*, in *Six Plays*, pp. 219–20.

28. "*Paradise Lost* and the Theatre of Frustration," *NT*, Jan. 1938, p. 8.

29. Quoted in *Fervent Years*, p. 158.

30. Ibid.

31. Ibid., p. 159.

32. See, for example, N.Y. *Times*, Apr. 3, 1936, sect. X, p. 4; Brooklyn *Eagle*, May 17, 1936, sect. C, p. 1.

33. N.Y. *World Telegram*, Mar. 19, 1935, p. 16.

34. "Odets' First Film," July 28, 1936, p. 12.

35. Selections from *The General Died at Dawn*, *NM*, July 28, 1936, pp. 12–13.

36. Odets, "Democratic Vistas in Drama," N.Y. *Times*, Nov. 21, 1937, sect. XI, p. 1.

37. Ibid.

38. Odets, *Golden Boy*, in *Six Plays*, p. 257.

39. After his first visit, he made several excursions between the years 1936 and 1941, once to make a film called *Gettysburg* and another time to write the screenplay for a film called *The River is Blue*, which later emerged, rewritten by Lawson, as *Blockade*. In 1943 Odets went to Hollywood for a period of slightly over four years, during which time he wrote and directed his most successful film, *None But the Lonely Heart*. During the latter part of his life he was a permanent resident of the movie colony.

40. Barbara Perch, interview, N.Y. *Times*, Aug. 27, 1944, sect. II, p. 3.

41. Odets, "On Coming Home," N.Y. *Times*, July 25, 1948, sect. II, p. 1.

42. Ibid.

43. Seymour Peck, interview, N.Y. *Times*, Feb. 20, 1949, sect. II, p. 1.

44. Odets, *The Big Knife* (New York, 1949), p. 146.

45. *Lies Like Truth* (New York, 1958), p. 52.

46. Ruth McKenney, "The New Odets Play," *NM*, Dec. 6, 1938, p. 28.

47. Odets, *Rocket to the Moon*, in *Six Plays*, p. 416.

48. Elliot Norton, interview, N.Y. *Times*, Nov. 5, 1950, sect. II, p. 3.

49. Quoted in Frederick Lumley, *Trends in Twentieth Century Drama* (London, 1956), p. 224.

50. Odets, *The Country Girl* (New York, 1951), p. 122.

51. "The Three New Yorks," N.Y. *Times*, Mar. 31, 1940, magazine sect., p. 6.

52. Odets, *Night Music* (New York, 1940), p. 160.

53. "Genesis of a Play," N.Y. *Times*, Feb. 1, 1942, sect. X, p. 3.

54. Odets, *Clash By Night* (New York, 1941), p. 218.

55. Herbert Mitgang, interview, N.Y. *Times*, Dec. 26, 1954, sect. II, p. 3.

56. Odets, selections from *The Flowering Peach*, in *The Best Plays of 1954-55*, ed. Louis Kronenberger (New York, 1955), p. 193. Since *The Flowering Peach* was never published, the quotations in this study are from the excerpted, synopsized version in the *Best Plays* series. My critical judgments, however, are not based solely upon this version, but also upon my recollection of the original Broadway production.

57. Mitgang interview, p. 3.

CHAPTER EIGHT

1. *Lies Like Truth*, p. 37.

2. S. N. Behrman, *The Second Man*, in *Four Plays* (New York, 1955), p. 75.

3. Behrman, *Rain from Heaven*, in *Four Plays*, p. 216.

4. Behrman, *End of Summer*, in *Four Plays*, p. 326.

5. Behrman, *No Time for Comedy* (New York, 1939), p. 101.

6. Behrman, *Biography*, in *Four Plays*, p. 94.

7. Behrman, *Wine of Choice* (New York, 1938), p. 84.

8. Behrman, *Meteor* (New York, 1934), p. 127.

9. Behrman, *Dunnigan's Daughter* (New York, 1945), p. 133.

10. Behrman, prefatory note to *Rain from Heaven* (New York, 1934), p. 11.

11. Behrman, *The Talley Method* (New York, 1941), p. 161.

CHAPTER NINE

1. "Elmer Rice Says Farewell to Broadway," N.Y. *Times*, Nov. 11, 1934, sect. IX, p. 1.
2. "Apologia Pro Vita Sua," N.Y. *Times*, Dec. 25, 1938, sect. IX, p. 1.
3. N.Y. *Times*, Nov. 11, 1934, sect. IX, p. 3.
4. Elmer Rice, *Not for Children*, in *Two Plays* (New York, 1935), pp. x-xi.
5. Ibid., p. xv.
6. Ibid., p. xii.
7. Ibid.
8. "Apologia," loc. cit.
9. Rice, *The Adding Machine*, in *Seven Plays* (New York, 1950), p. 95.
10. Rice, *The Subway* (New York, 1929), p. 95.
11. Rice, *Street Scene*, in *Seven Plays*, p. 146.
12. See, for example, "Elmer Rice Answers John J. Raskob," *NM*, Feb. 18, 1936, p. 15.
13. See N.Y. *Times*: Jan. 25, 1931, p. 25; Jan. 24, 1936, p. 20; Feb. 26, 1945, p. 21; Oct. 16, 1953, p. 33; Dec. 21, 1955, p. 20; July 6, 1956, p. 14.
14. "Project for a New Theatre," N.Y. *Times*, Oct. 8, 1933, sect. X, p. 1.
15. "Rice Sees Theatre Improved by WPA," N.Y. *Times*, Dec. 11, 1935, p. 29.
16. Murray Schumach, interview, N.Y. *Times*, Nov. 23, 1958, sect. II, p. 1.
17. Letter to the Drama Editor, N.Y. *Times*, Feb. 12, 1933, sect. III, p. 3.
18. Rice, *We the People* (New York, 1933), pp. 252–53.
19. "Fire in Leipzig," *Germany: A Self-Portrait*, ed. Harlan Crippen (New York, 1944), pp. 324–25.
20. Rice, *Judgment Day*, in *Seven Plays* (New York, 1950), p. 369.
21. Rice, *Between Two Worlds*, in *Two Plays* (New York, 1935), pp. 203-4.
22. "Apologia," p. 5.
23. See *We the People*, pp. 17–18, 70, 72, 236.
24. Rice, *Flight to the West* (New York, 1941), pp. 21–22.

CHAPTER TEN

1. Maxwell Anderson, *Off Broadway* (New York, 1947), p. 76.
2. Ibid., p. 48.
3. Ibid., p. 20.
4. Ibid., p. 43.
5. Ibid., pp. 15–16.
6. Maxwell Anderson and Harold Hickerson, *Gods of the Lightning* (New York, 1928), p. 79.
7. Anderson, *Winterset*, in *Eleven Verse Plays, 1929–1939* (New York, 1940), p. 70. The plays are paginated individually.
8. Reprinted in *Off Broadway*, p. 59.
9. Anderson, *Knickerbocker Holiday* (Washington, 1938), pp. v–vi.
10. Anderson, *Both Your Houses* (New York, 1933), p. 178.
11. Anderson, *Mary of Scotland*, in *Eleven Verse Plays*, p. 37.
12. Anderson, *The Feast of Ortolans*, in *Eleven Verse Plays*, p. 15.
13. Anderson, *Second Overture*, in *Eleven Verse Plays*, p. 5.
14. Anderson, *The Masque of Kings*, in *Eleven Verse Plays*, p. 105.
15. Anderson, *Valley Forge*, in *Eleven Verse Plays*, p. 50.
16. Anderson, *High Tor*, in *Eleven Verse Plays*, p. 54.
17. Anderson, *Key Largo*, in *Eleven Verse Plays*, p. 21.
18. Ibid., p. 89.

ELEVEN: EPILOGUE

1. "Ionesco: Man of Destiny?" June 22, 1958, p. 15.
2. "The Playwright's Role," June 29, 1958, p. 14.
3. Letter, July 6, 1958, p. 19.
4. Letter, July 13, 1958, p. 14.
5. *Brecht: the Man and His Work* (New York, 1960), p. 239.

INDEX